700.458 OEM

DEMOCRACY | A Project by Group Material

Dia Art Foundation

Discussions in Contemporary Culture

Number 5

DEMOCRACY | A Project by Group Material

Edited by Brian Wallis

BAY PRESS   SEATTLE   1990

Printed in the United States of America.
First Printing 1990
Second Printing 1996
Bay Press
115 West Denny Way
Seattle, Washington 98119

Design by Bethany Johns
Typesetting by The Sarabande Press, New York
Printing by BookCrafters, Chelsea, Michigan
Set in Sabon

Library of Congress Cataloging-in-Publication Data
(Revised for no. 5)
Discussions in Contemporary Culture
Nos. 1–2 edited by Hal Foster. No. 3 edited by Gary Garrels. No. 4 edited
by Barbara Kruger and Phil Mariani. Contents: no. 1 [no special title].
–no. 2. Vision and visuality. –no. 3. The work of Andy Warhol. –no. 4.
Remaking history. –no. 5. Democracy: A Project by Group Material. 1. Art
and Society. 2. Aesthetics, Modern–20th century. 3. Group Material. 4.
AIDS.
I. Brian Wallis. II. Dia Art Foundation.
N72.S6D57 1987   700'.1'03   89-650815
ISSN 1047-6806 (no. 5: pbk.)

Cover:
Jane Rosett, Civil disobedience against the Hardwick decision in front
of the Supreme Court Building, Washington, D.C., October 10, 1988.

Title Page:
Civil rights demonstration, August 28, 1963, Washington, D.C., view
from the top of the Lincoln Memorial toward the Washington Monument.

CONTENTS

EDUCATION AND DEMOCRACY

POLITICS AND ELECTION

CULTURAL PARTICIPATION

AIDS AND DEMOCRACY: A CASE STUDY

We dedicate this project and book to our friend Bill Olander, who died of AIDS in 1989. Bill was an exceptional person. His integrity, openness, and generosity are painfully missed. With this dedication, we acknowledge Bill's untiring support for cultural activism, his inclusive curatorial style, and his insistent "expression of doubt," always conveyed with uncommon thoughtfulness and an irrepressible sense of humor.

We extend this dedication to the many grass-roots organizations working against bigotry and social irresponsibility. These groups are models of self-empowerment and are creating vital methods for effecting social change.

A NOTE ON THE SERIES

This is the fifth publication in a series initiated by the Dia Art Foundation called "Discussions in Contemporary Culture." The series is based on an ongoing program of lectures and symposia held at Dia's performance space at 155 Mercer Street, New York, to explore topics relating to culture for diverse communities. We continue to rely on artists, scholars, and critics from outside Dia to initiate and develop these events with us.

As part of this process, especially in regard to the opening of a new center for exhibitions at 548 West 22nd Street, Dia invited five internationally recognized arts professionals to meet with our staff in New York in June 1987 to discuss the forthcoming schedule of exhibitions. By intention this group represented a diversity of informed opinions and positions and included: Harald Szeemann, Curator, Kunsthaus, Zurich and independent curator; Kaspar Koenig, Director of Portikus and Chancellor of the Städelsches Kunstinstitut, Frankfurt; Kathy Halbreich, Curator of Contemporary Art, Museum of Fine Arts, Boston and former Director, List Visual Arts Center, MIT; Yvonne Rainer, filmmaker and instructor, Whitney Independent Study Program; and Richard Bellamy, director of the Oil & Steel Gallery (1980s) and Green Gallery (1960s). Out of these discussions, particularly through the urging of Yvonne Rainer, emerged the need to support the work of artists engaged in exploring a broader range of art making than that generally presented in museums and galleries. The Dia staff at her recommendation approached socially engaged artists Group Material and Martha Rosler to consider projects at Dia. It quickly became clear that these projects could not be conventional exhibitions.

Rather than creating projects at 548 West 22nd Street, the decision was made with the artists to use the Dia spaces in Soho at 77 Wooster Street for installations and 155 Mercer Street for open, public discussions or "town meetings," tying the two together as much as possible. Situated at the geographic center of Soho and the New York art world, these spaces offered ready accessibility to the audience actively participating in this critical process as well as to the general public. The starting point for this publication thus was a series of events conceived and directed by the artists' collaborative Group Material over the course of more than two years (1987-89), including planning sessions; private roundtable discussions; a series of four exhibitions; and open public "town meetings." This composite form of "exhibition" or art project, under the project name "Democracy," explored the condition of democratic processes and democratic ideals in this country through specific issues of public education; politics and election; cultural participation; and the AIDS crisis.

Group Material's project "Democracy" formed the first half of a broader effort, as a whole called "Town Meeting." The second half, conceived and directed by Martha Rosler, addressed issues of housing, homelessness, and urban planning and will continue with a forthcoming companion volume to this one. The project has been too complex to be recorded faithfully in a single publication. Group Material in any case wanted this publication to function less as a distillation of many events and discussions and more as yet another, integral phase of this overall project (part process, part discussion, part display of objects, part exposition, part text). Much of the visual material in this book, the essays by Brian Wallis and David Deitcher, and the statements by Group Material and Yvonne Rainer represent significant new dimensions to the "Democracy" project.

Those familiar with Dia's "Discussions in Contemporary Culture" series of symposia and lectures at 155 Mercer Street found a very different tone and a new procedure at the town meetings. The usual relationship of lecturers and experts to an "audience," as interactive as these audiences have sometimes been, was overturned in the town meetings by an emphasis on the views of many, speaking to each other. This multiplying of voices comes through in the edited transcripts of the meetings, and in the spirit of the book as a whole in which, true to Group Material's method, the whole is greater than the sum of the richly contextualized parts.

With "Town Meeting," Group Material and Martha Rosler invented a program at Dia asserting, in its many phases and parts, social and political inquiries as the guiding principles of organization. This revises a system of values to which the Dia Art Foundation, as an arts organization, has grown accustomed. The rallying points for each installation and town meeting did not fall within the aesthetic or art-historical criteria that an arts organization is supposed to be able, in some advantaged way, to discern. Instead, these art-specific criteria were secondary (in the formulation of the public discussions as much as in organizing the installations of visual art), and were of value only to augment the focused arguments being made concerning aspects of the condition of democracy in this country.

Charles Wright, Executive Director
Gary Garrels, Director of Programs

ACKNOWLEDGMENTS

We owe a great debt to Yvonne Rainer, who brought us to Group Material, Martha Rosler, and to a new view of how our program can function. The artists' collaborative Group Material, including Doug Ashford, Julie Ault, Felix Gonzalez-Torres, and, in the end, Karen Ramspacher, who began her involvement in Town Meeting a part of Dia's staff and became a member of the collaborative midstream, together were a tireless and extremely dedicated leader in the project. We are grateful to Brian Wallis for his introductory essay, his thorough editing of the transcripts of town meetings and roundtable discussions, and for his essential guidance in the development of the book. David Deitcher's excellent essay gives a helpful perspective on Group Material's methods and aims. Gary Garrels, Director of Programs at Dia, coordinated this immensely complicated undertaking with the help of Karen Kelly, Programs Assistant, and the entire Dia staff. We are very grateful to the participants in the roundtable discussions and the public Town Meetings, including the many individuals who came to these events and publicly shared their opinions and concerns. We thank Bethany Johns who designed this publication working closely with Group Material. We also greatly appreciate our ongoing relationship with Thatcher Bailey at Bay Press, without whom this series of publications would not be possible for us.

Charles Wright

Yvonne Rainer

PREFACE: THE WORK OF ART IN THE (IMAGINED) AGE OF UNALIENATED EXHIBITION

Art that edifies and makes your spirit soar; art that gives you a taste of inspired madness; art that enhances and validates your superior taste; art that contains discomfiting messages in beautiful wrappings; art that testifies to the universality of the lone, suffering, melancholic artistic impulse. You didn't find such art in the shows curated by Group Material and Martha Rosler at the Dia Art Foundation's Wooster Street space from September 1988 through June 1989, or if you did, such expressions were imbued with very different meanings through their inclusion in these exhibitions. The artist's melancholy was here transformed into grief, rage, and social activism by and for those fallen to AIDS, civic neglect, homelessness, political mendacity.

The two separate series—"Democracy," organized by Group Material, and "If You Lived Here . . . ," organized by Martha Rosler—and their concomitant Town Meetings, have pushed the debates around art and politics into a new dimension. Although Group Material's shows included well-known artists, the sheer abundance of "unknown" participants, including children and the homeless, made for an exhilarating blowing-away, and more-than-implicit critique of the customary conserving-and-excluding strategies of museum- and gallery-sponsored art exhibitions. Needless to say, the governance of the art *market* was not in evidence here. And not unexpectedly, "pluralism," that ideological underside of market-value "one-of-a-kindness" and stanchion of cultural life in these United States, was not an operative factor despite the diversity of materials, styles, and origins of work shown. What surfaced again and again as one spent time in these shifting, seemingly chaotic installations was the conflict between official utterance and nonofficial representation of everyday life, between the exalted bromides of Western democracy and their thinly disguised "freedoms": to die of AIDS, to live on the streets in a cardboard box, to not learn to read, to speak without being heard, to make art that will never be seen.

For ten months the symbols of public and private identity and icons of presumed consensus—from flag to desk to hearth to hair—were paraded, trounced, and dissected, while their myriad misuses for capital and political profit were amply documented in film and video. Intermittently the eight Town Meetings provided a forum for the airing of opinions and reports from the various activist fronts. Issues of race, sex, and class inevitably collided. There were no resolutions—other than the one that was voted in at the "Cultural Participation" meeting, where it was resolved that hereafter, when invited to appear on panels, we would demand the inclusion of people of color. There were few people of color present at this particular meeting. The Town Meetings were remarkable for their capacity to accommodate disagreement, anger, crankiness, borderline psychosis, useful information, theoretical discourse, and productive networking, engaging people of all ages and from all walks of life. Their prevailing whiteness is indicative of the ongoing racial inequities in the art world.

I am occasionally struck by the memory of a pronouncement made in the mid-fifties by a painter friend of mind (a woman no less!): "The cream always rises to the top." Like all such analogies to "natural selection," this one evades the issue of who recognizes and separates the cream, and whose interests are served by such distinctions. The Group Material and Rosler projects are a vivid demonstration of how art exhibition can constitute a radically different approach, one that can offer not only a diversity of objects but can contextualize a social field in and from which the objects are produced and derive their meaning. In other words, art exhibition does not have to separate, or isolate, its objects from the conditions in and under which those objects have been produced. Most art exhibition obscures these conditions under the smoke screen of "quality," or the implicitly superior taste involved with selection. Someone standing behind me at the recent Velázquez show at the Met remarked, "The Inquisition was going on then." Yikes! Who would have known! Unobtrusively and tastefully placed notes at such exhibitions do little to mitigate the dominant impression that there has been a previous "separation of cream." Emphasis on quality has once again carried the day. The various modernist attempts to overturn these values— from dada to pop to minimalism—failed, not in the objects they produced, but at the site of their *exhibition,* which invariably focused—as most exhibitions continue to do—on the singular object alienated from its social context.

In light of Dia's longstanding and continuing commitment to cream separating, it behooves me to register my own lobbying effort on a five-person panel (convened by Dia, to its credit) as an initiating factor in the realization of these shows. One can only hope that the closing of the Wooster Street space that housed "Democracy" and "If You Lived Here . . ." does not signal the end of Dia's involvement with artist/activist-curated exhibitions, and that these particular projects have constituted a genuine precedent for future exhibitions sponsored by that commendable organization.

Meanwhile, these books are powerful testimony to the value of art as a social force in a time when progressive social consciousness at the institutional level needs all the prodding it can get.

Odilon Redon, *The Egg*, 1885.

ON DEMOCRACY

Participating in the system doesn't mean that we must identify with it, stop criticizing it, or stop improving the little piece of turf on which we operate.

—Judge Bruce Wright, Justice,
New York State Supreme Court

Ideally, democracy is a system in which political power rests with the people: all citizens actively participate in the process of self-representation and self-governing, an ongoing discussion in which a multitude of diverse voices converge. But in 1987, after almost two terms of the Reagan presidency and with another election year at hand, it was clear that the state of American democracy was in no way ideal. Access to political power was obstructed in complex ways, participation in politics had degenerated into passive and symbolic involvement, and the current of "official" politics precluded a diversity of viewpoints. When the Dia Art Foundation approached us with the idea of doing a project, it was immediately apparent to us that democracy should serve as the theme.

The subject of democracy not only became our content, but influenced our method of working. This theme prompted a greater awareness of our own process. One of the first questions we asked was: "Why are they asking us?" To us, the Dia Art Foundation signified "exclusive," "white," "esoteric," and "male," whereas we had always attempted to redefine culture around an opposing set of terms: "inclusive," "multicultural," "nonsexist," and "socially relevant." In general, we see ourselves as the outspoken distant relative at the annual reunion who can be counted on to bring up the one subject no one wants to talk about.

The subject that no one in the art world wants to talk about is usually politics. Yet, because every social or cultural relationship is a political one, we regard an understanding of the link between politics and culture as essential. "Politics" cannot be restricted to those arenas stipulated as such by professional politicians. Indeed, it is fundamental to our methodology to question every aspect of our cultural situation from a political point of view, to ask, "What politics inform accepted understandings of art and culture? Whose interests are served by such cultural conventions? How is culture made, and for whom is it made?"

In conceptualizing this project, therefore, we proposed a structure that differed from the conventional art exhibitions, lectures, and panels that Dia had previously sponsored. We identified four significant areas of the crisis in democracy: education, electoral politics, cultural participation, and AIDS. For each topic, we collaboratively organized a roundtable discussion, an exhibition, and a town meeting. For each roundtable we invited individual speakers from diverse professions and perspectives to participate in an informal conversation. These discussions helped us to prepare the installations and provided important information for planning the agendas for the town meetings.

Each of the four exhibitions that we installed at 77 Wooster Street reiterated the interrelatedness of our subjects and the necessity of our collaborative process. Our working method might best be described as painfully democratic, because so much of our process depends on the review, selection, and critical juxtaposition of innumerable cultural objects, adhering to a collective process is extremely time-consuming and difficult. However, the shared learning and ideas produce results that are often inaccessible to those who work alone.

Our exhibitions and projects are intended to be forums in which multiple points of view are represented in a variety of styles and methods. We believe, as the feminist writer bell hooks has said, that "we must focus on a policy of inclusion so as not to mirror oppressive structures." As a result, each exhibition is a veritable model of democracy. Mirroring the various forms of representation that structure our understanding of culture, our exhibitions bring together so-called fine art with products from supermarkets, mass-cultural artifacts with historical objects, factual documentation with homemade projects. We are not interested in making definitive evaluations or declarative statements, but in creating situations that offer our chosen subject as a complex and open-ended issue. We encourage greater audience participation through interpretation.

One form of participation was the town meeting held for each exhibition. These meetings were well publicized and were open to the public at large. In selecting the town meeting format, we meant not only to allude to the prototypical democratic experience but also to eliminate the demarcation between experts and the public so evident at most public lectures. For the town meetings all audience members were potential participants. Beyond the desire to erode such traditional categories, our expectations for these discussions were somewhat undefined. In the end, each town meeting had a life of its own, determined not only by the moderator, but by who was in the audience and who among them had the courage to speak up. Much of the public discussion built on issues raised in the roundtable meetings, and it was gratifying to hear different people discussing their relation to those issues.

The final part of "Democracy," and perhaps the most important, is this book. Through this book we tried to encapsulate many of the ideas that went into and came out of the Democracy Project in order to make them available to a far wider public than could attend the events. We organized this publication very much as we organize our exhibitions, bringing together a variety of voices and points of view to address the issues. In this case, we hope that the results provide a strong analysis of the current situation of democracy in America and suggest possible means for responding to its challenges.

This project and publication required the efforts of many people. We sincerely thank the artists, discussion participants, and contributors who are all listed elsewhere in this book. We are grateful to the galleries and lenders to the exhibitions and all the people who facilitated those loans.

It has been an extraordinary pleasure to work with the staff at Dia. Charles Wright was supportive from the beginning; Gary Garrels oversaw the project and consistently offered invaluable input; Karen Ramspacher's enthusiastic participation during the project led to her joining Group Material and we look forward to continued collaboration; Joan Duddy was always there for us, day and night; Karen Kelly devoted herself tirelessly to producing this book. We are grateful to the following people for their special assistance: Margaret Thatcher, Laura Fields, Isabel Stude, Camilla Fallon, Jim Schaeufele, Susan Walker, Fernanda Arujao, Deborah Meehan, Alexis Summer, Deborah Garwood, Eva Otterbeck, Sarah Rees, and Nancy Shaver.

The following people contributed in a number of ways: Eric Bemisderfer, Bill Dillworth, Hunter Reynolds, John Lindell, John Sprague, and David Nyzio installed the exhibitions; Rob Constantine and John Shuman creatively catered the opening receptions; Greg Davidek, Herb Perr, Mary Sabatino, Martha Rosler, Tom Klocke and Elizabeth Marks from Hospital Audiences, Rachel Romero, Materials for the Arts, and Kirsten Mosher generously gave varied assistance and support. We are indebted to Phil Mariani for her wise suggestions and helping hand. As individuals we are deeply appreciative of personal support from Ross Laycock, Sarah Safford, and Andres Serrano.

We gratefully acknowledge Tim Rollins, who was a member of Group Material until the fall of 1987. Tim was involved in the proposal stage of "Democracy." Because this project developed from the group's history of interests, Tim's ideas were present throughout, as were those of Mundy McLaughlin who left the group in 1986.

Doug Ashford, Julie Ault, Felix Gonzalez-Torres (Group Material)

Troops in riot formation line up in front of the Mall Entrance to the Pentagon on October 23, 1967, holding back thousands of demonstrators protesting the Vietnam War.

Brian Wallis

DEMOCRACY AND CULTURAL ACTIVISM

Today America faces a crisis of democracy. This is ironic, of course, since Americans, accustomed to being the international exemplars of democracy, have for the most part had to sit on the sidelines and watch as democratic reforms have erupted over the past several years in countries as different as Poland and the Philippines, in China (briefly), in El Salvador, in Nicaragua, and in the Soviet Union—of all places. In his first State of the Union address, in January 1990, President Bush drew attention to this phenomenon, going so far as to call 1989, his first year in office, the "Year of Democracy." And Bush assured the nation that Americans were not mere sideliners, but were in fact leaders in the international surge of democracy, providing the political model that other countries were now emulating.

Yet, despite the upbeat tenor of Bush's speech, his words rang hollow. Following two terms of the Reagan administration, the very concept of democracy seemed little more than a cliché used in magazine headlines and network specials to describe political developments elsewhere. At home democracy had been devastated by an eight-year siege; almost every principle of democracy had been inverted. If democracy meant equal rights for all citizens, the attack on the welfare system and the systematic transfer of wealth from the poor to the rich signaled a fundamental reconsolidation of the power of the elite. If democracy meant a participation of the citizenry in decision making, the perpetuation of policies opposed by a majority of the public (such as the illegal funding of the contras) signaled an expansion of presidential powers and an increase in the rule of the state. If democracy meant freedom of the press, Americans were faced with media that were increasingly owned by a small minority of corporations. And if democracy meant the enfranchisement of all voters, the 22.7 percent of the population that actually voted for Reagan's successor in 1988 signaled the disinterest of most of the population in the democratic process.

This woeful situation recalls a previous "crisis of democracy," one signaled by the title of a 1975 report by the Trilateral Commission, an elite panel of politicians and corporate chiefs brought together by David Rockefeller in 1973 to coordinate a political and economic partnership among the ruling elites of North America, Western Europe, and Japan. Their report,

The Crisis of Democracy, was an attempt to determine the root causes of the worldwide outbreak of civil unrest and demand for political participation that was creating international economic stagnation. What the report sought to understand and to control was the rise of "permissiveness" that propelled the unsavory "democratic upsurge of the 1960s."

For Samuel P. Huntington, noted professor of government at Harvard and author of the section of the report on the U.S., the crisis of democracy was a result of what he called "an excess of democracy." It was Huntington's belief that the events of the 1960s and early 1970s—protests, racial dissension, student takeovers, assaults on the power of the presidency—were a result of individuals and groups taking too literally the rhetoric of democracy. Without irony, Huntington observed that as more people became involved in the political process in the 1960s, challenges to authority, disappointments, and crises were inevitable because "democratic societies cannot work when the citizenry is not passive." Contrary to popular belief, Huntington stressed, "the arenas where democratic procedures are appropriate are limited." According to his account, all past democracies have been ruled by a small group of specialists who have participated most fully in politics. While admitting that the marginalization of all other segments of the citizenry is "inherently undemocratic," Huntington insisted on that necessity, writing that "the effective operation of a democratic political system usually requires some measure of apathy and noninvolvement." In other words, the function of the electorate was to passively ratify decisions of the executive branch of the government; if the citizens sought to actively participate in government, the political system was threatened.

The Crisis of Democracy was just one sign from corporate America that the foundation of liberal democracy would be restructured so as to be maintained by the ruling class. Symbolically, both the Carter and Reagan administrations sought—in very different ways—to act upon its lessons. Carter sought to institute a national austerity program, encouraging individuals to consume less and expect less from the government. Reagan encouraged private enterprise and the cult of the individual. This symbolic program was dramatized not only by singling out meritorious individuals (such as Joe Clark, Oliver North, or Whittaker Chambers), but by busting labor unions and opposing all collectives except the family and the nation.

Against the pressures of "special-interest groups" (a convenient euphemism for "the public"), Reagan sought to restore authority to the sullied prestige of the presidency. The symbolism of the "imperial presidency" that the Reagans so assiduously maintained in their personal style was even more fully realized in the administration's legislative programs. Central to Reagan's economic "revolution" was the argument that redirecting capital to the nation's wealthiest entrepreneurs would revitalize the economy. This "trickle-down theory" became the rationale for the Reagan administration's tax breaks for the wealthiest class, relaxation of corporate regulation, sweetheart deals with government and industry, and maintenance of a debilitating minimum wage (which remained at $3.35 an hour—or $6,900 a year— throughout the eight years of Reagan's administration). The much heralded "trickle-down" effect of these policies, the economic fallout that would have aided the middle and lower classes, never occurred.

Instead, throughout both terms of Reagan's presidency, the rich got richer and the poor got poorer. A succession of legislative maneuvers increased the already growing division between the wealthiest class in America and the growing ranks of the poor. Even though social programs for the poor constituted only 15 percent of the total federal budget in 1981, the Reagan administration launched an all-out offensive on welfare spending, which Reagan's conservative supporters regarded as a chief example of "permissiveness." As a result, the number of people living in poverty escalated to an all-time high—in all, approximately 11 million Americans joined the ranks of the poor during the Reagan years.

The trashing of democracy during this period was only most blatantly symbolized by the rapidly expanding chasm between classes. Voter apathy, the continued plight of the poor and the homeless, the neglect of health care for the vast majority of the population, the insensitivity to the needs of those affected by AIDS, the abandonment of the individual farmer, the disintegration of the education system: all represent further signs of the dysfunction of the democratic system that was once taken for granted. Reagan's vigorous assaults on the rights of the working class, the poor, blacks, women, immigrants, and gays and lesbians confirmed his administration's disdain for the conventional principles of democracy. By the end of Reagan's presidency, the disaffection of many marginalized groups had begun to erupt into public demonstrations of unrest. In the final year of Reagan's term, huge marches on Washington to protest inadequate AIDS funding and the Supreme Court's challenge to abortion rights signaled an end to the passivity that marked much of the decade and a return to an "excess of democracy."

In other words, one response to this latter-day crisis of democracy has been, in the past decade, a sharp rise in activism. On both ends of the political spectrum and on a number of pressing issues—the war in Central America, abortion, the environment, AIDS—citizens have banded together and taken to the streets in protest. Among the characteristics that these groups— left and right—share are their beliefs in the viability of civil disobedience, in the impact of media images on shaping public policy, and in the importance of symbolic protest. These protests often entail as well a participation in the practical aspects of the political process. But an overriding feature is the attempt to intervene in the political situation by providing striking visual representations. The 1980s abounded with examples of "mediacraft" and "photo opportunities," the staged demonstrations for the news media. These images were most skillfully engineered by the White House, but the techniques were also appropriated by protesters with less direct access to television. For demonstrators, it became essential to get images of their marches on television and to stress their own visual representations.

To the extent that such activism has, of necessity, become bound up with the creation of legible and effective images, this new style of politics might be called "cultural activism." Cultural activism might be defined simply as the use of cultural means to try to effect social change. Related to activist programs initiated by artists, musicians, writers, and other cultural producers, such activism signals the interrelatedness of cultural criticism and political engagement. Although the cultural means regarded as most widely effective is television, dramatic use has also been made of sophisticated graphics, slogans, videos, and films. The continued potency of even the most clichéd visual icon was demonstrated in 1989 by debates over the inviolability of the flag, the body, and the crucifix.

One irony of this struggle over representations is that it is conservative politicians and intellectuals who have most effectively colonized the use of culture as a site of ideological struggle in the 1980s. This is particularly ironic since their claim is generally that culture should be nonideological, free from politics. Given the moral conviction of the Reaganite cause and the reassertion of the role of the individual in democracy, the last great symbolic triumph of Reaganism may be said to have come with the small victory of Terry Rakolta, the housewife from Detroit who singlehandedly brought the networks to their knees. According to press accounts, Rakolta was so incensed by the overt suggestiveness and lewd humor of the television sitcom *Married With Children,* that she wrote letters to each of the show's sponsors demanding action. So effective was her one-woman campaign that on March 2, 1988, three of the show's eight sponsors announced that they were suspending all further advertising on the show.

But Rakolta's strategy was not an isolated one. This type of conservative cultural activism was a hallmark of the Reagan years. From the remarkably successful antiabortion film, *The Silent Scream,* to the massive protests by the American Family Association against the allegedly anti-Christian film *The Last Temptation of Christ,* conservative activists increasingly took their case to the public. Having learned from the student protests and civil rights demonstrations that had earlier signaled an "excess of democracy" to the Trilateral Commission, right-wing groups used mass protests, boycotts, civil disobedience, and congressional hearings to assert conservative causes. They often drew directly upon the examples of earlier, leftist strategies of symbolic, nonviolent protest. Randall Terry, the unofficial leader of the antiabortion group Operation Rescue, even claimed that his protesters were the contemporary moral equivalents to the 1960s civil rights activists (a claim that brought strong objections from civil rights groups).

What was significant about these right-wing protests is that many of them were directed toward specific cultural forms, principally television, but also rock music, MTV, films, pornography, and high art. Reverend Donald Wildmon of Tupelo, Mississippi, is typical in this regard. Shortly after Reagan's election in 1981, Wildmon gained prominence with a group called the Coalition for Better Television (CBTV). Upholding traditional Christian values, CBTV claimed that television promoted gratuitous sex, profanity, and violence. Threatening a boycott of sponsors' products, and claiming that five million followers were committed to joining him, Wildmon demanded that ten sponsors remove their support from series he cited as the "top sex-oriented." In June 1981, Proctor & Gamble, television's biggest sponsor (with $486 million in advertising), acceded to Wildmon's demands and withdrew its support from fifty made-for-TV movies and series episodes.

By 1984 Wildmon had changed the name of his organization to the American Family Association to reflect the broader intentions of his campaign to clean up television, film, and other forms of cultural expression. In 1986 he launched a campaign of boycotts against the film *The Last Temptation of Christ,* convincing several major movie chains to refuse to show the film. In 1988 he convinced Pepsi-Cola to drop a $10 million endorsement by the pop star Madonna on the grounds that her then popular single, "Like a Prayer," was anti-Christian.

Most notoriously, in 1989, Wildmon initiated a censorship campaign against the visual artist Andres Serrano for a photograph of a crucifix dipped in urine titled *Piss Christ.* When Wildmon's anti-Serrano campaign was subsequently taken up in Congress by Senator Jesse Helms as an example of the abuses of federal arts funding, it led (along with other controversial examples) to legislation to prohibit funding of visual arts deemed "obscene." But Wildmon's activities should not be isolated from other forms of right-wing activism. Right-wing cultural activism of the 1980s reasserted the power of the family, the church, and "the unborn," in addition to propping up conservative institutions and ideologies principally through the creation and control of symbolic images. As Reagan's former director of communications, Patrick Buchanan, has said, "Conservatives had best become interested in art if they wish to see civilization survive into the 21st century."

It is against the rise of this right-wing cultural activism and its effectivity that we must consider the work of many alternative groups active in the cultural field over the past several years. Building on the demonstrable structural and representational strategies of various struggles on the left, groups like Border Arts Workshop, ACT UP, PAD/D, Artists Call, and Gran Fury have redefined cultural production toward an activity that is collaborative, multicultural, and engaged with a community. This book offers a case study in the working methodology of Group Material, one such collective. Taking democracy at its word, these artists have attempted to reinstate the sort of "crisis" of democracy Samuel Huntington spoke of, a crisis brought about by too much participation, too much freedom of expression.

As for Group Material's methodology in this exhibition, several things need to be said. First, regarding audience: as Group Material acknowledges, and as I think should be patently clear, the principal audience for any exhibition at the Dia Art Foundation is going to be an art-world one. No amount of well-intentioned social heart-searching is going to bring the rest of the public in to see an art exhibition. The show was therefore organized to impress upon at least some of the audience that already exists for art the need to devise alternative strategies which would eventually also involve those at present unaffected by the work artists do.

Secondly, this new concept of audience carries the implication of a breakdown between the conventional notions of creator and viewer. Rather than an individual artist addressing a particular public, the issue should be a particular community creating both the need for and the form of a particular expression. This means generally that cultural work is not something bound to the galleries. As the exhibitions and discussions documented in this volume demonstrate, the production of culture is taking place around us all the time—not just in art studios, but in schools, in public spaces, in demonstrations, and on television. Group Material's project suggests that we can extract this cultural meaning only through the work of analysis, critical reading, and juxtaposition.

And finally, we should look closely at how Group Material frames the term "democracy" with three words: education, participation, and politics. These words, combined with an expanded notion of cultural production, suggest a new form of social engagement—less arrogant, less exclusive, a culture that is not made by the few but by the many. Democracy demands an active participation and this can only be achieved today with renewed cultural activism. As Noam Chomsky has made clear, "Meaningful democracy will involve popular takeover of decision making in the essential institutions. . . . They are what determine basically what our lives are."

"Anti-Bra Day," San Francisco, August 1, 1969. This particular protest was staged in front of one of the city's major department stores and called on women all over the world to send their bras to San Francisco for destruction.

David Deitcher

SOCIAL AESTHETICS

New York, September 14, 1989—Early this morning five members of ACT UP, an AIDS activist group, entered the New York Stock Exchange under cover of dark suits, crimson ties, and fake Bear, Stearns & Co. identification cards. They went up to the balcony and, just before the 9:30 a.m. opening bell, disrupted the start of trading for nearly five minutes by blasting horns and throwing a flurry of hundred-dollar bills to the trading room floor. This was not simply a belated tribute to the memory of Abbie Hoffman, who twenty years ago caused a near riot at the same location by tossing money to the bulls, the bears, and the pigs. ACT UP's C-notes, unlike Hoffman's dollars, were fake and were inscribed on the verso, "PEOPLE ARE DYING WHILE YOU PLAY BUSINESS." After chaining themselves to the bal-ustrade, today's demonstrators also unfurled a banner from the balcony; it read "SELL WELLCOME."

At high noon, several hours after these demonstrators were carted off to police headquarters, several hundred other AIDS activists took to the inter-section of Wall and Broad Streets. They formed a continuous circle of men and women more than two blocks long. Before the bolted doors of the Stock Exchange, and in the face of hundreds of cops, they raised a deafening clamor, blaring horns, drumming on cow bells, whistling, and raising their voices with chants to alert those who daily trade in the shares of Wellcome P.L.C. that they are profiting from blood money.

Wellcome P.L.C. is the British parent of the American company Bur-roughs Wellcome, which still charges ruinous sums for the drug Azidothymidine (AZT). Today it costs roughly $8,000 annually for a person with AIDS to slow the replication of the Human Immunodeficiency Virus (HIV) in his or her system by taking this drug. Of all drugs requiring daily dosage, AZT is the most expensive in history. This is true even though AZT was actually discovered as a possible anti-cancer agent in 1964 by Jerome Horwitz, a scientist at the federally funded Michigan Cancer Foundation, and despite the fact that the National Cancer Institute supplied Burroughs Wellcome with the raw ingredient required to make the first supplies of AZT. While Burroughs Wellcome has spent about $80 million to develop

Four members of ACT UP (AIDS Coalition To Unleash Power) arrested by deputies at the Burroughs Wellcome Co. offices in Research Triangle Park, Durham, North Carolina, 1989.

this drug—a modest sum by industry standards—an analyst with the British investment bank of Barclays Dezoete Wedd, Inc., in New York has estimated that the company's before-tax profit in 1989 was $100 million (on gross sales of $220 million to some 45,000 people with AIDS).

Recently scientists released data supporting the idea that AZT would benefit those who are infected with HIV, but who do not yet have AIDS. As a consequence, the FDA is on the verge of recommending that AZT be taken by the hundreds of thousands of people who fit that description in this country alone. As the ACT UP fact sheet accompanying today's demonstration asserted, "Wall Street is betting on AZT being the next drug to reach one billion dollars in annual sales." Over the past three weeks the price of stock in Wellcome P.L.C. has increased by over 40 percent.

Neither Wall Streeters nor Burroughs Wellcome are unfamiliar with ACT UP. Wall Street was the site of the AIDS activists' very first demonstration. On March 24, 1987, scores of protesters sat down in the middle of Wall Street while others distributed literature on AIDS and on how governmental indifference toward AIDS and corporate greed had turned the epidemic into a full-fledged health emergency. Two years later, on the morning of April 25, 1989, four members of ACT UP (two of whom were also arrested in today's action inside the Stock Exchange) donned business suits and briefcases and slipped by security personnel at Burroughs Wellcome's headquarters at Research Triangle Park outside Durham, North Carolina. Having equipped their briefcases with drills, bolts, a small TV, and enough food and drink to get by for three days, they sealed themselves inside a third-floor office in the company's South building. Then they telephoned local newspersons and national wire services to inform them—and the company—of their presence and their demands: that Burroughs Wellcome lower the price of AZT by 25 percent and that the company provide the drug to a federal program that distributes it to those who can't afford to buy it. Burroughs Wellcome promptly announced their intention to lower the price of AZT by 25 percent while claiming, no doubt disingenuously, that they had intended to do so anyway.

Among those Americans whose lives depend upon AZT and who were once solvent, many have since been forced into penury. This has not happened because a disability forced them to give up their jobs or because they had no medical insurance; but simply because their relative solvency (in New York, an after-tax annual income above $5,508) made them ineligible for Medicaid coverage and gave them no choice but to "choose" financial ruin. For these people—whose insurance coverage is inadequate or nonexistent, and who are not yet sufficiently destitute to qualify for Medicaid—the federal government begrudgingly instituted an AIDS drug reimbursement program as part of its Supplemental Appropriations Act for fiscal 1988. The

number of people enrolled in this program so far has averaged between seven and eight thousand. Funding for the program initially included $10 million that actually were redirected from elsewhere in the federal AIDS budget and $5 million from the always beneficent Burroughs Wellcome. Last March, when the funds were depleted, the federal government kicked in an additional $5 million. Now the time has come to renew this fund. Evidently fearing congressional opposition this time around, Senator Edward Kennedy has proposed that the program be restructured so that the federal government would henceforth disburse grants requiring matching state funds. Some states, no doubt, will be less than forthcoming with their halves, thus creating the preconditions for an exodus that will add an additional burden to states that already have a disproportionately high incidence of HIV infection.

New York, September 18, 1989—In a press release filled with obfuscation, self-justification, and feigned magnanimity, Burroughs Wellcome announced today that it would cut the price of AZT by 20 percent. On National Public Radio, a spokesperson for the company claimed that pressure from the international AIDS activists community had nothing whatsoever to do with their decision.

The AIDS epidemic has struck gay men, African-Americans, Hispanics, and the poor disproportionately. As a result, one's view of this health care emergency is forced to dilate and encompass racial, sexual, and economic privilege, issues from which the AIDS crisis is, after all, inseparable. Perhaps only the matter of reproductive rights shares with the AIDS crisis this capacity to prompt so multifaceted and broad-based a reflection on American social conditions today. Of all the developed nations in the West, only South Africa and the United States have no system of national health care. The costs of medical assistance in this country are notorious; the overcrowded public health facilities are inhumane, even lethal. These conditions of health care in America attest to the failure of our democracy to live up to its most basic principle: that it be government for the people, by the people.

"AIDS and Democracy: A Case Study," an exhibition organized by the artists' collective Group Material for the Dia Art Foundation in 1989, presupposed the capacity of the AIDS crisis to serve as a litmus test for democratic processes in the U.S. today. The failure of those processes to represent the interests of all Americans was symbolized in the rendering of the American flag that presided over the installation at Dia's Wooster Street space. Michael Jenkins's *June 30, 1986* resembles an inverted Old Glory, one that consists, however, entirely of stripes. The date used in the title of this work, and the use of nine rather than thirteen stripes in this flag, suggests Jenkins's concern with the nine Supreme Court justices who ruled (5-4) on June 30, 1986, that police had the right to invade a man's privacy in his home and jail him under a state antisodomy law. Where the blue field of white stars that symbolize the states of the union should be, Jenkins simply cut into his "flag." With the piece pinned to the wall—stripes down, the rectangular void at lower right—this flag seemed frozen in the midst of a continuous fall, as if the negative weight of those absent stars were just dragging it down.

"AIDS and Democracy" contained a considerable amount of educational and agitational printed matter. This was the result of Group Material's engagement with AIDS activists throughout the process of conceiving and organizing their installation. This material, most of which was contributed by ACT UP (New York), was piled neatly in roughly forty stacks on a very long table that bisected the room diagonally. At the opposite ends of these tables, large TV monitors faced clusters of folding chairs. These monitors showed a continuous program of eleven videotapes comprising a cross-section of the rapidly growing library of works in video by AIDS activists, video artists, and filmmakers. Produced over the past four or five years, these activist videos counter the repressive and ineffective educational material put out by federal, state, and city agencies, and refute the chronic misrepresentation by the mass media of AIDS, its modes of transmission, and the people who have it.

In this installation these videos and the graphics that constitute the ephemera of direct political activism (i.e., Gran Fury's posters, *READ MY LIPS* and *ALL PEOPLE WITH AIDS ARE INNOCENT*) were juxtaposed with works of "high" art. In many cases these art works could be understood to bear upon the AIDS crisis only within this context. For instance, Jannis Kounellis's untitled work (1975) consisted simply of an engraving of Jacques-Louis David's *Death of Marat* with a (real) black butterfly fixed to its surface. Andres Serrano's *Winged Victory*, a *Nike of Samothrace* photographed in piss, presided over the interior as the most luminous lament on display. Under more neutral circumstances it would have revitalized spiritual imagery that has been debased by organized religion by confronting the spectator with his or her anxiety about the body. Louise Lawler's *Them*, which targets the paucity of government spending on health research relative to defense spending in the U.S. and Europe, seemed tailor-made for the installation, but is a work that dates from 1986. Meanwhile, Don Moffett's illuminated box, *1988*, expressed a popular sentiment among visitors to the installation with its photograph of Reagan's departure, captioned in pink script, "So Long, Farewell, Auf Wiedersehen, Goodbye."

These heterogeneous juxtapositions took place in the midst of what had become a polarized situation among some artists and AIDS activists. By late 1988 this became evident in a contentious debate about what, if anything short of collective direct political action, constitutes a significant cultural response to the AIDS crisis.[1] In retrospect, "AIDS and Democracy" was more valuable as an opportunity to investigate the terms of this conflict than as an attempt to reconcile the two sides of the argument. By providing a forum in which fairly poetic individual art works shared space with a broad range of educational and political artifacts, the installation gave visitors a chance to decide for themselves what significance, if any, each work might have in dealing with this political, social, and personal crisis. It clarified, moreover, that in a situation where the lines are so clearly drawn between those who want to stop the dying and others who continue to exploit it to further a conservative political agenda, the Enemy is not to be found among those who created these works of art.

Finally, there were emotional reasons for joining together art that reflects on death and loss, that questions institutional authority, and that militates for political change. This deep emotional purpose was stated upfront in a statement that Group Material displayed near the entrance. This statement, which outlined the rationale behind this installation in terms of the motivation for AIDS activism itself, dedicated "Democracy" in its entirety to Bill Olander, who, though gravely ill at the time, attended the opening. No less moving, however, were the little touches: the presence of a ramp that the artists procured for placement outside the door to the gallery to guarantee smooth entry for all visitors, including those using wheelchairs.

The title "Social Aesthetics" is not mine. My friend Bill Olander coined it back in 1982 as the title of his essay in the catalogue for "Art and Social Change," an exhibition he organized for the Allen Memorial Art Museum at Oberlin College. Bill was supposed to have written the essay that I am now writing, but on March 18, 1989, he died of AIDS. I borrow his title for two reasons: first, to emphasize the loss that I and the members of Group Material feel in his absence; and second, because the concept of a socially based aesthetic corresponds with the terms of a "cultural activism" that can encompass both the radical militancy of ACT UP and other activists and the work of artists who, like Group Material, use the symbolic sphere of culture to effect social and political change.

It is now almost a decade since the twelve original members of Group Material decided to reject the conventional options open to them as artists just out of school, to work outside the art marketplace, and to adopt a collective identity. Intent on developing an art that could deal critically with cultural, political, and social issues, Group Material decided to use collaborative methods and to engage, whenever possible, with other community-based and activist groups. This allowed them to extend their encounter with political and social issues well beyond the traditional limits of aesthetic form and content.

During the 1980s, the term "cultural activist" has been applied— sometimes generously, sometimes exclusively—to a variety of cultural practices that criticize mainstream culture and the institutions that regulate it, often embodying the cultural expressions of nonmainstream communities. A conjunction of theoretical, cultural, and historical circumstances made this reclassification of oppositional culture into cultural activism possible. On a theoretical level, this shift was in part a result of debates about the Marxist theory of ideology which took place in France in the late 1960s. The political theorist Louis Althusser was central to this critical reformulation.

In his essay "Ideology and Ideological State Apparatuses," Althusser reiterated the traditional Marxist understanding that the ruling ideology, which is manifest in cultural production, facilitates the perpetuation of existing dispositions of power and privilege in society. But departing from more parochial Marxists, Althusser insisted that the dominant ideology is not simply a passive, "superstructural" reflection of social relations determined by the economic "base" of material production; rather, he emphasized, ideology and the social relations of production are joined together by a complex, reciprocal action of mutual determination. What is more, Althusser envisioned the cultural sites of ideological production and reproduction as zones of symbolic contestation, not only emblematic of, but crucial to, class struggle. Oppositional or critical cultural practices, he argued, have the power to destabilize and hinder the reproductive powers of the dominant ideology. Al-

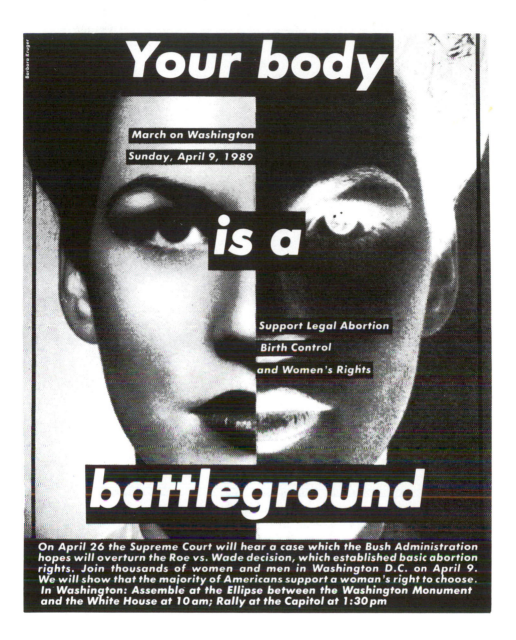

Barbara Kruger, poster for the March for Women's Lives (march for reproductive freedom) in Washington, D.C., April 9, 1989.

thusser's acknowledgment that cultural practices can possess critical powers, and that these are of direct consequence to class struggle, provided the theoretical precondition for conferring "activist" status onto cultural production.[2]

Since Althusser's day, issues of race and sexual difference have been recognized by many (though not, alas, by all) on the left to be as important as class is in any social transformation that is worthy of the term "revolutionary." The anticolonial uprisings in North Africa, Southeast Asia, and elsewhere from the 1950s on, and the rise of a massive American civil rights movement during the 1960s expanded the basis for a critique of Euro-American culture to include institutionalized racism that colonizes, distorts, and in other ways renders invisible people of color and their forms of cultural expression. From the mid to late sixties, the rise of the feminist movement, and, from the end of the sixties, the struggle for lesbian and gay rights forceably added the issue of sexual difference to the critique of Western "humanist" culture. Thus critiques arising out of these struggles that centered on the issues of race and gender, as well as class, led to the multifaceted assault on modernist culture that emerged during the 1960s. No great synthesis between these issues ever emerged, nor is it likely that anything more synthetic than a coalition is theoretically practicable. To this day, women, gays, and lesbians have to argue for the political status of their struggle, which many men on the left continue to dismiss as mere "personal" matters, which detract from what they insist is the only truly revolutionary concern—class struggle.

Intent upon the creation, organization and promotion of an art dedicated to social communication and political change, Group Material has used a variety of strategies to explore issues that bear directly or indirectly upon class, race, and gender, and their interface with culture. When the collective inquires, as it often does, "How is culture made, and who is it for?" it presumes the ideological inscription of oppressive social relations within the dominant culture. Group Material proceeds from the assumption that conventional definitions of culture can and should be exposed as conservative instruments of social reproduction. The idealist view of history and aesthetics, which has determined the organizational and discursive practices of museum culture since its formation, highlights the transhistorical over the concretely historical, the eternal over the contingent, and the apolitical over the political in whatever museums put on display. In this way the aestheticism of the museum corresponds with the interests of the ruling elite that supports these institutions while they, in turn, legitimate the power of that elite.

Most of Group Material's projects can be understood as attempts to endow the question, "How is culture made, and who is it for?" with a seductive physical dimension that prompts the spectator to interrogate the relation between the dominant culture and specific social and political issues. At the same time, Group Material's collaborative, heterodox method results in situations that afford glimpses of a very different "culture," one that privileges pluralism and social justice over the maintenance of canonical laws and social privilege.

Most often their projects result in installations, as the ones they initiated in their storefront space at 244 East 13th Street in September 1980. From the start this collective used the art of exhibition as a form of montage, one that recalls the historical avant-gardist tradition. If their art evokes the spirit of Berlin Dada, however, it is not so much individual works by John Heartfield, Hannah Höch, and Raoul Haussmann that it summons, as the kaleidoscopic installation of the 1920 International Dada Fair in Berlin. In the manner of montage, Group Material's installations create a friction between elements—a productive, discursive friction that sparks improbable insights into a given theme. Yet unlike the 1920 Dada Fair, Group Material's installations always proceed from the choice of a socially significant theme to the selection of cultural artifacts that will, ideally, illuminate that theme and provoke debate.

Thus, in December 1980, Group Material analyzed "alienation" from a Marxist perspective, with an installation of works that helped not only to "express" this ubiquitous malaise but to reveal its dependence upon capitalist social relations. As the announcement for *Alienation* put it:

[We get up in the morning][But the morning isn't ours][We get ready for work][But the work isn't ours][We go to the workplace][But the workplace isn't ours][We work all day][But the day isn't ours][We produce a lot of wealth][But the wealth isn't ours][We get paid some money][But the money isn't ours][We go back home][But the home isn't ours][We would like to be social][But society isn't ours]

In addition to the art installation, Group Material also staged an "Alienation Film Festival," which included premieres of works by local independent filmmakers, and a screening of James Whale's 1931 classic, *Frankenstein*. As part of the project they invited Bertell Ollman, a professor of politics at New York University and author of a book on alienation, to speak before an audience at the Group Material storefront about alienation and its significance in advanced capitalist societies.

Staging this film festival, and inviting a teacher to speak at their space suggest the special role that social interaction has played within Group Material's collaborative method. Whereas modern artists have an especially high regard for works of art that seem to be the organic embodiment of their interactive material processes, Group Material engages in interactive cultural processes in order to effect social communication in the hopes of facilitating social and political change. Thus, when Group Material decided to rent their storefront space, they intended their gallery to become part of the social fabric of the existing neighborhood. This was evident not only in the film screenings, parties, and discussions that they held there from time to time, but in the strong populist element that their installations possessed. The most striking manifestation of this populist impulse—and of the desire to identify with their neighbors and their concerns—was the exhibition "The People's Choice" (later renamed "Arroz con Mango").

The first part of "Arroz con Mango" consisted of a letter that Group Material distributed among their "friends and neighbors of 13th Street." Dated December 22, 1980, the letter began, "Group Material is the gallery that opened this October at 244 East 13th Street. We are a group of young people who have been organizing different kinds of events in our storefront. We've had parties, art shows, movies and art classes for the kids who are always rushing in and out." After breaking the ice they came right to the point. They were interested in showing "things that might not usually find their way into an art gallery: the things that you personally find beautiful, the objects that you keep for your own pleasure, the objects that have meaning for you, your family and your friends." The resulting installation included religious imagery, dolls in fancy dresses, family photos, amateur paintings, and clay bowls; it featured a knitted bag from Guatemala, a collection of PEZ candy dispensers, a Rembrandt reproduction, and a poster of Robert Morris, oiled up and posing with chains as a crypto-fascist, S&M dreamboat. Notwithstanding its anarchic potential, everything was exhibited with that deference to order and clarity that are the *ne plus ultra* of aesthetic display—and of the much more heterodox displays of Group Material as well.

At best, the populist impulse reveals a determination to open the domain of "culture" to forms of expression that belong to culturally and economically marginalized groups. It can also effect transformations of the cultural site in a somewhat different sense. Group Material created art for spaces that, in an era of wholesale privatization, are in few ways worthy of the designation "public." In projects like "DA ZI BAOS" (March 1982) and "Subculture" (September 1983) Group Material attempted to restore the public dimension to such spaces by temporarily transforming the terms of the discourse that usually takes place there.

"DA ZI BAOS" consisted of alternating red and yellow monochromatic posters that were illegally wheatpasted to the facade of the defunct S. Klein's department store on Union Square. The posters featured statements solicited by Group Material from people in the area around Union Square—a public space whose ethnic and economic diversity and rich history of political struggle were being threatened with eradication at the time by aggressive private

Group Material, *DA ZI BAOS*, 1982. Union Square, New York City.

"development." Group Material also collected statements from six political
and service organizations. CISPES (Committee in Solidarity with the People
of El Salvador) contributed the following: "'If they kill me I will rise again
in the Salvadoran people, in the mass organizations.'—Archbishop Romero,
assassinated by the junta 3/24/80. 'They have risen up and asked the American people for their solidarity because their struggle is our struggle.'"

"Subculture" consisted of sometimes trenchant, often amusing, artist-
designed posters which Group Material commissioned to provide temporary
relief from the advertising one commonly encounters in the ad space above
the windows of New York subway cars. The artist Vanalyne Green, who was
then working as a secretary, contributed a poster showing grimy coffee cups
photographed from above, to which she added the following narrative caption: "Sometimes when he asks me to bring him a cup of coffee I do so. But
I pour the coffee in a dirty cup that has a ring of dried coffee around the inside of the cup. And I smile as I hand it to him."

The members of Group Material dealt with the issue of American racism when, in June 1981 they staged "Atlanta: An Emergency Exhibition."
This show explored the social ramifications of the murder in Atlanta of
twenty-eight black children over a period of two years. The collective intended, in the words of the press release, to go "beyond the shock, beyond
the sensationalism, beyond the anger, the guilt and the ribbons," to find the

"history" and the "sense" behind the killings.[3] Among the powerful works that were lent to this show were those by Faith Ringgold, Candace Hill-Montgomery, Jerry Kearns, and the Madame Binh Graphics Collective. That part of Group Material's process that entails interaction with communities of interest was especially strong in this instance. Fifty local schoolchildren who were enrolled in a program called "Arts and Education: Learning to Read through the Arts," in which Tim Rollins (then a member of Group Material) taught, created paintings in response to the question, "Who's Killing the Kids?" Those paintings, which in many cases went beyond the crime to consider its social context, were a focal point of the installation.

In 1984 Group Material installed "Timeline: A Chronicle of U.S. Intervention in Central and Latin America" at P.S.1 in Queens. Three years after they abandoned their attempt to interact with a specific working-class community by giving up their storefront space on East 13th Street, they still interacted with groups, such as those who were militating against U.S. interference in Central and Latin America.[4] "Timeline" was their contribution to "Artists Call," a community-wide artists' response to American intervention in El Salvador and Nicaragua. CISPES provided Group Material with a list of American interventions, which the artists translated into characteristically striking pictorial and sculptural terms. Among these, a pile of ground coffee, a bunch of bananas, and copper plates suggested the nature of American "interests" in the region. One year later, Group Material joined with the art community again, but in an altogether different sense. They were invited to participate in the Whitney Biennial. The immediate result was *Americana*, a radically eclectic blend of appliances, commercial designs, art, and other forms of decor. Isolated from the rest of the Biennial in the Whitney's ground floor gallery, it commented wryly on the strictly retail biennial survey of American art by offering a self-contained alternative to it. The long-term result of the Whitney invitation was that, as the decade proceeded, Group Material, like so many other activist-artists, became part of the international contemporary art circuit, for which they were asked to devise works in situations that are as far removed from the realm of community-based and grass-roots political activism as the concept of "arts and leisure" suggests. Such a transformation of the institutional circumstances that frame their project threatened to trivialize and neutralize it.

In this sense, the Dia Art Foundation—once better known for its commitment to the abstract and spiritual in art—presented Group Material with a considerable challenge when it invited the collective to organize an ambitious project. How could the collective—then consisting of Doug Ashford, Julie Ault, and Felix Gonzalez-Torres—maintain the edge to their cultural critique? How could they preserve the emancipatory intent and meaningful community interaction that had typified their original project while moving at the behest of a rich cultural foundation to the very heart of Soho, the torpid and trendy shopping district in lower Manhattan? How, under these conditions, could they ensure that their characteristic engagement with groups involved in potentially life-and-death struggles would not degenerate into a form of cultural colonization and exploitation? How, indeed.

Group Material responded to this challenge by relying upon collaborative processes as they had all along. First they selected the theme of democracy in America and divided it into smaller topics from which this unwieldy object of investigation might be interrogated. For reasons that have as much if not more to do with the artists' lived experience as they do with expertise and study, the collective decided upon the following four topics: "Education and Democracy," "Politics and Election," "Cultural Participation," and "AIDS and Democracy: A Case Study."

The first manifestations of "Democracy" were the roundtable discussions, in which Group Material invited people from pertinent communities of interest to gather at Dia for an informal discussion; one roundtable discussion was held for each of the four subtopics. These were opportunities for the collective to reach out to representatives of particular interest groups, while engaging them as participants in and coproducers of Group Material's cultural process. As the transcripts from the roundtable discussions reveal, the artists listened far more than they spoke. This is entirely consistent with their ongoing desire to learn about the central issues of, say, the public school system from those who are engaged in the day-to-day struggles of trying to educate.[5] In this way the artists came away from the discussions with insights into how best to proceed with the job of organizing the second manifestation of "Democracy," the installations.

The roundtable discussions also helped Group Material to map out the third part of "Democracy," the town meetings. Like the roundtable discussions, one town meeting was scheduled to coincide with each of the four installations. As befits the designation, these meetings were open fora for public discussion. Envisioning the town meetings from the beginning as indispensable parts of "Democracy," Group Material ensured that the installations would not be taken for the whole of their project, and that their project, moreover, would not be construed as an extended diagnostic session during which three participants in an artists' collective take the national pulse in four ways and find it erratic. As it turns out, however, there was never any great danger that the installations, even taken on their own, would have led to this conclusion.

Group Material installation at the Dia Art Foundation, New York, *Education and Democracy*,
September 14–October 8, 1988.

Group Material installation at the Dia Art Foundation, New York, *Politics and Election*,
October 15–November 12, 1988.

Group Material installation at the Dia Art Foundation, New York, *Cultural Participation*, November 19–December 10, 1988.

Group Material installation at the Dia Art Foundation, New York, *AIDS & Democracy: A Case Study,* December 17, 1988–January 14, 1989.

Public education in America today—especially in our inner cities—is best known for gross inequities in the quality of education, for functionally illiterate high school graduates, for truancy, for wholesale physical deterioration of schools, for the violence in and around schools, and for its Byzantine administrative structures. Under these conditions it seems certain that a considerable proportion of tomorrow's electorate—like today's—will be ill-equipped to protect what democratic freedoms it has. The press release for "Education and Democracy," the first installment of Group Material's "Democracy," contained the following quotation from Thomas Jefferson:

In every government on earth is some trace of human weakness, some germ of corruption and degeneracy, which cunning will discover, and wickedness insensibly open, cultivate and improve. Every government degenerates when trusted to the rulers of the people alone. The people themselves therefore are its only safe depositories. And to render even them safe, their minds must be improved to a certain degree. This indeed is not all that is necessary, though it be essentially necessary. An amendment of our constitution must here come in aid of the public education. The influence over government must be shared among all the people.

To take Jefferson at his word is to conclude that democracy in America is in jeopardy, and has been for some time. Of course, education alone cannot be held accountable for the fact that so few Americans are moved to participate in the electoral process. But neither the consensus that American public education today is in crisis, nor the fact that only 20 percent of those eligible to vote in this country did so in the last election can prevent the talking heads of the mass media from taking every opportunity to brag about our flawless system of government. Who, for example, can forget the spectacle of Dan Rather, beaming from among the youthful throngs in Tiananmen Square last June, as if the song the demonstrators were singing were "America the Beautiful" and not "The Internationale"?

Despite their decidedly critical viewpoint, Group Material managed to avoid the pitfall of assuming the smug posture of condemnation and superiority that has proven irresistible to many on the embattled left. The installation of "Education and Democracy" was a case in point. The room contained four rows of classroom chairs arranged on a bias, as if in perpetual salute to the American flag that hung from the wall nearby. The walls were painted black, with the title of the show written directly on the wall in a well-rounded chalk script. Other samples of writing in chalk—and erasure—added to the scholastic decor. This pedagogical theater avoided didacticism in part through the playfulness of the installation, and in part through the inclusion of largely ambiguous artworks by Peter Halley, Mitchell Syrop, John Ahearn, Lorna Simpson, and Andy Warhol, among others. Mixing school and art-gallery props removed the possibility that the installation would be dominated either by argument or irony. This cut both ways: the thematic context and the presence of numerous objects that are not conventionally classified as art imposed decidedly unorthodox readings on the "Art." At the same time, many of the objects that were conceived and executed by students and teachers conveyed their message in bold and expressive forms. Take, for example, *Question Mark(s)* by Meryl Meisler and the Drop Ins of Roland Hays Intermediary School. This collaborative work framed the southwest corner of the space with two giant question marks: one backwards, the other upside-down. The surfaces of the question marks consisted of a continuous layer of photographic testimony, produced by the students, that literally underscored in red the school's ongoing physical deterioration. This collaboration between students and teachers—only one among many collaborations in the show—confirmed the presence within the school system of innovative teaching methods, methods that go well beyond the limits of colorful children's drawings.

"Education and Democracy" also provided a historical framework, pointing to some of the social conditions that spurred the progressive movement in American teaching that flourished from the 1930s until the Cold War. Three Lewis Hine photographs in the show documented the living conditions for uneducated working-class children during the second decade of this century. By no coincidence, this was precisely the historical moment when John Dewey outlined the basis for modern American progressive education in the book he titled, significantly, *Democracy and Education* (1916). The social conditions substantiated by Hine's photographs were among those that lent urgency to Dewey's project. In Group Material's installation, these photographs were placed near four small paintings by students in Keith Rambert's class at Brooklyn's Boys and Girls High School. The point of these paintings was clear from the words inscribed across their surfaces: "School gives a sense of direction. (Study! Study!)," "Class is long," and "LEARN TO EARN." The juxtaposition of Hine's photographs and Rambert's small paintings brought to mind one underlying, yet fundamental and recurring aspect of the discourse on education: the degree to which public education is governed by a productive imperative that will dominate people's lives long after they graduate school.

Thomas Jefferson understood—as did many Enlightenment thinkers—that any public instruction that hoped to protect democracy would have to balance practical training with other forms of edification and stimulation. Nearly a century later John Dewey sought to recast this more or less "organic" concept of education. Regarding democracy as a "mode of associated living, of conjoint communicated experience," Dewey argued that the more numerous and socially diverse the citizens of a nation are, the more worthy of the name "democracy" that nation becomes. Democracy, for Dewey, was a dynamic social process that could, indeed must, be advanced by continuously "breaking down . . . those barriers of class, race, and national territory which [keep] men from perceiving the full import of their activity."[6]

During the second half of the nineteenth century—that is, between Jefferson and Dewey—popular education really emerged in the industrialized nations of the West. From the start, it was the site of a discursive conflict. To one side were those for whom education simply meant the preparation of an entire class of people for efficient and docile labor. On the other side were reformers, who saw education as a means of helping people to rise from the class into which they were born, and as a means of combating the increasing atomization of individual life in an era of massive industrialization. Latter-day pragmatist that he was, Dewey claimed to reject the "organic" Rousseauean (or Jeffersonian) model and set out to redefine instrumental logic more radically than had previous reformers. Henceforth, he hoped, the meaning of "efficiency" would no longer be divorced from broader social and personal considerations.

When social efficiency as measured by product or output is urged as an ideal in a would-be democratic society, it means that the depreciatory estimate of the masses characteristic of an aristocratic community is accepted and carried over. But if democracy has a moral and ideal meaning, it is that a social return be demanded from all and that opportunity for development of distinctive capacities be afforded all. The separation of the two aims in education is fatal to democracy; the adoption of the narrower meaning of efficiency deprives it of its essential justification.[7]

During the Reagan era conservative ideologues in Washington sought to restore the means-ends logic that Dewey decried—and the authoritarian methods that correspond with it—in order to "reform" the American public school system. Former secretary of education William Bennett couched his assault on the existing approaches to public education in the sort of devious language that became a hallmark of Reagan appointees. "Anti-determinism" and "anti-relativism" were the names he used to describe the practice he advocated—no longer making allowances for childrens' socioeconomic, ethnic, or racial background, whether in the material used to teach them or in the standards applied to determine their success and failure. Teaching was going to get tough.[8]

Content, character, and choice—Mr. Bennett's "three C's"—identified his formula for successful schools. "Content" designated an insistence on materials that derive from our "common" (read: Western, white, and largely male) cultural heritage. "Character" denoted Mr. Bennett's plan to infuse our schools with patriarchal, Judeo-Christian family values, and the kind of discipline epitomized by one of the education secretary's favorite role models, Joe Clark.[9] "Choice," in this case, should not be confused with reproductive rights, since Mr. Bennett intended that sex education become moral education, in which lessons in sexual abstinence are taught with a liberal sprinkling of such words as "modesty" and "chastity."[10] By "choice," Mr. Bennett referred to the parents' (the plural, Bennett's own, denotes his disapproval of single-parent families) ability to decide which school their children should attend; a laudable idea in theory which, in the absence of massive infusions of funds for the redevelopment of inner-city schools, would condemn certain children to very long rides in buses, assuming that there would be room for them in school at the other end.

Other considerations that have fueled the conservative educational agenda were also alluded to in Group Material's installation. The struggle over bilingual teaching was mapped out in a diagrammatic, visually striking work called *U.S. English No Pasara*, which was created by Ed Morales, Tom McGlynn, Diana Caballero, Elaine Ruiz, and the Committee for a Multilingual New York. Consisting of strategically aligned quotations from those involved, as well as their names and political affiliations, *U.S. English No Pasara* delineated a startling genealogy of contemporary American xenophobia. It exposed the ideological basis for "U.S. English," a nonprofit organization that seeks to ensure monolingual education in America. Among those quoted are Phyllis Schlafly, Norman Podhoretz, the members of the Council for Inter-American Security (i.e., John Singlaub, Adolfo Calero, and other belligerent patriots), and—always my personal favorite—the congenitally macho former secretary of education, chain smoker, and current drug czar, William Bennett. Bennett's testimony consisted of the following: "The evidence has become increasingly clear that bilingual education is doing very little to help students learn English." If ideology can be defined as that which passes unnoticed as common sense, then this nugget is ideology in its crystalline form.[11]

Group Material's education installation was a model of its kind. Its juxtapositions prompted a broad range of insights into its theme, foregrounding the relationship between education and social destiny, while offering proof of imaginative approaches to teaching in a climate of political torpor and bureaucratic intransigence. It also fulfilled that aspect of the group's mandate that concerns the definition of culture and its consequences. By placing art works by well-known artists in these circumstances—and thereby extracting new meanings from them—Group Material revealed once again how contingent meaning is upon the circumstances of display. Finally, the installation

Ed Morales with Tom McGlynn, Diana Caballero, Elaine Ruiz and the Committee for a ▶
Multilingual New York, and Victory Arts, *U.S. English No Pasara*, 1988.

Conservative Mandate

Phyllis Schlafly
conservative activist

Bilingual education is a device to provide jobs to Spanish-speaking school personnel

Dr. Robert Rossier
Accuracy in Academia

Bilingual students are required to know a great deal about left-wing union leaders

Norman Podhoretz
editor, *Commentary*

One does a great disservice to the children of immigrants if one doesn't force them to learn English

William Bennett
Secretary of Education

The evidence has become increasingly clear that bilingual education is doing very little to help students learn English

U.S. English

S.I. Hayakawa
co-founder, U.S. English

Tens of thousands of so-called bilingual teachers with temporary certifications cannot even speak English

Linda Chavez
President, U.S. English
(Highest-ranking Hispanic in the Reagan Administration)

I got a "C" in the only Spanish class I took

William Everdell
History Teacher, St. Ann's School, Brooklyn

Bilingual education keeps minorities ignorant in a way just short of preventing them from reading and writing at all, which is one way black slavery was maintained in the American South

Steven Symms
Senator from Idaho

Many Americans feel like strangers in their own neighborhood, aliens in their own country

Council for Inter-American Security
Bilingual education is a threat to national security

Members Include:
Adolfo Calero, FDN
John Singlaub, World Anti-Communist League
Col. Lawrence Tracey, Low-Intensity Warfare Specialist
L. Francis Douchey, author, The Communist Connection & Guatemala

English First

Rusty Butler
Council for Inter-American Security

The language situation in the U.S. could feed and guide terrorism and has serious implications for national security

Larry Pratt
president of English First, a project of Committee to Protect the Family

There is a moral obligation to learn English. These radicals (supporters of bilingual ed) make a good living from the misery and suffering of their countrymen.

Lou Zaeske
American Ethnic Coalition

Hispanic leaders are political padrones who are exploiting their own people by keeping them less well-educated in English so they'll always have a group to represent

John Tanton
co-founder, U.S. English

The language question is derivative of immigration policy. Large numbers of immigrants create communities where English is not spoken, language ghettos used by self-serving ethnic politicians

Dan Alexander
Save Our Schools
Convicted in Dec. 1986 of racketeering and extortion

Imagine a first-rate chemistry teacher who also must be fluent in Vietnamese or Swahili?

Population Environmental Balance
(John Tanton sits on board)

Ran an ad in San Francisco Chronicle blaming traffic jams on immigration

"U.S. English No Pasara"
an Installation by Ed Morales

proved that to redefine "culture" more inclusively, as a social process rather than an ossified canon, is not to throw out the proverbial baby with the bath water—a claim that conservatives who favor the traditional, canonical view of culture invariably level at their opponents.[12]

It would be more difficult to make such undivided claims for the two subsequent installations, "Politics and Election" and "Cultural Participation." I imagine my dissatisfaction with the former was partly unfair, having something to do with displaced anger, with my personal feeling that presidential elections have become wasteful burlesques. But if that's the way I feel, then why wouldn't I have relished an installation that revived the Iran-Contra Scandal and raked Ollie North over the coals, that mocked politicians and state power, that criticized the national love affair with symbolism and its impatience with substance, that ridiculed the electoral orchestration of corn pone and sentiment? Somehow it just seemed arch and, sadly, ineffectual.

But what would have been "effectual" under the circumstances? After all, this installation contained some remarkable artworks: Leon Golub's appropriately diminutive portraits of our petty masters (1976); Hans Haacke's *MoMA Poll* (1970); Mike Glier's prickly symbols of male power (*Fancy Men's Clubs*, 1988); Christian Marclay's electric cord that joins a microphone at one end with a hangman's noose at the other (*Hangman's Noose*, 1987); three of Christy Rupp's *Rubble Rats* (1979); and more. "Politics and Election" also included signs of Group Material's finesse. Upon entering, the viewer was confronted by the glow of the great communicator—a TV tuned in to network broadcasting—propped anthropomorphically on a white pedestal that, painted with bands of red and blue, looked more like a speaker's podium than a pedestal. Behind it was a massive forty-foot American flag. Together, they effectively sent up the rhetorical excess of the electoral potlatch.

In retrospect, this juxtaposition may have been the most significant one in the installation. The 1988 election will be remembered as the year television staged the theatrical transformation of George Bush. In the space of one short interview, when Dan Rather ineffectually broached the subject of Bush's role in the Iran-contra fiasco, the well-coached, not to say eager, vice president transformed himself from a reticent Northeastern Dr. Jekyll to the ever pugnacious Mr. Hyde that he remains today. The 1988 election was also the one in which television, in the hands of the Republican National Committee and its master of the grotesque, Roger Ailes, gave birth to the "negative" campaign ad. With little resistance from an inept Democratic party, the racist appeal of the revolving-door-justice pitch and the sublime environmental rhetoric of the Boston Harbor ad effectively manipulated the electorate to turn the tide and clinch the Republican victory.

Would Group Material's installation have seemed more "effectual" had it appeared somewhere other than at the epicenter of the downtown art scene? Perhaps. I can imagine that if it had been located where a more heterogeneous public could have seen it, the visitors' responses would have consisted of something other than heads bobbing in assent. Even so, the show still could have ventured further afield. There are, for example, ways to address the interface between American consumer culture, the construction of consensus, and the procurement of consent. Group Material is hardly oblivious to such issues and has touched on them in other circumstances. One solution to the problems with "Politics and Election" was implicit in the artists' decision to follow it with the one called "Cultural Participation."

Whereas "Politics and Election" represented the American electoral politics too simply as a travesty, "Cultural Participation"—an ambiguous name at best—set its sights on the effects of consumer culture on American life. Upon entering the installation, my eyes fixed upon a long line of little cellophane bags that circumnavigated much of the interior like a dado from hell. These snackfood bags—the result of Group Material's visit to a single supermarket—carried brand names and bore designs that, consistent with advanced capitalist marketing strategies, target consumers, identifying them according to their ethnicity, class, and age. The display of snack foods suggested one possible interpretation of the title, "Cultural Participation." Cultural participation consists to a very great extent in the seemingly insignificant decisions that Americans make by the score every day when they engage in individual acts of consumerism. Cultural identity is not arrived at genetically, nor is it only the result of learning. We define ourselves culturally every day in our seemingly involuntary and intuitive responses to a closed circuit of cultural representations. Fueled by an economically motivated compulsion to expand, consumer industries tap our desire and offer to accommodate our every wish; but first, they create those wishes. Though numbering in the dozens (with no two bags alike), this decorative product line could but hint at our national good fortune, at the abundance of our freedom to choose.

The theme of democracy as a tainted cornucopia was elaborated further by the inclusion of individual art works. Thus there was a product-line sculpture by the compulsively shopping formalist Haim Steinbach. One of Richard Prince's photographs of Marlboro men suggested the lasting imaginary appeal of Western mythology. Six color photographs by Lance Carlson examined the representation of classy consumer goods by a local upscale department store. Four photographs by Vikky Alexander of the West Edmonton Mall in Alberta attested to the horror that is the world's largest shopping center. But an especially significant presence in "Cultural Participation," one

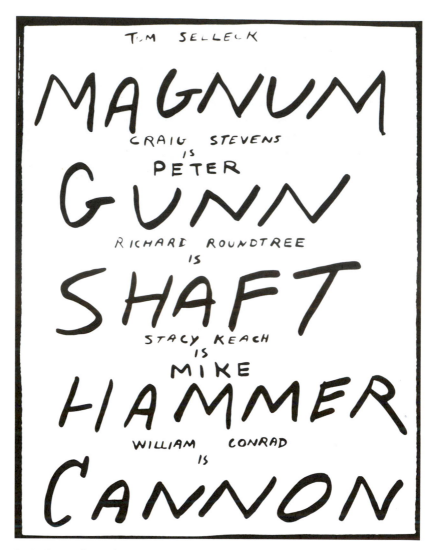

Jessica Diamond, *5 Dicks,* 1988-89.

which indicated the pertinence of consumer culture to democracy and to electoral politics, was a film that Group Material screened continuously throughout the exhibition. That film was George Romero's 1979 paean to the suburban shopping mall and its implicit effects on people, *Dawn of the Dead*.

The myriad seductions of this consumer culture tend to level difference and discourage dissent. With television as its principal conveyor of messages and the primary purveyor of acceptable, functional social types, consumer culture holds out the continuous promise of fulfillment. To enter paradise all you need is to interpolate yourself as the voluntary subject of the dominant ideology, whip out your wallet, and make another purchase. With such bliss at your fingertips, who needs politics? In his book *Captains of Consciousness*, Stuart Ewen locates in the 1920s the emergence of the historical processes that made it possible for American consumer culture to inhibit the expression of mass political dissent.[13] At that time advertising joined with the concept of buying on credit to erode the collective social identity of those who had been commodity producers; henceforth they would gaze into the adman's mirror and see themselves as consumers. But the realization of this social transformation had to await the postwar era, when a wartime economy functioning at capacity shifted from arms production to production of consumer goods. The middle class—which had expanded considerably with full employment during the war and savings compelled by rationing—was pressed into service sustaining the growth of the consumer economy. As the construction of postwar suburbs proved, the captains of industry understood that building and selling homes was the most crucial element if the economy were to continue to grow. And as the "captains of consciousness" knew, the ideological lubricant that was essential to this machinery was a compound of the nuclear family and the American Dream. To be sure, the suppression of political dissent in this country was not exclusively the product of the new consumerism. The Cold War atmosphere of fear and rabid anticommunism also restricted social resistance. And the history of the Congress of Industrial Organizations (C.I.O.) during the later 1940s, culminating in its reunion with the A.F. of L. in 1955, describes the often brutal suppression of progressive forces within the American labor movement.[14]

Group Material's "Cultural Participation" tended to outline only the contemporary consequences of this history. The gallery was appointed with four sets of redwood picnic tables, piled with magazines, others appointed with fast-food menus, still others sporting air fresheners. Amidst the piles of mass-circulation magazines there were also some deviant titles like *Anarchy Comics* and *Artpolice*. Group Material found other ways to make sure that recreation and the quick fix did not dominate the space unimpeded. A color photograph by Tina Barney of indolent rich kids lounging in a tony interior was given edge, if not substance, by its installation across the room from five altogether more modest black and white shots of old buildings in ruinous states marked, "DEMOLISHED BY NEGLECT." The latter were taken by members of Detroit's Urban Center for Photography as part of their collaborative work intended to stop such "neglect." The project was initiated when a local photographer, Keith Piascezny, tried to deliver a picture of a woman and her baby to her at home where he shot it. Discovering that she had been evicted, he decided to fix the large print to the facade of the building.

"Cultural Participation," like "Politics and Election" before it, found novel ways to articulate its theme. Yet both shows ultimately lacked the capacity to resonate historically; or to reveal the complexity of the issues involved as "Education and Democracy" had. My point can be stated simply: "Politics and Election" and "Cultural Participation" may each have been less successful on its own than had they been reconceived as a single installation. Had that been possible—and more than scheduling problems would have made this difficult—the interdependence between the failure of electoral politics in this country and the history of American consumer culture could have been disclosed.

Accompanying each of these exhibitions was an open forum where anyone could speak out on the designated subject. What could Group Material have intended by these "town meetings"? Was there irony in that title? Would it have mattered if there was? While organizing a multifaceted examination of democracy in America, it must have seemed important to artists as committed as these to extending the limits of cultural discourse to offer a forum in which real discussion could take place. Since panel discussions inhibit debate by reinforcing the separation between those who speak from one side of a table to those who listen on the other, the idea of an open forum for discussion must have been appealing. And after all, isn't "Town Meeting" just a catchy name to give it? Well, no. As Group Material has helped many people to understand, for everything there is a context, one that determines meaning, sometimes overwhelmingly.

The townsmen's words were heard and weighed, for all knew that it was a petitioner that could not be slighted; it was the river, or the winter, or famine, or Pequots, that spoke through them to the Governor and Council of Massachusetts Bay.

In a town meeting the roots of society were reached. Here the rich gave council, but the poor also; and moreover, the just and the unjust. In this open democracy every opinion had utterance; every objection, every fact, every acre of land, every bushel of rye, its entire weight. The moderator was the passive mouthpiece, and the vote of the town, like the vane on the turret overhead, free for every wind to turn, and always turned by the last and strongest breath."[15]

Written over a century ago by Ralph Waldo Emerson, this idyll to the town meeting is already steeped in nostalgia. This sentiment is apparent in the notion of a method of government that is the perfect and inescapable product of natural forces—of rivers overflowing their banks and harsh New England winters; and of human forces that are, in Emerson's writing, tantamount to

Freedom of Speech

Norman Rockwell, *Freedom of Speech*, 1943.

natural ones at their most uncontrollable: those native Americans that he casts as aggressors. Emerson's enthusiasm for the town meeting echoed the sentiments of Alexis de Tocqueville and Thomas Jefferson, whose comments are excerpted in the published version of the address he delivered to the people of Concord, Massachusetts, in 1835.

Nostalgia for simpler, arguably more innocent times has lost none of its appeal. "Town meetings" are in vogue today, like many other manifestations of American vernacular taste that now possess the auratic appeal of the vaguely historical and the historically vague. Ted Koppel now stages "town meetings" for the global village on ABC television, most famously when he brought together Israelis and Palestinians in the Holy City to partake of New England's governmental legacy to the world. Frequently with the financial assistance of the Annenberg CPB Project, Fred Friendly has produced ten thirteen-part programs on a variety of topics including the constitution, ethics in America, terrorism, AIDS, and health care. As broadcast on NET, these shows partake heavily in the code of the town meeting. (The Annenberg CPB Project also distributes them as complete college courses.) Nor is the current electronic infatuation with the town meeting unprecedented. Starting in 1935, a man named George V. Denny conducted a radio show called "America's Town Meeting of the Air," which stayed on the air until ABC dropped it in 1956.

Is it only a coincidence that the "town meeting"—such as it is—should undergo a revival at a time when the range of political debate has been narrowed, and when political discussion has been sacrificed in favor of telegenic sloganeering? Ben H. Bagdikian has noted that the "lords of the global village" today are but a small fraction of the corporate and state-run entities that controlled our sources of information as little as six years ago. He has argued that satellite technology, combined with a tendency among conservative world leaders to further privatize the airwaves, has endowed these companies with unprecedented power. And yet Bagdikian claims that it is not "free enterprise," as such, that is incompatible with the purposes of public information and debate. Rather, as he points out, "It was assumed that once governments got out of the way, the 'free flow of information' and power of the public 'to ascertain and appraise events' would be made possible by free-enterprise media. They were correct. The problem today is not free enterprise but the lack of it."

In other words, the problem is that the monopolistic practices of the Murdochs, Maxwells, and Time/Warners now "exert a homogenizing power over ideas, culture, and commerce that affects populations larger than any in history." These media giants, Bagdikian continues, have two sources of enormous leverage: "They control the public image of national leaders who, as a result, fear and favor the media magnates' political agendas; and they control the information and entertainment that help establish the social, political and cultural attitudes of increasingly larger populations."[16]

This is the context that dictates the mythic function and fetishistic character of the town meeting's renascence. Still, I do not mean to claim that it is delusional for people to assemble in groups to oppose government policies and oppressive social attitudes, or to try to seize control over some crucial aspect of their lives. Clearly, the recent history of AIDS activist groups, from the People with AIDS Coalition to ACT UP and the Community Research Initiative, has disproven that bit of sophistry. But despite the best of intentions, those who traffic in a highly mythologized language are bound to some extent to become the instruments of its use. By calling these open discussions "Town Meetings," Group Material opened themselves up to the criticism that they risked playing into the hands of people who harp on the idea that, "We, at least have such open discussions in this country." And "that's democracy, and that's all there is to it."

On a less parochial note, what seemed most striking about the town meetings was just how disconcerting and contradictory they were. This was due in large part to the fact that they were understood from the beginning as symbolic events: as manifestations of the vanguard world of art. "AIDS and Democracy," which one might have expected to be a vital forum given the presence of a large and successful local activist movement, was no more vital than any other. In fact, perhaps because ACT UP holds its own public meetings every Monday at 7:30 p.m. to deal with the AIDS crisis, this town meeting contained fewer illuminating moments than others. A good deal was said about how individuals can make a difference in the face of this devastating crisis, how important and difficult it is to persevere in forging coalitions when the people you are rallying to the assistance of are considered expendable by the dominant culture. To those AIDS activists who came that night hoping to hear new voices, to learn new strategies to combat government intractability and corporate greed, or to reach new constituencies, however, the meeting was clearly a disappointment. The town meetings stopped well short of effecting that widespread sense of "empowerment" that many people in attendance considered to be their goal. And then there were individuals on hand who complained about the inappropriateness of the "art context." At "AIDS and Democracy" this took place for the fourth time in as many town meetings, thus turning it into something more like the town crier's refrain.

Through it all, the wheels of the tape recorders kept turning, provoking the vague sensation that these not-quite-public proceedings were taking place inside an institutional bubble; that at any moment, as in the great dinner party scene that concludes Luis Buñuel's *The Discreet Charm of the Bourgeoisie*, the massive garage door to the Dia space might suddenly and unceremoniously rise, revealing Mercer Street, the audience for whose benefit all of this was taking place, and the absurdity of our gesture.

Given these circumstances it was hard not to think of Jean Baudrillard, whose theory of the simulacrum (as is all too widely known in the New York art community) implicitly argues against the logical viability of political activism today. It would be hard to refute its relevance to this situation.[17] Finally, the sense of participating in something token, in something staged and recorded, of partaking in a process that, for most of those present, plays little or no part in their daily lives, foregrounded that nostalgic and mythic aspect of the "town meeting's" currency. In this way Group Material's town meetings demonstrated the danger of staging such assemblies from above, as it were. They proved, once again, how intractable are the obstacles in this society to widening the range of political debate, to opening lines of communication between constituencies with divergent interests, and, finally, to effecting a sense of urgency in the midst of a culture that militates in so many sophisticated ways against change.

---

1. When Dennis Cooper and Richard Hawkins organized the exhibition "Against Nature: A Group Show of Work by Homosexual Men" for Los Angeles Contemporary Exhibitions (Jan. 6–Feb. 12, 1988) pressure was applied by some AIDS activists, who regarded the show as irresponsible and retrograde, to prevent individuals from participating in it. A panel discussion that coincided with the exhibition "AIDS: The Artists' Response," organized by Jan Zita Grover for the Hoyt L. Sherman Gallery at Ohio State University was marked by heated debate about what constitutes a legitimate response to the AIDS crisis. In November, Gran Fury executed a piece for The Kitchen in New York that stated, "WITH 42,000 DEAD OF AIDS ART IS NOT ENOUGH." They produced variations of this piece in the window of Printed Matter in New York, in the catalogue to the Ohio State University exhibition, and in the pages of the *Village Voice*—with the mortality figures increasing with every reappearance. For a discussion of this work, see my interview with Gran Fury in Russell Ferguson et al., eds., *Discourses: Conversations in Postmodern Art and Culture* (Cambridge, Mass.: MIT Press, 1990). For a more playful analysis of the entire debate, see John Greyson, "Parma Violets: A Video Script," in Dennis Cooper and Richard Hawkins, eds., *Against Nature: A Show By Homosexual Men*, exhibition catalogue (Los Angeles: Los Angeles Contemporary Exhibitions, 1988), pp. 10-15; also see my "Ideas and Emotions," *Artforum* 27, no. 29 (May 1989), pp. 122-27.

2. "In fact, the class struggle in the ISAs (Ideological State Apparatuses) is indeed an aspect of the class struggle, sometimes an important and symptomatic one: e.g. the antireligious struggle in the eighteenth century, or the 'crisis' of the educational ISA in every capitalist country today." See Louis Althusser, "Ideology and Ideological State Apparatuses (Notes Towards an Investigation)," in Louis Althusser, *Lenin and Philosophy and Other Essays*, trans. Ben Brewster (New York: Monthly Review Press, 1971), p. 185.

3. I want to thank Julie Ault for providing me with access to this press release, as well as to other Group Material documents that made it possible for me to write this essay. This documentation has recently been donated to the Museum of Modern Art library, where it can be found within the archive of Political Art Documentation/Distribution (PAD/D).

4. Affiliation with the Latino community associated with the Taller Latinamericano, for example, was crucial to the success of the June 1982 show "Luchar! An exhibition for the People of Central America . . ." See William Olander, "Material World," *Art In America* 77, no. 1 (January 1989), p. 127.

5. Sometimes there is overlap. Doug Ashford of Group Material is a teacher in the New York City school system and therefore has firsthand knowledge of the issues.

6. John Dewey, *Democracy and Education* (New York: Macmillan Company, 1916; first Free Press Paperback Edition, 1966), p. 87.

7. Ibid., p. 122.

8. See William J. Bennett, "Educating Disadvantaged Children," in *Our Children and Our Country: Improving America's Schools and Affirming the Common Culture* (New York: Simon & Schuster, 1988), esp. pp. 32-33.

9. See Mr. Bennett's tribute to the principal with the baseball bat and the bullhorn in "Let Us Now Praise Good Schools," a title whose evocation of James Agee and Walker Evans's Depression-era tribute to the rural poor, *Let Us Now Praise Famous Men* is an interesting example of conservative appropriations of liberal and left signifiers to suit their diametrically opposed social agenda. Ibid., pp. 37-45.

10. See Bennett, "Sex and the Education of Our Children," in ibid., pp. 98-101.

11. Bennett has also written, "In the last two decades common sense had been beaten, shoved, and kicked around." See "Let Us Now Praise Good Schools," p. 40.

12. Mr. Bennett opposes tampering with the Western cultural canon. See Lillian S. Robinson, "What Culture Should Mean," *Nation* 249, no. 9 (September 25, 1989), pp. 319-21.

13. Stuart Ewen, *Captains of Consciousness: Advertising and the Social Roots of the Consumer Culture* (New York: McGraw-Hill Book Company, 1976).

14. See William H. Chafe, *The Unfinished Journey: America Since World War II* (New York: Oxford University Press, 1986), p. 105ff.

15. Ralph Waldo Emerson, "The Town Meeting," in Ralph Waldo Emerson's Concord Address, *Old South Leaflets*, first series, no. 4 (1883), pp. 1-2.

16. Ben H. Bagdikian, "The Lords of the Global Village," *Nation* 248, no. 23 (June 12, 1989), pp. 820, 807, 811.

17. In January 1987 Group Material organized a show that was critical of this implication in Baudrillard's work, entitled "Resistance, Anti-Baudrillard," at White Columns in New York. The pertinent texts by Baudrillard are: *Simulations*, trans. Paul Foss et al. (New York: Semiotext(e), Inc., 1983), and *In the Shadow of the Silent Majorities*, trans. Paul Foss et al. (New York: Semiotext(e), Inc., 1983).

EDUCATION AND DEMOCRACY

John Ahearn, *Tiger*, 1983.

EDUCATION AND DEMOCRACY

Participants in the roundtable discussion of May 21, 1988:

John Deveaux, executive director of Bronx Educational Services
Rodney Harris, teacher and administrator, Boys and Girls High School, Brooklyn, New York
Catherine Lord, dean of the art department, California Institute of the Arts
Tim Rollins, artist and director of Art & Knowledge Workshop, Bronx, New York
Ira Shor, professor of English at the College of Staten Island and author of several books on education.
Group Material: Doug Ashford, Julie Ault, Felix Gonzalez-Torres

Tim Rollins Let's start with a general question, a paradox really. And that is: one of the most cherished ideas in America, the rationale for compulsory education and public schooling in this country, is the belief that a genuine democracy cannot exist without the full education of all its citizens. So how do you explain our obvious failure in this regard? Even the most optimistic people in government have to admit that the public school system in this country is failing. So the question is this: Does this relationship between democracy and mass education still exist, or is it simply an outdated, romantic notion? Or, to put it another way, is knowledge really power anymore?

Ira Shor I have a few practical things to say based on my experiences this past year as an educator. People who work in isolation should come together to develop a common agenda on education; I think that is the right goal to set right now. Your plan to make the town meeting interdisciplinary and multicultural, and to cross the borders that separate not only people who work in education and art but also people who work at different levels *within* education is important. We must take education seriously as a field with a genuine impact on democracy. But many powerful divisions exist that undermine it. First, the crisis in schools is a very real crisis. And we must recognize that the crisis in urban school systems is very different from the crisis in suburban schools. This urban/suburban distinction often has its roots in class and racial division. Then you have another division between private and public schools. So we have three different types of schools, three different types of education really, to talk about. We can't talk about education generally because what we say about District 5 in urban Manhattan would not be the same for suburban schools. And what we say about public schools in suburban areas would be different for Manhattan schools.

Urban schools face the greatest crisis. Since Reagan was elected in 1980, money has been withdrawn from the public sector, including public health, public housing, mass transit, and public education. Wealth has been transferred to the private sector and to the military, away from needed public programs. The situation is worse where the tax base is the poorest. In rich school districts where the tax base can make up for the withdrawal of federal funds, like in suburbia (where property values are high, family incomes are high, and volunteerism among parents is high), the community itself can supply resources that you simply won't find in urban school districts. In the urban school districts the decline of the public sector has created dramatic effects. High schools especially are in a crisis in urban areas throughout the country. Suburban school districts have different problems. So we might talk about democracy in this context. Can we live with a dual system: a private sector that offers small classes and luxurious environments for rich kids and a public sector that offers those conditions only in the wealthier school districts while poorer, urban school districts are allowed to disintegrate? A town meeting on education and democracy must focus on these several, very different experiences that are offered by American education, depending on where you're born, how much your family earns, what your skin color is, or what your sex is.

Doug Ashford But we also have to consider the community context of schools. There is no way any decision can be made in the school if it isn't a decision of the whole community. That's one of the reasons why progressive principals are trying to institute later hours, weekend openings, and adult education in high schools to make them more community based. But because of the overall structure of a city like New York, such ideas obviously mean restructuring the school system, the school board, and a lot of other bureaucratic baggage. The schools will not change until that happens.

Shor Well, in the sixties we were able to win a lot of things in the public sector. In fact, one thing saving education today is the programs, those liberal programs, started in the sixties, like Head Start for example. They have been successful; the record so far has been good. Head Start is a good example. There is a study called "The Ypsilanti Study" that came out a few years ago that traced the effects of the Head Start program on students over a fifteen- or eighteen-year period. Among those students there is a lower rate of teenage pregnancy, a lower rate of drug addiction, a lower rate of incar-

Diane Neumaier, 1988, *Street Graphic Interventions.* Documentation of informational campaign clandestinely posted throughout the New York subway system by the Metropolitan Health Association.

ceration, a higher rate of high school graduation, and a higher rate of college attendance. All the things that we would hope for were actually achieved by investment in that highly contested program. That's a good example of investing from the bottom up, instead of from the top down. We have to turn priorities on their head, we have to invest in the bottom — which is what the public sector is all about.

Felix Gonzalez-Torres Which goes back to what Tim was asking before: "Is knowledge still power?" Yeah, it is power. The amount of knowledge is a matter of life and death right now for some minorities.

Shor What has happened to the public sector in the last twenty years, in this long conservative period from Nixon through Reagan and Bush, is at the heart of the crisis in education. Public schools that should be promoting democracy are crippled in doing so because of cutbacks and overcrowded classrooms, shabby working conditions, and inadequate wages. Public teachers' salaries were virtually frozen for a period of fifteen years. When they fell behind other professionals, public teaching became less attractive to the most ambitious and aspiring young people. They went elsewhere, into computers, accounting, business, marketing, Wall Street. In general, the idea of public service died because salaries and working conditions became bad in public education.

Another indicator of the crisis in education is the fact that although the black drop-out rate from high schools has been declining over the last ten years, the black attendance rate in college has also been declining. In other words, the percentage of black high school graduates going on to college is decreasing. That's because of the deterioration of the public sector. As tuition has gone up and federal aid has gone down, the cost of state college has become harder for working people and poor people to afford. It's harder to go to college and harder to stay in college. When the door of public higher education is closing, it limits people's aspirations. You think, "What has staying in school got to offer?"

Rollins Not only that, but the school system itself limits students' perceived potential. The kids that I work with have already been "diagnosed" as learning disabled, dyslexic, academic risks, emotionally handicapped — they've been stamped quite firmly. But we also get some kids who are genuinely gifted and read in the top 90 percent of all kids in the country. It's always these "gifted" kids who are the first to get scholarships to a private academy. As the most valuable members of the community, though, it would be great if they could stay here and continue to be part of the community instead of being plucked out. The hidden message is that your neighborhood is someplace to leave. It's surplus baggage and because of your special skill you will transcend it. And this is how the private sector plucks from minority communities the most talented members. Of course, it's good P.R. for business and it tends to be quite dramatic for the kid, but it doesn't help the community.

Shor   There is a word in education called "creaming." There is a 2 percent cream from the top of the bottle. You take the cream and you leave everything else. Then, you can move up a few people from poor backgrounds to demonstrate that the system is democratic. Creaming off some lower-class students for success supports the mythology of an open system. At the bottom, the great ocean of students remains without adequate resources delivered to them. Part of the democratic theme should be a criticism of "creaming."

In 1971 a New York State Supreme Court decision called *Serrano* v. *Priest* said that unequal investment in children's education was unconstitutional and so ordered the state to equalize the amount spent on education of each schoolchild regardless of what neighborhood he or she came from. That decision has never been implemented, but it is now being pushed in about ten states around the country. The unequal investment in schoolchildren has been declared unconstitutional in Kentucky, Texas, and Minnesota.

Ashford   One of the more interesting things about this new empowerment movement is cutting through the psychological dimension that makes communities and people see themselves as one, victims, or two, passive recipients for whatever comes down the pike in terms of government aid. This state of mind has resulted in a lack of responsibility in the communities and a lack of involvement by parents in the schools. So, you have a parent-teacher night, for instance, and the parents who come are parents of the students who are doing well. But what about single-parent families or the working poor? They don't come because of this weird embarrassment that schools have created. In other words, at some point we must talk about community responsibility and empowerment.

Rodney Harris   Our school is 100 percent black or Hispanic; in other words, there is not one white student who attends the school. The principal of our school has actually indicated that he is from the neighborhood. So he has a strong personality. You need that sort of personality in Bedford-Stuyvesant. I mean, high schools in predominantly black neighborhoods are usually dumping grounds for all the students no one else wants. Johnny is misbehaving so they send him to District 17, to this particular high school. What our principal has done in this situation is put in at least twelve hours a day, every day, and I understand he is the only principal who does this. He comes in at 7:30 every morning and doesn't leave school until eleven o'clock

Michael Boane with the Arts Workshop Program of Hospital Audiences Inc., *Untitled*, 1986.

at night. He personally reviews the records of every student who is going to be transferred into the school. Now, if the student is a total knucklehead, if he has a prison record, if he has been thrown out of other schools several times for various reasons, he will deny the student admission to the school. Needless to say, the people downtown, the central school board and the superintendents, are giving him a lot of trouble about that.

Rollins Sounds like the "Joe Clark Syndrome."

Harris It's similar but not the same. Joe Clark has a tendency to criticize people in a very negative fashion. This principal doesn't use negative terms to describe people. Joe Clark has called students leeches and welfare recipients. I saw Joe Clark on the Donahue show once and he had the father of one of his students in the audience and he actually said, "You bum. You just run around in a Cadillac getting welfare checks with four or five wives." You know, the stereotypes people have of black people. Joe Clark emphasizes the negative and that sets a certain type of atmosphere in the school. Our principal simply tries to make sure that negative students don't get into the building and he gets rid of those students who are not interested in an education. And I think that's the right approach. When I came into education, I thought I could save everybody, but obviously you become realistic after a while and realize, as a friend of mine once told me, you can't save everybody. If you save one out of ten you are doing a good job.

Shor   Why can't you save everybody? What stands in the way?

Harris   The street. The street gets hold of many of these students, especially in a neighborhood like Bedford-Stuyvesant. We live in a society where you are nothing unless you possess certain material objects—sneakers, gold chains, VCRs, stereos, Walkmans, or what have you.

Rollins   They are symbolic.

Harris   Yeah, they're symbols of success. A lot of students see crack dealers who have all these beautiful things that you have to have to be somebody and they say, "Why should I come to school every day, work hard, and put up with the teachers and the administration, when I can just go out there, stand on a corner, sell crack, and buy everything I ever wanted?"

John Deveaux   What always amazes me is how many people *don't* sell crack. I think it's testimony to how good people basically are, because that money sure must be tempting and it sure would be easy to make it. I agree that there are lots of incentives not to go to school, but there must also be a strong incentive to stay in school. I have no doubt that your school is as strong as you say, Rodney, because your principal is beginning to say, "There is a reason to be in school. Take some responsibility. You are somebody."

You've got to be so careful about blaming the victim. I always hear, "Why don't those parents come to student-teacher night?" But there isn't always someone to pay their babysitter or they're afraid they won't be able to read the signs or whatever. There are so many reasons why parents don't come. And then even if they do come in and say they want some help, the teacher's going to say, "Man, I've got thirty-five kids in class," or "Your kid's a clown," or "There is no after-school tutoring. I know you'd like the kid to come here in the afternoons so you could work or he could be safe and get extra help, but the janitors won't let us open it up because it's too damned expensive." So it's a tough one, and I think we have to stay away from blaming the victim.

Ashford   Of course we do, but you have to look at where these different complaints come from. It is one thing for someone like William Bennett to say I want all the schools in urban America to kick out the knuckleheads, it's another thing for a group of parents or concerned teachers to decide that they're not going to allow their community's high school to become an academic dumping ground. Then it becomes not just an educational agenda but a social agenda for a whole class and a whole group of people.

Rollins   The level of education is very low, miserably low, in the urban centers, but the level is also extraordinarily low in suburban areas. Sure, in the top private schools you get a great education, but that's about it. I think the only reason the right is so upset about the educational system is because of economic competition from foreign markets. So, for example, the art department of the school gets a thousand dollars for the whole year, but all of a sudden there is this great new computer system and you have thirty Apple computers lined up. You go in there and it looks like the kids are training for the new sweatshop. They say, "You gotta get a job. I don't want to do art, I don't want to read literature, I want to do computers so I can get a job." What is education really about? What is it for?

Harris   But most people when they go to college say, "I'm going to college so that when I get out I'll get a good job." They're not going for an education. They're going to college to get a job. So then they go on to get an MBA saying, "I got to get an MBA, so I can get that $48,000 job." These institutions become nothing more than factories producing robots that fit right in, perfect pieces that fit right into the continuum.

Shor   But there is a difference between urban and suburban schools. The intellectual level is not at the ceiling in the suburban school system, but the difference is that the working conditions are good. And now 96 percent of all teachers coming out of the teachers' colleges want a good job in a suburban school; only 4 percent say they will work in an inner city school. So you have a crisis of teacher shortages in the inner city schools, primarily because the working conditions are terrible. Second, the drop-out rates are extremely high in urban schools, and much lower in the suburban schools. So even though the jobs at the end of the school pipeline are not great, even for the suburban kids, they have a leg up on the urban kids in whatever job market does exist. And right now the market is deteriorating because high tech is leading to lower wages, fewer skilled jobs, fewer unionized jobs, and more dull routine jobs on Silicon Valley-type assembly lines.

Rollins It's like back to the nineteenth century.

Ashford But I think that in a way the students are right. Kids are taught to see education as some kind of step toward social gain, you know, something that makes them more economically viable. Knowledge in itself is rarely represented for them as important. This coincides with the original agenda of public education in New York: to socialize people coming to the city from different backgrounds. The first school boards were organized by rich philanthropists in response to the perceived dangers of Irish immigration. From that point in the early nineteenth century public education has been designed to socialize people, to normalize people who are a threat to the status quo.

Deveaux Tim, you began with a statement about compulsory education being tied to democracy, and yet some of the statements you are quoting are tied to the fact that kids were no longer allowed to work but needed to go to school to work. Maybe that is something to be looked at. Education for what? It's the acquisition of knowledge for knowledge's sake that often is fun when you are allowed to learn. There is a difference between learning and schooling. Being allowed to learn is what isn't happening in our schools.

Shor Before the 1960s, the drop-out rate in high schools was much higher than it is now. It was 70 or 80 percent in the twenties, thirties, and forties. It wasn't called a problem because we didn't expect everyone to finish high school. The latest statistics report that nationally about 28 percent of all students drop out of high school. But if you break that figure down by race, the highest drop-out rate—around 60 to 65 percent—is among Hispanics; slightly lower is the black drop-out rate—about 55 to 60 percent; and the white drop-out rate is about 20 percent. In the cities it's worse: 60 to 70 percent of the nonwhite students drop out before they graduate. But the point is you can't even talk about a national drop-out rate unless you break it down by race.

There wasn't a crisis in the thirties, forties, and fifties even with high drop-out rates because the economy was expanding and people left school to take jobs. My father left school at fourteen and went into a trade. Now when you drop out, the jobs in basic industries like steel, oil, and manufacturing simply don't exist. We had an enormous tool-and-dye industry in New York City that disappeared after World War II and has gone to Germany and Japan. All that industrial training you could learn on the job and all those highly skilled, well-paying, unionized jobs have been sent to cheap-labor countries abroad. So when you drop out, the job market can't receive you. So you become a social threat.

Gonzalez-Torres So basically what you're saying is that every time a kid drops out of school, he becomes a threat to capitalism.

Shor No, he doesn't necessarily threaten the system but he does become a judicial problem, a social-work problem, a community problem. But that's in the urban schools where students drop out to a job market with wages that can't even support a life. On the suburban side, what is upsetting people — the so-called crisis of a nation at risk — is that white kids are underperform- ing. They feel compelled to say that they're very upset about inadequate mi- nority education, but mainly they want more from white kids. The mediocrity, the lack of interest in education is spreading from places where you think there is no point in going to school to places where there should be a point in going to school. Even in the best school districts they're not able to motivate enough kids to take school seriously.

In the twenty-first century there is going to be a whole new world sup- posedly full of high-tech careers. The experts claim that the future is going to be wide open for workers in these highly skilled, high-paying jobs, though no report has been able to document those jobs. What the reports do predict for the future is a lot of low-skill, high-tech jobs. In the near future we are going to have voice-activated computer terminals which will mean you don't even have to type.

Rollins All these sorts of promises are very lucrative to the big business of education. Tools and terminals can be sold to schools. It's a megabillion- dollar business that uses kids as an excuse for the production line.

Deveaux In adult education in New York, or in almost any place for that matter, there are very few native-born people, white, black, or Hispanic. And there are so many immigrants who can speak the language but don't want to. To get to those adults has a lot to do with outreach and real effort. Our most successful way to reach students is a twenty-second spot on all-news radio. It says, "If you are one of the one million New Yorkers who can't read, you can learn, call this number." It's anonymous, and it says we're talking to you, we're talking to people who can't read. Everybody in the school takes responsibility for those who call in, no matter how pissed off, tired, or hot they are. It's like a hotline for some people because they feel so lousy about not being able to read. Out of the six hundred calls we get, three hundred will come, three hundred won't.

It's almost like Alcoholics Anonymous. Although illiteracy is not a disease, there is an embarrassment, a closet factor. There's one story that does it for me. There are a lot of wonderful quotes by students; we go around the room and everyone says why they are here and why they want to learn to read. So, there are a lot of great stories. This one fellow says, "I'm here because of women." He looks at me and says, "I'm forty years old and I've been dating for a long time. I'm tired of getting to the point where I have to say, 'No, I can't read the menu. Would you order for me?' Finally I was with this woman I really like. It was our fourth date. She didn't know I couldn't read. But she said she had a nice time, she liked me. She said, 'Do you want to come back to my place?' I thought, 'This is it.'" The whole class eases in. "She says, 'Do you want a drink?' I say, 'Yeah, great, I'll have a drink.' I'm thinking, 'This is it. Tonight is the night.'" The class is a little bit more perked up. "Then," he says, "she turns to me and pops the question. She says, 'Do you want to play Scrabble?'" The whole room cracks up.

There are credible techniques for how you teach and how you bring people out and how you work with people that I think others can use. Hopefully you understand where they're at. Our staff has a lot of nonreaders on it now. But because of the amount of staff development involved it's expensive, it does cost money. I'm worried right now because we didn't get a grant for $3,000 which would have let us go to museums and art shows.

If you think back upon your own education you may remember that you had pretty good teachers for twelve years. It takes a long time to learn to read. There are the quick-fix people out there, the bureaucrats, but it took most people at least six years, three hours a day, every day, to learn to read, six years to reach a sixth-grade reading level. But the legislators don't even think about that. They forget. There is a lot of mythmaking about what you can do if you try hard enough, and a lot of forgetting about how hard it is to learn to read.

Rollins Also, your point about education being expensive—nothing is more expensive than bad education. That costs more in the end. We pay $4,000 per student for remedial education, and then you can't even get a pencil, you can't even get paper. You could bring in a very high-quality, cost-effective education for under that, I'm certain.

Ashford That's the point. It's cheaper in the long run to pay for good schools than to pay for all the other things when they fail.

Rollins That raises the central question: How useful does this society consider well-educated people?

Shor Part of the town meeting has to include another dimension, between suburban and urban, between public and private. The other question is that about 40 percent of all public school budgets are absorbed by bureaucracy. So if the New York City public school system spends $5 billion a year, $2 billion goes just to support 110 Livingston Street, the central administration. Good education means that the poorest school districts have to be funded the same as the handsomest. But now, even inside the schools, resources are wasted on administration and bureaucracy, as well as on dull commercial textbooks and standardized tests. To talk about power and democracy, we have to discuss that. There is no democratic governance inside the school system for teachers, students, or parents. Right now it's a hierarchy that is dominated by managers, called school administrators, who take up the most desk space and money, but don't even take part in the educational process.

Deveaux If the concept of knowledge for knowledge's sake is accepted by people other than tenured academics, perhaps every idealistic program or youth program won't be judged solely by whether it helps people get jobs. Maybe you can let people come in, excite their minds, and develop their ideas and thoughts. I think the failure to see education this way is tied to why there isn't democracy in the schools. If you are going to talk about democracy in education, that is a very good place to start.

Shor This is a great time to push this issue because I think we are at a turning point. In April 1983, the White House released "A Nation at Risk," a report saying that "a tide of mediocrity" was washing over the schools. According to this report, we were committing "unilateral educational disarmament"; we were losing to the Soviet Union in security and to Japan and Germany in economic trade wars. Since that report appeared, official reformers have proposed punitive and bureaucratic remedies for the school: more traditional courses to graduate from high school, more standardized testing—test the teachers, test the five-year-olds. Reform has been punitive and bureaucratic for a while but it hasn't really worked. So we are at a turning point now.

Now even Albert Shanker, the head of the American Federation of Teachers, is endorsing learner-centered schools. He used to support the bureaucratic machinery, the standardized tests, and the reforms of recent years. Now he's talking about learning-centered schools, teacher autonomy, and restructuring education—the three themes which are emerging now as an opening for the left. They open a window onto a different agenda about what education reforms should be.

I gave a talk two weeks ago at City College on teacher empowerment. It's important to talk about teacher-student-parent empowerment in relation to the school bureaucracy and in relation to the curriculum and society at large. If we take a comprehensive view of empowerment, one that takes into account not just teacher autonomy or teacher empowerment but also includes parents, students, and community members in relationship to power and society, then we're pushing it through an opening in the right direction.

Julie Ault Democracy isn't one day a week, one month a year, one Tuesday in November, voting or not voting. It would give me hope to think that democracy involves education. In schools with courage, where voting takes place, issues should be discussed and debated, ideas approved or not approved. That kind of participation could ultimately mean that 60 percent or more of the people vote. How can you get excited about "some of the people" electing a president? The education process has a place in this election. We need to read, we need to discuss, we need to have opportunities to talk about it. That would be better than a media that glosses over everything and reduces it to surface.

Harris This is the essence of cultural deprivation. In a sense this is where nonwhite students for the most part have no exposure to their history or their culture beyond the issues of the United States. If you want to refer to cultural deprivation, it exists in every single course taught in these public and private schools. The education system is obviously Eurocentric, totally Eurocentric, whether you are teaching science, history, math, or what have you. If we are going to discuss cultural deprivation we are going to have to discuss the fact that half of us are totally eliminated from what they call world history. You go to the school to take a world history class and all you are talking about is Europe. This is another thing that will keep students out of school and will increase the drop-out rate because the students come to school and they can't relate to anything that is taking place. No role models, everything is European.

Rollins I don't think it's that they have no role models, it's just boring. Ralph Waldo Emerson said the idea of reading books is not just to read them but to be inspired to make something. And I think one of the most important problems—particularly within public schools but even in private schools—is a methodological problem. The best way to keep anyone marginal in a society, whether it's old people, kids, people surviving on welfare, is to pull them out of production, pull them out of making things that have meaning in the world.

What the kids and I produce together means a lot. It has completely changed the fiber, the psychological fiber of the kids and what they think is possible. Not only that, but this belief in what is possible spreads to the parents and to the community as a whole. We operate in the art world. Predominantly white audiences come in and see the stuff that we make. So for the last seven years I have been making my work collaboratively with a steady group of kids. They call themselves K.O.S. (Kids of Survival) and they are kids ranging from thirteen to eighteen years old, black and Hispanic kids, predominantly from the South Bronx. We paint on book pages and books, making these epic paintings that people have started to become interested in. We have works in the collections of the Philadelphia Museum of Art and MoMA. The kids have traveled to Madrid and Germany, and this summer we're going to work with kids in Northern Ireland making a painting in Derry, *The Red Badge of Courage.*

Catherine Lord   One of the things that's very important to your program is that you paint on books that the kids have read.

Rollins   Not in the beginning, though, because particularly for my kids the book is the enemy. The book is the thing that makes you feel inferior. It is the thing that you can't deal with, it is the outsider.

We take the content of a book like *The Scarlet Letter,* which you would think would have no relevance to a group of teenagers in the Bronx, to talk about the "A" and about stigma and about transcending stigma. What we do is reuse the book. We've also done *The Autobiography of Malcolm X;* I mean this stuff isn't taught to our kids. You know what books they teach? They still teach *Catcher in the Rye.* I mean this is mediocre literature, this is not great literature.

The whole expectation of the literature program is astonishing. It's more than astonishing, it's patronizing and it's oppression in its vilest form. It's one thing to say we don't want to teach you this stuff because you're never going to use it or we don't think you'll understand it. But to presume that these books are valueless to people is a kind of intellectual fascism.

Shor   I think part of this project should make clear that your students are inventing their own language to understand this culture. They are making the confrontation in their own words. They have to. Now let's suppose that you speak black English—American black English, standard black English—which is a different variety of English than standard white English. Can the school acknowledge that you have a right to that language? You have a right to speak your community language. White working-class students don't speak standard English, either. They speak a different language than the dominant groups, and they're not allowed to talk in school in their street language. Every group that is not standard, whether it's white or black or Hispanic or Asian, speaks a form of English that is different from the school language.

Part of the democracy and education project has to acknowledge the language that people actually express themselves in and what they are confronting in schools. Many African-American students who are coming in now are effectively silenced because they don't speak like the Secretary of Education. Current practice requires them to stay silent and to memorize and respond in a foreign idiom. The key to dealing with it, it seems to me, is something like what Tim said before: the class produces a product. This is a good approach. It might mean producing a newspaper that's actually bidialectical, one side in standard English and the opposite side in the community language. But we must acknowledge that the community language is not "broken English." It's simply a different language. Community languages have their own vocabularies, their own grammatical structures, their own histories. We already have some experiences accumulating about how to deal with this, how to bring community language to school, not only use it for the street but also to find a voice. That is one of the legs of democracy inside the schools.

Rollins But those aren't issues that are discussed in teacher training.

Lord What *are* teachers trained for?

Rollins How to manage a classroom, write a lesson plan.

Harris In this day of teacher shortages, the only thing the schools are concerned with is having the body in front of the class. They show no interest in properly preparing the teachers to go into this class, much less in dealing with different languages. Most teachers thrown into this situation have never been in front of a class before, and they don't know what to do.

Deveaux It's partly a problem of how the curriculum is structured. Staff meetings should begin with teachers from the school talking about their theories of education and sharing ideas. This is a fundamental democratic point; the structure must allow people to speak to one another—that is what people do in democracies. Someone was saying that they have their class critically analyze our culture, Western and non-Western. In that is the excitement of education. Education *is* criticism. It's thinking, it's using your ideas; it's forming ideas, expressing ideas, talking about your own ideas. This is the essence of education: discourse. There can be no democracy without informed discourse.

Shor When we take up the idea of restructuring education, we have to include in the school day time set aside for teacher conferences. How can you be a competent professional unless you talk about teacher autonomy, learne -

Agnes George with teacher, Keith Rambert, of Boys and Girls High School, *Class is Long,* 1988.

centered schools, and restructuring education? These are now becoming accepted as legitimate themes. They can be discussed openly and we can say this is what we need. But who is going to define what democracy and empowerment mean? The battle is on to define school-based policy from these grand themes.

We need rank-and-file teacher activism. The bureaucracy will reform itself only as a last resort, because of pressure from below. I know there are some fine people in the administration, but they are the minority, they are not the system as a whole. We must look to those people as powerful allies for what children and teachers really need in school. But most important is the rank-and-file teacher activism that will push the union and school bureaucracies in democratic directions that they don't want to go. Parents have to be mobilized to join with activist teachers to make education work for their kids. Community activism and school activism are the two huge constituencies. There are 2 million public school teachers and parents of 40 million public school children. These are powerful constituencies that can move the bureaucracy, if they are aroused.

Rollins This connects with the innovations going on at Boys and Girls High School since there the principal is from the community. One major problem in the public school system in New York is an incredible alienation between teachers and the school. Very few teachers choose to go into a school like Boys and Girls or IS 52 in the Bronx; their connection with the community is the twenty yards from the car to the front door at eight o'clock in the morning and three o'clock in the afternoon. They don't patronize the local merchants, they don't eat in the restaurants in the area. You have to get into the community, start spending your money there, be there, put something in.

Harris It would shake up the entire teaching community if they were to require teachers to live in their school districts. If that happened, you couldn't let Johnny come into your classroom and stand on the desk because if he lived next door to you, you wouldn't want him to do that to your property. So you're working to teach Johnny to respect property, to keep his area of the classroom clean, to keep the school clean. You're going to teach Johnny to read and write because he is your neighbor.

Ashford There is a law on the books that will propose that teachers in the New York City public high school system have to be living in the city. Now that law has been contested by many. Would you get enough teachers from each community?

Harris That means the teachers would have to move into the community. It would force their hands. They would be forced to deal with a lot of issues they don't want to deal with basically because they want to punch in at eight o'clock and out at three o'clock, and go on with their business. They couldn't care less what happens in the neighborhood, even during those six hours and twenty minutes they're supposed to put in. People have to understand what is taking place in these high schools. If you go in some of these schools, they actually let some of these kids run rampant. You wouldn't believe it. These teachers let some of these kids do whatever they want in the classroom. And it affects the students. They see it as a lack of concern. They can tell which teachers have a concern for them and which don't. One of the major arguments we hear from drop-outs is that teachers don't really care what we do, whether we're there.

Shor There is a real opportunity for us at this time because over the next decade half of the current teachers are going to retire or leave the profession. There will be a million teachers needed in the system throughout the country over the next decade. The teacher core will virtually turn over in the next ten years. New York state alone will need 100,000 new teachers, which is half the teachers we have now. That means that many of the teachers coming up will probably be young and less entrenched in the worst way of doing things. The system probably will lose them if things don't change. One reason the school system decided to open the door to learner-centered schools and restructuring is because they can't attract the teachers they need under the present poor conditions.

Harris Well, we have to think about why people became teachers in the first place. You should never become a teacher because of the salary, or the time you get off. You should be a teacher for the love of teaching students. If you don't love students, or teaching, don't become a teacher. That should be emphasized in any teacher training program: don't come into this program and don't become a teacher unless you love students and you want to teach.

Deveaux The system is obliged to create conditions where your love of learning can work. The system is now set up to destroy that love of learning and your commitment to children. You come into education because you love children and you love learning but then you have to ask, is the system worthy of you? If we have an unworthy system then we lose the people who have the strongest convictions. Right now, in the urban areas, we have schools that convince people to change careers as soon as possible. If you stay in the school system, people think you were not ambitious enough to try to make it somewhere in another career.

Harris Also, a lot of teachers don't know how to deal with the system as it is. One of the reasons you have so many black and Hispanics in special-ed classes is that the teachers go in there and they say that these students are not interested in learning, we can't discipline them, they're hyperactive; they say the students should be evaluated for special education. This happens because teachers more or less rule from their own sociological background in which everybody is separated, blacks in one area, whites in another. The only contact these white teachers have with black people is what they see on TV—on the news they see black people handcuffed, arrested for some crime or other, or they see programs like *Good Times,* where blacks are portrayed as comedians. They have no contact with black people outside of work. So they think these kids have no interest in education. Teachers' expectations are one of the most important factors.

Ashford There are teachers in our public school system, paid by our tax dollars, who tell students that they will never produce, never go anywhere, never be successful, never do anything. And unfortunately, at least at my school, these are predominantly the white teachers. And if Ira says they are all going to retire in the next ten years, I say great. It can't be too soon.

Harris If you analyze how well the students are performing, the community is one problem but the teacher attitudes are also a problem, especially when you are talking about negative incentives. When I was in high school, my math teacher took me aside and said, "Rodney, forget it. You'll never learn this." That is exactly what he told me.

Rollins It's not only racial, though. There's also a class element to it. I've seen black upper-middle-class or middle-class teachers tell black kids from really poor families the same sort of thing.

Harris But you have to understand they are coming out of the same educational system. Education is structured to teach you to hate yourself if you are a black person, and to love everything European. They are only doing what they are taught to do.

Ashford There are two different lines. Many black teachers talking to kids say, "I got mine, you get yours." And many white teachers say, "I've always had mine, you'll never get yours." It's an angry relationship of authority, and it will only be broken down when the student agenda is addressed. This is what I think is really important about Tim's project among others. As Ira pointed out, the language is not coming from a curriculum specialist or even a teacher. The language is from the students themselves.

Deveaux What's coming through strongly from Doug and Rodney and Tim is that education doesn't educate to deal with a democracy. It doesn't educate kids to deal with the racism that is wrecking democracy, and it doesn't recognize that the U.S. is a multicultural society.

Lord Actually, we don't have democracy and we never did. We only speak as if we had one. Maybe we should deal conceptually with the society we have.

Shor A school should be democratic and multicultural, ideally. We can't have a democracy unless schools reflect our multicultural society. People have to see themselves as citizens and fight for these things in places where the big decisions are made. Whether there are jobs or not for graduates or dropouts does not depend on schools; those economic decisions are made in other places. How can a school or education produce jobs? It can't. It can only overproduce skilled, knowledgeable people if the economy underproduces jobs. A democratic education should direct people's attention to where power really is in this society.

Lord One of the key differences is between production and consumption. We must teach people to produce culture, not just consume it.

Rollins   Good education changes the quality of your life, and to have the quality of your life change in America means the disruption of a lot of markets.

Harris   An educated person is dangerous to a capitalistic society like this one. When too many people become educated they will demand better housing, adequate health care, better education for their kids, politicians who are more responsive, and an overall improvement of the system. This system cannot absorb all these demands, so obviously they have to keep a certain percent of the population uneducated.

Lord   The expediency of escalations in the number of people who are not uneducated, but simply undereducated also means a class of educational consumers wanting to make up for what they should have had earlier.

Deveaux   What about the undereducated still in school? Why isn't there more Board of Education support for independent initiatives in school? Can't they give a little—10 percent of their budget—to little independent educational institutions without controlling them?

Rollins   That has actually happened in a lot of communities. I know Banana Kelly's doing that; they have their own independent program for high school drop-outs, mostly knuckleheads, who are not able to function within the system. Kelly is making the first step by bringing in Board of Ed teachers who want to help the kids to learn how to work in this situation. The kids do the normal amount of course work, which they are not particularly interested in, but then they spend the rest of the day renovating buildings, learning general construction skills, and redoing the neighborhood. This is one way of working with the system but in defiance of the system.

Deveaux   That's interesting. Board of Ed teachers get to go and work in community-based situations but the community never has any control over anything that they do. The next step for me is the community saying, "OK, you're hired. These are going to be your people. We are giving you the money to do this since our tax dollars are paying for it, but you must work with us, be accountable to us, and learn from us." Then we are getting somewhere.

Shor   Finally, how can a project like this one that you're proposing at Dia, an art project about democracy, play some role in pushing forward a democratic agenda for education? It's very difficult to take on the whole system,

the force you need is enormous. So, I think it makes sense to seriously caucus with the existing activist groups and bring them together like this. You
need people who are already in the field in activist groups pushing campaigns around specific issue to see what kind of comprehensive agenda can
be developed. That would also raise new themes to add to the agenda. In the
field of political activism, one and one does not equal two. One and one
equals more than two because combining groups have a social chemistry and
working together allows them to do more.

John Ahearn, *Thomas*, 1983.

The Cosby Show visits Lena Horne.

Henry Louis Gates, Jr.

WHOSE CANON IS IT, ANYWAY?

William Bennett and Allan Bloom, the dynamic duo of the new cultural right, have become the easy targets of the cultural left, which I am defining here loosely and generously as that uneasy, shifting set of alliances formed by feminist critics, critics of so-called minority culture, and Marxist and poststructuralist critics generally—in short, the rainbow coalition of contemporary critical theory. These two men (one a former United States Secretary of Education and now President Bush's "drug czar," the other a professor at the University of Chicago and author of *The Closing of the American Mind*) symbolize the nostalgic return to what I think of as the "antebellum aesthetic position," when men were men and men were white, when scholar-critics were white men and when women and people of color were voiceless, faceless servants and laborers, pouring tea and filling brandy snifters in the boardrooms of old boys' clubs. Inevitably, these two men have come to play the roles that George Wallace and Orville Faubus played for the civil rights movement, or that Richard Nixon and Henry Kissinger played during Vietnam—the "feel good" targets who, despite internal differences and contradictions, the cultural left loves to hate.

And how tempting it is to juxtapose their "civilizing mission" to the racial violence that has swept through our campuses since 1986—at traditionally liberal Northern institutions such as the University of Massachusetts at Amherst, Mount Holyoke College, Smith College, the University of Chicago, Columbia, the University of Pennsylvania, and at Southern institutions such as the University of Alabama, the University of Texas, and the Citadel. Add to this the fact that affirmative action programs on campus have become window dressing operations, necessary "evils" maintained to preserve the fiction of racial fairness and openness but deprived of the power to enforce their stated principles. When unemployment among black youth is 40 percent, when 44 percent of black Americans can't read the front page of a newspaper, when less than 2 percent of the faculty on campuses is black, and when only 40 percent of black students in higher education are men, well, you look for targets close at hand.

And yet there's a real danger of localizing our grievances, of the easy personification, assigning celebrated faces to the forces of reaction and so giving too much credit to a few men who are really symptomatic of a larger political current. (In a similar vein, our rhetoric sometimes depicts the high canonical as the reading matter of the power elite. You have to imagine James Baker curling up with the *Pisan Cantos,* Dan Quayle leafing through *The Princess Casamassima.*) Maybe our eagerness to do so reflects a certain vanity that academic cultural critics are prone to. We make dire predictions, and when they come true, we think we've changed the world.

It's a tendency that puts me in mind of my father's favorite story about Father Divine, that historic con man of the cloth. In the 1930s, he was put on trial and convicted for using the mails to defraud. At sentencing, Father Divine stood up and told the judge: I'm warning you, you send me to jail, something terrible is going to happen to you. Father Divine, of course, was sent to prison, and a week later, by sheer coincidence, the judge had a heart attack and died. When the warden and the guards found out about it in the middle of the night, they raced to Father Divine's cell and woke him up. "Father Divine," they said, "your judge just dropped dead of a heart attack." Without missing a beat, Father Divine lifted his head and told them: "I *hated* to do it."

As writers, teachers, or intellectuals, most of us would like to claim greater efficacy for our labors than we're entitled to. These days, literary criticism likes to think of itself as "war by other means." But it should start to wonder: have its victories come too easily? The recent turn toward politics and history in literary studies has turned the analysis of texts into a marionette theater of the political, to which we bring all the passions of our real-world commitments. And that's why it is sometimes necessary to remind ourselves of the distance from the classroom to the streets. Academic critics write essays, "readings" of literature, where the bad guys (you know, racism or patriarchy) lose, where the forces of oppression are subverted by the boundless powers of irony and allegory that no prison can contain, and we glow with hard-won triumph. We pay homage to the marginalized and de-monized, and it feels almost as if we've righted an actual injustice. (Aca-demic battles are so fierce—the received wisdom has it—because so little is truly at stake.) I always think of the folk tale about the fellow who killed seven with one blow: flies, not giants.

Ours was the generation that took over buildings in the late 1960s and demanded the creation of black and women's studies programs and now, like the return of the repressed, has come back to challenge the traditional cur-riculum. And some of us are even attempting to redefine the canon by edit-ing anthologies. Yet it sometimes seems that blacks are doing better in the college curriculum than they are in the streets or even on the campuses.

This is not a defeatist moan, just an acknowledgment that the relation between our critical postures and the social struggles they reflect is far from transparent. That doesn't mean there's no relation, of course, only that it's a highly mediated one. In all events, I do think we should be clear about when we've swatted a fly and when we've toppled a giant. Still, you can't expect people who spend their lives teaching literature to be dispassionate about the texts they teach; no one went into literature out of an interest in literature-in-general.

I suppose the literary canon is, in no very grand sense, the common-place book of our shared culture, the archive of those texts and titles we wish to remember. And how else did those of us who teach literature fall in love with our subject than through our very own commonplace books, in which we inscribed secretly, as we might in a private diary, those passages of books that named for us what we had deeply felt, but could not say?

I kept mine from the age of twelve, turning to it to repeat those mar-velous words that named me in some private way. From H. H. Munro to Dickens and Austen, to Hugo and de Maupassant, each resonant sentence would find its way into my book. (There's no point in avoiding the narciss-ism here: we are always transfixed by those passages that seem to read *us*.) Finding James Baldwin and writing him down at an Episcopal church camp in 1965—I was fifteen, and the Watts riots were raging—probably deter-mined the direction of my intellectual life more than anything else I could name. I wrote and rewrote verbatim his elegantly framed paragraphs, full of sentences that were somehow both Henry Jamesian and King Jamesian, garbed as they were in the figures and cadences of the spirituals. Of course, we forget the private pleasures that brought us to the subject in the first place once we adopt the alienating strategies of formal analysis; our profes-sional vanity is to insist that the study of literature be both beauty and truth, style and politics, and everything in between.

In the swaddling clothes of our academic complacencies, then, few of us are prepared when we bump against something hard, and sooner or later, we do. One of the first talks I ever gave was to a packed audience at a college honors seminar, and it was one of those mistakes you don't make twice. Fresh out of graduate school, immersed in the arcane technicalities of con-temporary literary theory, I was going to deliver a crunchy structuralist analysis of a slave narrative by Frederick Douglass, tracing the intricate play of its "binary oppositions." Everything was neatly schematized, formalized, analyzed; this was my Sunday-best structuralism: crisp white shirt and shiny black shoes. And it wasn't playing. If you've seen an audience glaze over, this was double glazing. Bravely, I finished my talk and, of course, asked for questions. "Yeah, brother," said a young man in the very back of the room, breaking the silence that ensued, "all we want to know is, was Booker T. Washington an Uncle Tom or not?"

The funny thing is, this happens to be an interesting question, a lot more interesting than my talk was. It raised all the big issues about the poli-tics of style: about what it means to speak for another, about how you were to distinguish between canny subversion and simple co-optation—who was manipulating whom? And while I didn't exactly appreciate it at the time, the exchange did draw my attention, a little rudely perhaps, to the yawning chasm between our critical discourse and the traditions they discourse upon.

Obviously, some of what I am saying is by way of *mea culpa,* because I'm speaking here as a participant in a moment of canon formation in a so-called marginal tradition. As it happens, W. W. Norton, the "canonical" anthology publisher, will be publishing *The Norton Anthology of Afro-American Literatu e.* The editing of this anthology has been a great dream of mine for a long time, and it represents, in the most concrete way, the project of black canon formation. But my pursuit of this project has required me to negotiate a position between those on the cultural right who claim that black literature can have no canon, no masterpieces, and those on the cultural left who wonder why anyone wants to establish the existence of a canon, any canon, in the first place.

We face the outraged reactions of those custodians of Western culture who protest that the canon, that transparent decanter of Western values, may become—breathe the word—*politicized.* That people can maintain a straight face while they protest the irruption of politics into something that has always been political—well, it says something about how remarkably successful official literary histories have been in presenting themselves as natural objects, untainted by worldly interests.

I agree with those conservatives who have raised the alarm about our students' ignorance of history. But part of the history we need to teach has to be the history of the very idea of the "canon," which involves the history both of literary pedagogy and of the very institution of the school. One function of literary history is then to conceal all connections between institutionalized interests and the literature we remember. Pay no attention to the men behind the curtain, booms the Great Oz of literary history.

Cynthia Ozick once chastised feminists by warning that strategies become institutions. But isn't that really another way of warning that their strategies, Heaven forfend, may *succeed*?

Here we approach the scruples of those on the cultural left who worry about, well, the price of success. "Who's co-opting whom?" might be their slogan. To them, the very idea of the canon is hierarchical, patriarchal, and otherwise politically suspect. They'd like us to disavow it altogether.

But history and its institutions are not just something we study, they're also something we live, and live through. And how effective and how durable our interventions in contemporary cultural politics will be depends upon our ability to mobilize the institutions that buttress and reproduce that culture. We could seclude ourselves from the real world and keep our hands clean, free from the taint of history. But that is to pay obeisance to the status quo, to the entrenched arsenal of sexual and racial authority, to say that things shouldn't change, become something other and, let's hope, better.

Indeed, this is one case where we've got to borrow a leaf from the right, which is exemplarily aware of the role of education in the reproduction of values. We must engage in this sort of canon reformation precisely because Mr. Bennett is correct: the teaching of literature *is* the teaching of values, not inherently, no, but contingently, yes, it is—it has become—the teaching of an aesthetic and political order, in which no person of color, no woman, was ever able to discover the reflection or representation of his or her cultural image or voice. The return of "the" canon, the high canon of Western masterpieces, represents the return of an order in which my people were the subjugated, the voiceless, the invisible, the unpresented, and the unrepresentable.

Let me be specific. Those of us working in my own tradition confront the hegemony of the Western tradition, generally, and of the larger American tradition, more locally, as we theorize about our tradition and engage in canon formation. Long after white American literature has been anthologized and canonized, and recanonized, our efforts to define a black American canon are often decried as racist, separatist, nationalist, or "essentialist." Attempts to derive theories about our literary tradition from the black tradition—a tradition, I might add, that must include black vernacular forms as well as written literary forms—are often greeted by our colleagues in traditional literature departments as a misguided desire to secede from a union that only recently, and with considerable kicking and screaming, has been forged. "What is *wrong* with you people?" our friends ask us in genuine passion and concern; after all, aren't we all just citizens of literature here?

Well, yes and no. Every black American text must confess to a complex ancestry, one high and low (that is, literary and vernacular) but also one white and black. There can be no doubt that white texts inform and influence black texts (and vice versa), so that a thoroughly integrated canon of American literature is not only politically sound, it is intellectually sound as well. But the attempts of black scholars to define a black American canon, and to derive indigenous theories of interpretation from within this canon, are not meant to refute the soundness of these gestures of integration. Rather, it is a question of perspective, a question of emphasis. Just as we can and must cite a black text within the larger American tradition, we can and must cite it within its own tradition, a tradition not defined by a pseudo-science of racial biology, or a mystically shared essence called blackness, but by the repetition and revision of shared themes, topoi, and tropes, the call and response of voices, their music and cacophony.

And this is our special legacy: what in 1849 Frederick Douglass called the "live, calm, grave, clear, pointed, warm, sweet, melodious and powerful

Photocopy of Malcolm X anonymously distributed in many New York City high schools.

human voice." The presence of the past in the African-American tradition comes to us most powerfully as *voice*, a voice that is never quite our own— or *only* our own—however much we want it to be. One of my earliest childhood memories tells this story clearly.

I remember my first public performance, which I gave at the age of four in the all-black Methodist church that my mother attended, and that her mother had attended for fifty years. It was a religious program, at which each of the children of the Sunday school was to deliver a "piece"—as the people in our church referred to a religious recitation. Mine was the couplet "Jesus was a boy like me/ And like Him I want to be." Not much of a recitation, but then I *was* only four. So, after weeks of practice in elocution, hair pressed and greased down, shirt starched and pants pressed, I was ready to give my piece. I remember skipping along to the church with all of the other kids, driving everyone crazy, repeating that couplet over and over: "Jesus was a boy like me/ And like Him I want to be."

Finally we made it to the church, and it was packed—bulging and glistening with black people, eager to hear pieces, despite the fact that they had heard all of the pieces already, year after year, like bits and fragments of a repeated master text. Because I was the youngest child on the program, I was the first to go. Miss Sarah Russell (whom we called Sister Holy Ghost—behind her back, of course) started the program with a prayer, then asked if little Skippy Gates would step forward. I did so.

And then the worst happened: I completely forgot the words of my piece. Standing there, pressed and starched, just as clean as I could be, in front of just about everybody in our part of town, I could not for the life of me remember one word of that piece.

After standing there I don't know how long, struck dumb and captivated by all of those staring eyes, I heard a voice from near the back of the church proclaim, "Jesus was a boy like me/ And like Him I want to be."

And my mother, having arisen to find my voice, smoothed her dress and sat down again. The congregation's applause lasted as long as its laughter as I crawled back to my seat.

What this moment crystallizes for me is how much of my scholarly and critical work has been an attempt to learn how to speak in the strong, compelling cadences of my mother's voice. As the black feminist scholar Hortense Spillers has recently insisted, in moving words that first occasioned this very recollection, it is "the heritage of the *mother* that the African-American male must regain as an aspect of his own personhood—the power of 'yes' to the 'female' within."

To reform core curricula, to account for the comparable eloquence of the African, the Asian, and the Middle Eastern traditions, is to begin to prepare our students for the roles of citizens of a world culture, educated through a truly human notion of "the humanities," rather than—as Mr. Bennett and Mr. Bloom would have it—as guardians at the last frontier outpost of white male Western culture, the keepers of the master's pieces. And for us as scholar-critics, learning to speak in the voice of the black mother is perhaps the ultimate challenge of producing a discourse of the Other.

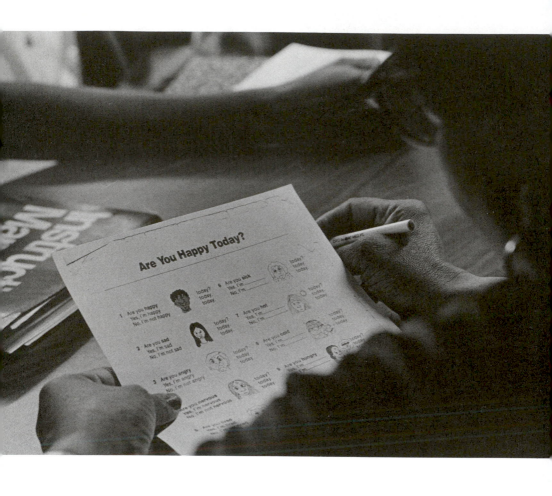

Catherine Lord

LETTER TO GROUP MATERIAL

January 1990

Dear Group Material,

At our roundtable discussion there was so much to be said about public education, especially high school education, that we never touched on a couple of key developments in art education and state arts funding. That these developments in many ways represent battles over the symbols of high culture doesn't mean they are irrelevant to ideas of democracy. On the contrary, the right has been far more astute than the left in picking symbolic fights and using them to its ends. With conservatives like Patrick Buchanan calling for a cultural revolution in the next decade, the issue now is who gets to define culture, and who is enabled to produce it.

The agenda of two Reagan appointees to key cultural positions are pertinent in looking at how the right has gone about reclaiming culture for the privileged in the last decade. Appointed chairman of the National Endowment for the Humanities shortly after Reagan's election, William Bennett began by defunding projects oriented to left politics, women, and people of color. At the same time, by means of a 1985 report titled *To Reclaim a Legacy,* Bennett ostentatiously promoted a return-to-excellence agenda that effectively narrowed the humanities to the history of dead, white, Western men. Bennett proved so steadfast in the scholarly arena that in time he was rewarded with the entire U.S. Department of Education. There, he dramatically magnified the same conservative agenda, targeting those below the upper-middle class by cutting deeply into student aid programs, while simultaneously ridiculing any choice of "faddish" progressive education over "the best Western civilization has to offer," as he succinctly put it at a 1987 Getty conference on education in the arts. (Now, of course, as Bush's drug czar, these ideological struggles have taken on a new dimension for Bennett; rather than debating the canon, he can command the artillery.)

Frank Hodsoll, who was Bennett's counterpart at the National Endowment for the Arts, also did his bit in implementing a conservative cultural agenda. More was involved here than Hodsoll's relatively well-publicized vetoes of proposed grants to projects too left-wing to suit his taste in art, or too specialized in their focus on women or people of color. Hodsoll, like Bennett, decided to use the clout of his agency to address the matter of arts education; this took the form of a 1988 document modestly titled *Toward*

Civilization. Lamenting the minor place of arts education in American schools, Hodsoll sought to revitalize it by consolidating a one-dimensional past and foreclosing social change. His goal was to transmit the "central core" of American civilization—mostly white, mostly male, and (without apology) mostly European. However, admirable though these goals are, he was obligated to demonstrate that art education is no mere frill. Noting Japan's commitment to extensive K-12 art education, Hodsoll thus reasons that improving basic arts skills will surely increase the productivity of American workers by developing their problem-solving abilities. Art education would also foster effective communication, an asset in the corporate boardroom as well as for ordinary folk bombarded by the messages of television. Finally, according to Hodsoll, more art education would produce "discriminating consumers," who can, in addition to making wise product choices, change the course of broadcast television by affecting the Nielsen ratings.

This, then, is the general context for the steady consolidation of a conservative cultural canon now occurring in conventional visual arts teaching, in many public and private schools, from kindergarten to college level. Let me say, though, that we must be careful not to romanticize our losses. The scope of art teaching has never been very inclusive in this country, given the post-1945 infatuation with notions of high art. (Symptomatically, "teaching art" means, with equal ease, teaching people either to produce the stuff "professionally," as artists, or to "appreciate" it better, as consumers.) By the end of the 1970s, however, the feminist movement, gay and lesbian politics, anticolonial and antiracist struggles, as well as critiques of communications and commodities monopolies, had made visible breaches in the monolith of traditional Eurocentric, phallocentric curricula. By the mid-1980s, "alternatives" to conventional art education had become fairly popular, especially as the graduates of such programs were picked up by an art market hungry for new products.

In the visual arts, the symbolic leader of the move to contain culture as a province of the privileged has been the J. Paul Getty Trust, specifically a branch called the Getty center for Education in the Arts. Since its founding in 1982, the center has aspired to reform visual arts teaching by implementing in various American schools a K-12 curriculum program portentously called Discipline Based Arts Education (DBAE). This program seeks to make art more appealing to what the Getty invariably portrays as cost-conscious, conservative educational bureaucrats by insisting that studio art be taught in conjunction with art history, art criticism, and aesthetics. Not only will these four disciplines be taught together, but the curriculum will be written, sequential, and capable of evaluation by standardized testing.

To understand the full ambition of DBAE, however, it's important to understand it tactically, within the self-imposed scope of the Getty Trust.

Setting itself the task of making a "quantum" difference in the fine arts, the Getty in 1982 added to the faux-Roman villa that is its Malibu museum a set of related programs. These departments were devoted not merely to restructuring the teaching of art in the U.S., but also to projects designed to further art-history research, develop sophisticated conservation practices, systematize previously incompatible art-history data bases in assorted countries, and inventory all the films ever made about art. What the Getty means by making a difference in the fine arts has nothing to do with the production of contemporary art, or culture, but with the acquisition, restoration, preservation, and promotion of (mostly) Western art and its history.

The Getty won't divulge what the Center gets each year to promote DBAE, but the Getty Trust, legally obliged to give away some $110 million a year through its eight programs, is not a shoestring operation. As one of the Trust's eight programs, the Center for Arts Education has the plushest aura to be found in art-ed circles. This is not a world of desktop published newsletters, but one of free conferences, grant programs to sizeable school districts, big-name consultants, and a steady stream of quietly elegant publications, free, or almost, for the asking.

Oddly, despite the money poured into the program, the Getty's interest in art education hasn't gotten much attention, either in the art press or the general press, and the DBAE program hasn't figured heavily in current debates about reforming the canon. Perhaps this is because the acronym is unpronounceable, perhaps because the program is a lot more boring in art circles than, say, censorship brouhahas. Or perhaps it's because the Getty's mode of operation is to go forward by political networking, making alliances with education bureaucrats, with appropriate state officials, and most important, with all those underpaid art teachers thrilled by a prestigious foundation going to bat for them. And probably the restraint in questioning DBAE's premises has something to do with the fact that dreaming about just a teeny cut of those millions tends to dull the critical faculties.

The kind of arts education the Getty advocates is nicely encapsulated by the title of an early DBAE report, "Beyond Creating." Here, art is explicitly defined as a repository of culture, and since culture is seen as largely dead, the DBAE program manifests an enormous skepticism about the potential contributions of working artists. This sentiment becomes distaste in the face of any notion of cultural production that doesn't assume professionalizing the notion of the artist. The word "artist" is rarely used in DBAE circles. Rather than risk suggesting that art is produced by individuals who actually work at it, DBAE dwells on "art," "the arts," "art works," "art history," "art criticism," and "art education." These subjects are taught by "art specialists," who may teach *about* artists, but are scarcely required, or even encouraged, to *be* artists themselves. (Getty staff have confessed their distrust about artists' reliability in teaching all-important subjects like art history.) The DBAE approach is, instead, to teach students basic art "skills," like mixing colors and drawing lines, along with the vocabulary for talking about that art deemed to be significant. Thus, one DBAE staple is a classroom activity called "aesthetic scanning," in which students look at a Great Work and inventory elements of its appearance. In some regions, art specialists have refined this strategy by using flash cards literally to put the right words in their students' mouths. (For example, the right Matisse card would read "vibrant" not "tranquil.") Not surprisingly, contemporary artists who question culture through their own production are nowhere in evidence. Neither are artists who make art as well as art criticism. In the DBAE universe, artists make and other people get to talk. Ansel Adams and David Hockney are, from everything I've seen, about as hip as the Getty gets.

Finally, though the Getty's model of an integrated curriculum sounds very reasonable at first to those who believe in the importance of a social context for art, it's actually a model which divorces art from any understanding of politics, economics, or history. (Presumably, these topics are taught by the "generalists" in other classrooms.) When such connections are made, they are made in the safely distant past—about, say, medieval life. The DBAE agenda, protestations to the contrary, is aimed at a white, middle-class, provincial America, where problems of housing, food, employment, and medical care have been wished out of existence. It's not just that the Getty's notion of art is conservative, it's that their conception of children ("the little tykes," as one Getty staffer called them in welcoming guests to a 1989 conference) is imaginary.

If the specifics of the DBAE program appear to be related to the NEA's approach, it's not a coincidence. The director of the Center for Education in the Arts, as well as several DBAE luminaries, served as Hodsoll's advisors. Relations between the federal agency and the Getty Trust are sufficiently chummy that the NEA helped the Getty to fund a public television series for children about art. Given these connections, it's interesting to observe that the budget increase George Bush proposed for the NEA in January 1990— the first significant increase in ten years—is earmarked for arts education.

This latest symptom of a significant shift in the NEA agenda directly follows last year's battles in the arts community over punitive sanctions taken against three institutions who sponsored exhibitions of work offensive to the right's agenda because of homoerotic, supposedly anti-Christian, or explicitly antifascist content. The exhibitions involved, all funded in part by the NEA, included work by Robert Mapplethorpe and Andres Serrano, as well as an exhibition of work about AIDS entitled "Against Our Vanishing." (The latter was actually produced in direct response to an NEA call for thematic responses to issues of AIDS.) These shows became symbolic targets that could serve the right's desire to reinstate "the best Western civilization has to offer" by fanning public ire about the alleged extremes of contemporary art. The NEA under Frank Hodsoll had witch-hunted only work with left politics, and had generally ignored the question of sexually explicit art. Last year's events represented a move to eliminate state subsidies for any work perceived as "obscene" in the specific sense that it threatened religious or "family" values.

The ploy was largely successful. Faced with images that required a complicated and *politicized* defense, the arts community managed to unify only around a vague "freedom of expression" slogan, rather than to take the offensive in critiquing the conservative agenda that had led to the attacks. When put in the position of having to choose between their own NEA funding or disavowing homoerotic work, many proved all too willing to live with the "compromise" of defunding work defined as obscene. In other words, the gay-bashing conducted by Jesse Helms & Co. was echoed in the arts community response to threats of funding cutoffs. And all in all, the nature of the response served to discredit the power of the U.S. arts community to defend *contemporary* work. This, naturally, will make it easier to alter the flow of state arts funding determined by the NEA, shifting it to more blatantly bolster a restrictive culture of blockbuster presentations, big organizations, decorative arts, and the education necessary to produce trained consumers of these things. As Congress moves into reauthorization hearings for the legislation that enables both Endowments, I can't help but feel pessimistic about the new "compromises" that will be exacted.

Too bad to end on a downer, as we say in sunny Southern California, but there it is.

Catherine Lord
Los Angeles

TOWN MEETING!
EDUCATION & DEMOCRACY
ORGANIZED BY GROUP MATERIAL
Tuesday, September 27, 8 pm
DIA ART FOUNDATION • 155 Mercer St.
AGENDA

Meeting Chairperson: Tim Rollins, Director, Art & Knowledge Workshop, Bronx

I. Welcome and introductory remarks by Tim Rollins for Group Material

II. Brief summary of issues raised during a panel on Education & Democracy organized by Group Material*

III. Open to the floor: Discussion on the following questions --

A.   What are some aspects of the present crisis in education in the U.S.?

B.   Education for whom? -- Who has the greates access to organized forms of education? Who is denied access to these same institutions? How is democracy served by current educational policies? Is a Eurocentric curriculum suitable for the increasingly multicultural nature of contemporary American society?

C.   Education beyond schooling? -- What is the state of forms of education beyond public and private institutions? What are community-based, alternative, adult, ethnic and religious programs currently doing? What are the problems and solutions presented by these grass-roots organizations?

D.   Education for what? -- Is Jefferson's conviction that education is the most important project of a democratic society still binding or has it degenerated into a myth? What is the role of education for democracy in the current cultural, political and economic climate of the U.S.?

E.   What is to be done? -- Could this Town Meeting and its participants be organized to build education for democracy coalitions in New York City and beyond?

Please come prepared to speak on these issues. The Town Meeting on Education & Democracy will be recorded, transcribed and incorporated into a publication organized by Group Material for the Dia Art Foundation.

*Education & Democracy panel held in May 1988: John Deveaux, Bronx Educational Services; Rodney Harris, Boys & Girls High School, Brooklyn; Catherine Lord, California Institute of the Arts; Tim Rollins; Ira Shor, City University of New York.

This project is supported in part by public funds from the National Endowment for the Arts, a federal agency, and the New York State Council on the Arts.

EDUCATION AND DEMOCRACY

Chairperson, Tim Rollins I was raised in a very small working-class town in Maine called Pittsfield. And I can vividly recall the phenomenon of the town meeting, even from when I was a kid. The town meeting was a very serious and dramatic gathering that everyone would eagerly anticipate before it happened and complain and gossip about afterward. In the New England tradition, no one under eighteen was allowed to attend. So I dreamed that when I reached voting age the very first privilege that I would exercise—after drinking, of course—would be attendance at the town meeting. I was certain that with the clarity of my convictions and the passion and the fire of my youth, I would move the crowd. But in 1971, shortly before I turned eighteen, the town voted to stop meeting altogether.

I never knew why the town meetings were abandoned. So, as I was preparing my comments for tonight, I called the Pittsfield town registrar, Mrs. Bemis. She has been the registrar for forty years, and she remembered me. She offered me some pretty wise opinions about why the town meetings were canceled. She said people seemed increasingly unwilling to assume the responsibilities of democracy and of empowerment and self-determination. And she said the meetings were becoming free-for-alls, dominated by people more interested in spouting their own opinions than in constructive dialogue. Also, in the context of Maine, the town meeting was seen as an old-fashioned, provincial, and inefficient form of government. So the few participants in that last town meeting elected to form a town council, and they hired selectmen. In the end, the biggest reason for the demise of the town meeting was that people simply stopped coming.

So tonight is my first town meeting. And it is very exciting to see everybody attending. Here, the town is not determined by geographic lines. Ours is a community of concern. And tonight our focus is on the current crisis in American education, with particular emphasis on the situation here in New York City. Thomas Jefferson said that every government degenerates when trusted to the rulers of the people alone, and that the people themselves therefore are its only safe depositories; to render even them safe, their minds must be improved to a certain degree. This self-education is not all that is necessary, though it is essential. In addition, for example, an amendment to the constitution should be proposed to aid public education. But the point is, the influence of government must be shared among all the people. So all of us here tonight are about to engage in an act of critical imagination. This sort of act has been described by Paulo Freire as going beyond tomorrow without being naively idealistic, anticipating tomorrow by dreaming today.

May I encourage us to think out loud tonight? Let's not be afraid of disagreements or contradictions. We're going to have a dialogue with lessons that we can take back to work tomorrow. The first issue we have is: What are some of the aspects of the present crisis in education in the U.S.? If anyone can speak from experience or has a position on this issue, now is the time to talk.

Geno Rodriguez My name is Geno Rodriguez. I'm director of the Alternative Museum. And I'm wondering how we can talk about American education when the audience does not seem to reflect the total spectrum of Americans. That is to say, I don't see very many blacks, I don't see very many Hispanics or Asians, and those whom I do see are mostly artists or art-oriented people, often removed from the concerns of their own community. I think that the first thing we have to do—before we start discussing education—is find out from within ourselves why we are unable to make the cultural bridge functional. Nobody is really getting the people to come across the bridge; there is something wrong and it is reflected in the constitution of our arts community. Our arts community has only the weakest links with the concerns of most Americans. Instead it has links with itself, self-indulgence, and, at the most negative level, a self-aggrandizing version of liberalism.

John Contini I want to expand on that issue. My name is John Contini. I am a teacher in the New York City public school system. Originally I worked in Harlem at a junior high school on 129th Street. Then I worked for a project for homeless children that was started last April at the Martinique Hotel. Now I am working in the Lower East Side to help kids who have dropped out of high school. I think one reason we don't see many black and Hispanic and Asian people here tonight is because of the unequal standards of education in this country. In 1896 there was a Supreme Court decision called *Plessy* v. *Ferguson* that said separate and equal facilities were constitutional. In 1954 that ruling was knocked down by *Brown* v. *Board of Education,* which held that separate but equal school systems were unconstitutional; you must have integrated facilities, particularly schools. However, if you take a look around the New York City school system, you will find that it is not integrated at all. There are thirty-two school districts in New York City. Of those thirty-two districts, seventeen have a minority population of 92 percent or higher; eight of the school districts have virtually a 100 percent minority population. That leaves the fifteen remaining school districts

And, down on the dust speck, the scared little Mayor
Quick called a big meeting in Who-ville Town Square.
And his people cried loudly. They cried out in fear:
"We are here! We are here! We are here! We are here!"

Dr. Seuss, illustration of Whoville from *Horton Hears a Who*, 1954.

with the 88 percent of the city's white population. So what is happening is
that those fifteen predominantly white school districts are better funded, better integrated, and better supplied with resources than the seventeen districts
that have more than 92 percent minority population. (And obviously there is
no real effort at integration when you have eight districts with 100 percent
minority population.) How can we encourage racial harmony, or inter-
cultural understanding when our city's black and Hispanic students see virtually no white faces in their classrooms for nine years? If you have an
unequal education system, it's not surprising that there are fewer Hispanics
or other minorities here than whites.

Rodriguez Now wait a minute! I think that it is very important to understand what's going on here. This kind of dialogue, in which we are presum-
ing to find solutions for people, has a farcical side to it. This shows the
worst of our left-wing liberal personalities. What we really have to do is stop
talking abstractly and start dealing with the difficult job of getting people
together. And that's not easy. For instance, in my case, I grew up in a ghetto
in New York City. And it wasn't easy to not only make the jump out of the
ghetto to study in Europe, but also to come back here and start the first
artist-founded museum in the country. But most difficult of all was to be
able to socialize with people like yourselves. That required a constant effort.

I had to say, "I'm not afraid of those people." I wondered if I could work myself into your mainstream and put forth my agenda and my perspective as an equal. Now, whether you accept me as an equal or not, I consider myself an equal. But I have a lot of anger in me against the type of people here. You have to do less of this liberal talking and do more about getting your hands down into it, getting out there with people.

Felix Gonzalez-Torres Hi, my name is Felix Gonzalez-Torres, and I am a member of Group Material. I really feel like I should reply to the comments that were just made. When Group Material tried to organize this town meeting, it was an honest attempt to avoid doing just an exhibition about "the Other." All that stuff that you are talking about is so familiar. And I really dislike the "farcical" tag you put on this discussion. I dislike that very much. Our project is about inclusion and not about exclusion. And to start the town meeting with so much anger really puts me off. Perhaps it's a good question why there are not that many blacks and Hispanics here. But I guess with blacks it is easy to see; he's black, he's not white. But with Hispanics that idea of visual identification is a little racist. I mean, what am I supposed to do, wear a flowered shirt?

Allen Rosenberg Hi, my name is Allen Rosenberg. I'm an artist and a student at Hunter College. It seems to me that Hunter has an extremely high minority population, but that the way the classes are divided up is a completely different story. The art history department, which I am in, is almost entirely white, but departments like health sciences or physical education have a much higher minority population. It all comes down to economic necessity. I also went to F.I.T. [Fashion Institute of Technology], which has a far better endowment than Hunter, but it is also far more integrated. All of my classes had high minority populations in them. The reason that F.I.T. is so well integrated is clear: people are there to learn out of economic necessity. Students are majoring in fashion design and they want to go into the fashion business because they see it as economically viable. People are drawn to health sciences for the same reason; they perceive a lot of job opportunities there. Art history, on the other hand, has a lot of middle-class and upper-class white students for whom the economic question is not an issue. So, I think that we always have to remember the economic question as well.

Herb Perr I teach at Hunter College, and I'd like to talk about something slightly different. If you look at William Bennett, the former secretary of education, I think you can understand part of the reason for the crisis in education today. Bennett believes that education should be structured around white, male, European history and knowledge. For instance, when the faculty at Stanford University tried to change the core curriculum and have students read texts by women and so-called Third World authors, Bennett sharply criticized this as a move away from the white European classics.

The other thing I think is very important in relation to education is the whole issue of segregation. Recently I went to a talk by a woman who is publishing a book on educational segregation. She researched colleges and high schools that were either all black or all women, and she found that the black students excelled when they were separated from whites and the women excelled when they were separated from men. Now we're not just talking about New York City here. Nationwide, women and blacks excelled and they had higher self-esteem. I am not advocating segregation, I am just raising this as an interesting problem. It points out that integration is not a simple solution to the problems in the educational system. And, similarly, in the art world, we can't necessarily think that if you bring more blacks, Hispanics, or Asian-Americans into a situation like this or anywhere, that it will automatically solve the problem of inequality. We've got to go deeper than that.

Rollins We've kind of naturally moved into Item B on the agenda, that is "Education for whom?"

Mario Asaro I can address that. My name is Mario Asaro and I'm presently co-chairing a group called Artists/Teachers Concerned. We are trying to cut through some of this bullshit, to get kids into the public eye so they can show what they are doing. We are now an official subcommittee of the New York City Art Teachers Association. How did this happen? I went to board meetings and got us accepted. Now the NYCATA is going to give us funding, mailing, and all kinds of great stuff. We call for all teachers to come and meet with us, especially art teachers who want to exhibit their students' work or share with us their lessons. That way we can all grow, as a team, as a whole. We're dedicated to incorporating socially relevant lesson plans into the classroom and into the community. If you are interested in making a difference, in teaching children not just the aesthetics of art but what is really important in art and what is really important in their life, and in showing kids how they can say what they think and bring it out, I would urge you—especially you art teachers—to pick up one of these flyers on the way out and mail it back to us. Then we will contact you to be a part of what we are doing.

Our current project is a show we have coming up on March 3 in a Brooklyn-based gallery called Minor Injury. We're also trying to start a network of people on the state as well as the national level. We want the National Art Education Association to present the work we are doing. Hopefully this will be the first big step of the networking process we are

Meryl Meisler and the Drop Ins, *Question Marks,* 1988. Students from IS 291 in Brooklyn document the failing building structure of their school.

talking about. But if you are teaching, please get back to us so we can include your kids' work in what we are doing. Let them know that you care and that the community at large cares about what they have to say.

Contini Another important thing is alternative education. As you can read in the newspaper almost every day, the drop-out rate in traditional educational settings is phenomenal and just continues to escalate, so alternative education is a necessary option. The Board of Education has several alternative projects. Two alternative high schools are doing some wonderful work with children who just don't fit into what the board of ed considers a traditional school setting. I left a job teaching at a junior high school in Harlem to work on a program of alternative education for homeless children at the Martinique Hotel. The problem with these homeless children was—because of adverse conditions that they were living in—they were not going to school. Once you stepped into the Martinique Hotel you understood immediately why those children lacked the enthusiasm or self-esteem to get along in a conventional school setting. They weren't being fed properly, they were up all night, there were no adequate cleaning facilities for clothes or anything else. So you could walk into the hotel on any given school day and there would be about a thousand kids around the hotel who should have been in school.

So after about a year or so of trying to get the kids to go to school and realizing that wasn't going to work, the Board of Education in their infinite wisdom decided to bring the school to the kids. They hired a couple of teachers—me and another teacher—and a couple of professional counselors and said, "Okay, you want to have a program to educate the kids inside the hotel. Go to it."

Now, bringing in two teachers and a couple of professionals to educate students is, under these conditions, not the ideal situation. But the idea was basically a good one: if students aren't going to go to school, then we must reach out to those students. And part of reaching out is going to them, wherever they may be. If that is the Martinique Hotel, so be it. We can't just sit back and say, "Hey, these kids aren't going to school, they dropped out of school, but they made that choice. They are eighteen years old, just let them be." We are going to have to do more than that, because the system as it exists is not working, as we know from the curriculum, and as we know from segregating the cultures. So the alternative has to be more outreach. We have to get the kids and say, "Hey, we really care."

Rollins Thank you, John. At this time I want to focus on an issue that I am very concerned with as a teacher, and which I think relates to the general course of this discussion. I am sure there are people in the audience who have very strong opinions about this. We are asking a question, a rhetorical question, of course: "Education for whom?" But now I would like to expand on that a bit and ask, "Is a Eurocentric curriculum suitable for the increasingly multicultural nature of contemporary American society, and particularly in the context of New York City?"

Jorge Cortero   Hi, I'm Jorge Cortero. I'm an artist and also an art educator at P.S. 87. "Education for whom?" Ideally it is supposed to be for everyone. So they say. But the bottom line is that if you have money, then you or your children have the possibility of going to the best schools—you have that opportunity. Information, knowledge, personal growth in whatever field are all available to you. "Who has the greatest access to that organized form of education?" People with money. "Who is denied access to those same institutions?" People who can't afford school. "How is democracy served by current educational policies?" Well, if you conform to a certain quota requirement, you might have the opportunity to win a scholarship, but that still doesn't guarantee you an education. "Is a Eurocentric curriculum suitable for the increasingly multicultural nature of contemporary American society?" [laughter] No. [more laughter] No, let's face it, just here in New York City we've got all kinds of groups of people from Latinos to Greeks to Italians to Chinese to Koreans. Are their cultural needs being met? I don't think so. I know personally, as a Puerto Rican having studied in the city's educational system, that many of my needs were never met. I did learn about great European painters in my art studies here and in Europe. In elementary school I learned about Lincoln and other great people, but I never learned about Muerdo Medin or other great historical figures of Puerto Rico. That probably would have helped me to develop some form of self-esteem. But that kind of culturally specific teaching is lacking. And I am not just talking about Puerto Rican programs or black programs. It goes without saying that the curriculum is primarily Eurocentric. But I'm saying that the problem here is really about economics. Education should be something that everyone has access to; it shouldn't be based on economics.

Rollins   Eurocentric? I'll give you my definition of it as a public school teacher. Intentionally or unintentionally most of the curriculum *does* tend to concentrate on the cultures of Europe, particularly in the fine arts. That's clear. But the same is true of literature, mathematics, and philosophy. There is no Latin American philosophy, there is no African philosophy. It's basically Eurocentric. Instead, you have Puerto Rico Day, you have Black History Week, but even these are token gestures. I remember once in my first year of teaching all the teachers were told that we had to do a week-long lesson on a black leader or a black hero for Black History Day. So I said, "I'll

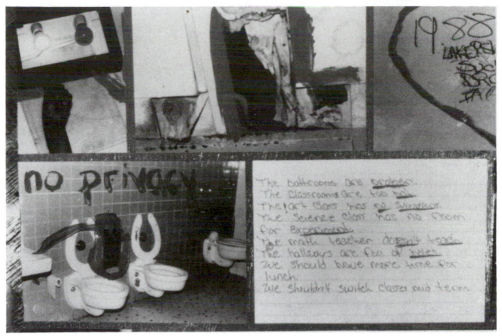

The bathrooms are broken.
The classrooms are too [illegible]
The [art] class has [no windows].
The science class has no room
for experiments.
The math teacher doesn't [read].
The hallways are full of [holes].
We should have more [time for]
lunch.
We shouldn't switch classes mid term.

Meryl Meisler and the Drop Ins, *Question Marks* (detail), 1988.

do Malcolm X." And they said, "Well no, we really don't want you to do
someone who is dead." [laughter] So I said, "Well, I'll do James Brown."
And they said, "He's *too* alive." [laughter] I think the point is that one of
the main reasons that you might not see a lot of blacks and Hispanics and
Chinese and all the other minority cultures here today is because this is not
really their turf.

I have worked in the South Bronx for ten years now. But I am the minority there, you see. To recognize and to cross those boundaries is very important, even within the curriculum. Often it's not so much a racial thing as
a class thing; you have upper-middle-class black and Hispanic teachers still
pushing *The Pearl* down the kids' throats and never ever introducing a poem
by Neruda or Marquez or any of these other people. So it's not only this
general idea of what culture is, or what education is, but the very fundamental awareness that it is not a democratic culture that we are talking about,
and it's therefore not a democratic curriculum.

One of the main things that is lost in all this is the community itself.
The community is completely shut out of the curriculum. I'm not talking
about the abstract community, but the actual community surrounding the
school. For example, Clifford Odets was born on Southern Boulevard, right
around the corner from our school, and he went to I.S. 52. Is there a book
by Clifford Odets in the library? No. I mean, you could go a year on
Clifford Odets. It's just amazing. And not only that, but Ishmel Okyme used

to live on Kelly Street (which has now become Kelly Street Park), and he wrote some of his greatest short stories right there. There is history right in the neighborhood, and although you may not think that black and Hispanic kids would relate to Clifford Odets or Okyme, if it's in the neighborhood they can. For instance, if it's part of the neighborhood, there are probably old people around who can remember these writers. Then that knowledge comes alive for the kids.

I don't think there is a diabolical monster at the board of ed saying let's cut out all the black and Hispanic studies in our curriculum. Rather, it has to do with culture as a whole. School and education and fine art *do* reflect the culture as a whole, that is a connection we have to make. The question is: How do we penetrate this larger culture through our work as educators, artists, musicians, fashion designers, construction people, critics, and all the other people I see in this room?

Betti-Sue Hertz   Hi, my name is Betti-Sue Hertz. I'm on the staff of the Bronx Council for the Arts and I'm also a visual artist. I would like to pick up on something Tim said about neighborhoods and the schools. I've also found that there is a tremendously rich traditional culture being passed down—in the form of tales, history, mythology, a sense of value and ethics—by people who are seniors in the neighborhood where the students live. But that cultural heritage is not being picked up by the school system. At the same time there is an enormous amount of resentment, hostility, and fear directed at the school by people in the community. In a lot of cases parents do not relate to what is being taught in the school, so there is a split and the child is in the middle. Often what the student is learning in school has nothing to do with the experience at home or in the streets.

The other part of this issue is that the educational system doesn't understand, or does understand and doesn't know how to deal with the enormous pressures of poverty that these people are enduring. Survival is first. If you can't survive in your community and you don't have your basic needs taken care of—emotional care and protection and health—you are not going to be able to learn.

Rodney Harris   My name is Rodney Harris. I teach at Boys and Girls High School. First of all, Eurocentricity suggests that all knowledge comes out of Europe—all the history, all the sciences, all the arts. What does this have to do with the average student? It creates a false sense of superiority among white students, and a false sense of inferiority among students of non-European ancestry. Boys and Girls High School is in Bed-Stuy; the school is 100 percent nonwhite: black and Hispanic. Last year, I was the coordinator of a program called "college-bound." For this, I was in charge of developing literature for the English department. So I had to meet with the chairman of the English department, who happens to be a lady of European descent. Taking into consideration that the education curriculum is purely Eurocentric but the school is almost 100 percent Afrocentric, I suggested to the chairman that we should have more books that our students could actually relate to. She disagreed, of course, and we got into a little argument. Finally she said, "Well, look, 70 percent of the books in this school are from a European point of view." "But 100 percent of the student population is Afrocentric. Why is it that we cannot at least have a fifty-fifty split?" She said, "That wouldn't make any sense because we are not educating these students to remain in Bed-Stuy. We are educating these students for the world."

It sounds crazy but if you think about this statement it indicates very clearly how disturbed our perceptions are because, in fact, 92 percent of the world's population is nonwhite. So if this teacher is "educating the students for the world," why is 70 percent of the literature available to the students admittedly—deliberately—Eurocentric? We have already been overexposed to Eurocentric education. Now I think there should be more of a balance. Of course, it is going to take years upon years upon years to make up that difference. What Eurocentric education does is reinforce the racism that already exists in this country and in this city. This city's school system is obviously segregated even though it is against the law. *Brown* v. *Board of Education* in 1954 supposedly eliminated that, but if you look from district to district in New York, you'll notice that the schools are purely segregated. And I would say if they are going to teach Eurocentric education in the all-black districts, they should also teach an Afrocentric education in the white districts. This would more or less balance things out, because a lot of white students have a negative view of all things that are black because of this Eurocentric education. In order to bring us back to what would be a more civilized society, we should try to balance these things out.

Unidentified Speaker Something underlying what everyone has been saying about Eurocentric education implies that it is really superior. How could it be superior if the world is now threatened by a catastrophic Greenhouse Effect? How can white male education be superior if people who graduate from school with this type of education are illiterate, able to read words but not to understand their meanings? How can it be superior if people think that the knowledge that they are learning doesn't relate to their bodies? How can this type of education be superior when people just don't help each other? How can such an education be superior if it produces people who are just out for themselves? We have to have a sense of common goals. Isn't that what education should be about?

Susan Cahan I'm Susan Cahan, and I'm the education coordinator at the New Museum of Contemporary Art. I think that while questions about the curriculum are very important, we should recognize that we are not just talking about a Eurocentric curriculum, but we are also talking about a phallocentric curriculum. It's really a dilemma because you want to develop in people a cultural vocabulary that will enable them to converse and communicate with other people in society. That is the argument for a consistent curriculum: the belief that this "common ground" will empower them and enable them to function more effectively. But I would advocate not only a greater integration of the curriculum, but also getting the students to *analyze* the Eurocentric and phallocentric materials that are being put before them. They need the tools to understand how those cultural objects exert their power and create our sense of identity. It's not enough for me to stand up and say that Picasso's *Demoiselles d'Avignon* does violence to women. I have to explain *how* it does that and *why* it does that. And that's a component that hasn't been discussed here.

Karen Hornick My name is Karen Hornick. I've been teaching freshman composition at Columbia University. It is a bastion of white male Eurocentrism, but I also have a few students from Boys and Girls High School in Brooklyn, ones who went through the higher education opportunities program. It seems to me that we keep raising the paradoxes and dichotomies of teaching without addressing the underlying philosophical questions. If we take a historical view, for instance, we would have to say that as long as there have been systematic attempts to create democracy there has been an effort to create a public school system. But at the same time there has always been a problem of trying to decide whether public schools should produce students who are all alike, or whether public schools should encourage cultural and ethnic differences. Now, as has been said, this question really has to get *outside* the school, and the school-community relationship is crucial. And it seems to me that people in the art and intellectual communities can really address this issue. There has been a lot of research at Columbia, for instance, on this subject. Shirley Brice Heath has done important anthropological field work on the education of Southern blacks in rural communities. Her research shows that even before they get to school, they learn a lot of things from their parents, especially their mothers, since it is primarily the women who raise the children. Not only do they learn specific facts from those mothers, but they learn how they learn, how to develop patterns, how to absorb information, how to think critically. But when they get to school there is this democratic urge to mainstream, and no one credits their preschool training. There has been some success recently, however, in taking this into account in certain Southern communities. My point is: we have to

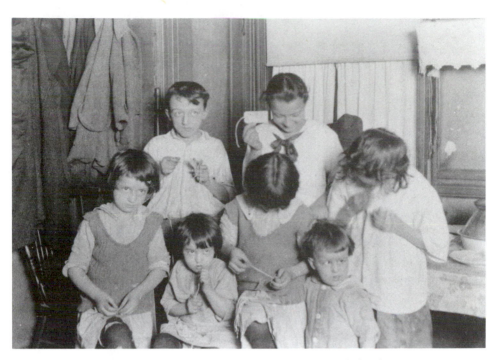

Lewis Hine, *Untitled*, ca. 1910. Children at work in the United States before the institution of child-labor laws.

think about starting the education of children by starting the education of parents.

Rollins   This connects with our next topic: "Education for what?" In the 1920s, when Horace Mann was devising the rationale for compulsory public schooling, mainly as a reaction to the child-labor laws (when the question was: What do we do with the kids now?), the whole idea harked back to Thomas Jefferson. Mann believed that a well-educated person was a more responsible person and was better able to determine the course of his or her own life, as well as that of the community. I'm not sure that is how education is viewed today. All of a sudden the Reagan administration is very concerned about education, not because they want to see individuals or communities empowered, but because they're threatened by the success of foreign markets. And it is becoming obvious that American kids are dummies. They're dummies not only in terms of what they don't know, but also in terms of their lack of job skills and their limited goals in life, beyond getting a TV or a VCR, and things like that. So that's another issue to explore. Personally, I tend to think that the solutions lie outside the public school system, in alternative situations like worker education, adult education, and elderly education. We need to hear from people involved in these kinds of projects.

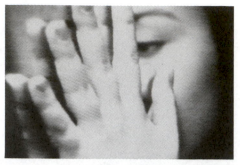

Rise and Shine Productions, video still from *The Power in our Hands*, 1988. Produced with Cyrille Phipps and the students of Mr. Miraglia's English class at Park West High School, New York, with Sean Russell, Ali Muhammad, Cathy Barreto, Carmen Cruise, Carmen Rivera and poet Kurt Lamkin.

Amy Snider My name is Amy Snider. I'm an art educator at Pratt Institute in Brooklyn. I just want to say something positive. I started teaching art in 1961 in New York City. This is my home. I have always lived here. But when I started teaching all my friends were artists or in the art world and what I did wasn't considered creative or important. It wasn't valued and so I felt alone. I had nobody to validate what I did. So tonight I am very heartened by the fact that so many of you from the art world are here. And I think we should stop worrying about all the problems and start talking about education as an arena for doing creative things. We are wasting time and time is short.

Unidentified Speaker I have recognized that fine arts is not a real popular subject, even though in the educational system they try to make it seem like one. But the bottom line is: it's in the school environment where we have to reach the kids. Yet some schools have no painting whatsoever. What I have done is to start up a mural program. The mural program gives everyone the opportunity to experience art and talk about art, from decorating auditoriums or any other space that is available, to looking for spaces in the community that we could have permission to paint. As far as themes or subject matter, it is collaborative. We try to get the community and the students involved together. We open up the subject matter to a lot of things, and not just themes dealing with culture; there are other social issues that mean a lot to the children. The mural program has been a very successful way of tackling this issue of the separation of education and democracy in the community.

Perr I want to elaborate on what Amy said. I would suggest that teaching is more than giving a lesson or developing a curriculum (although most teachers don't even have the opportunity to develop the materials that they are going to teach). We can change the system if as educators we begin to convene and have a discourse with administrators and we begin to have a dialogue with other teachers—meet after school, stay for the union meetings when they exist. Another thing to do is to meet the students outside of school. Don't run home, back to Soho or wherever you live, stay in the community and see what they're doing. The key word here is "advocacy." Most teachers that I know or I have observed are so broken down by the system that they don't realize that they can make changes. We can be active in advocating what we think is right.

Rollins Thank you, Herb. I think it's clear that the responsibility is ours. I suggest that everyone reread and think about agenda Item E which asks, "What is to be done?" and remember that all the models that are offering really strong alternatives in education, particularly arts education—I'm thinking of Bronx River Project or Harlem School of the Arts, or Jamaica Art Center, or Art & Knowledge Workshop—started from nothing.

My God!

Illustration by William Stieg as specified by Wilhelm Reich for his book, *Listen, Little Man,* 1948.

A CONVERSATION WITH
PAULO FREIRE

Paulo Freire The criticism that liberating education has to offer emphatically is not the criticism that ends at the subsystem of education. On the contrary, the criticism in the liberatory class goes beyond the subsystem of education and becomes a criticism of society. Undoubtedly, the New School Movement, the Progressive or Modern School Movement, brought many good contributions to the education process, but generally the criticism from the New School Movement stayed at the level of the school and did not extend into the larger society.

For me, one characteristic of a serious position in liberating education is to stimulate criticism that goes beyond the walls of the school—that is, in the last analysis, by criticizing traditional schools, what we have to criticize is the capitalist system that shaped these schools. Education did not create the economic base in society. Nevertheless, in being shaped by the economy, education can become a force that influences economic life. In terms of the limits of liberating education, we must understand the very subsystem of education. That is, how is systematic education constituted or constructed in the overall picture of capitalist development? We need to understand the systematic nature of education to act effectively within the space of the schools.

We know that it's not education that shapes society, but on the contrary, it is society that shapes education according to the interests of those who have power. If this is true, we cannot expect education to be the lever for the transformation of those who have power and are in power. It would be tremendously naive to ask the ruling class in power to put into practice a kind of education which can work against it. If education was left alone to develop without political supervision, it would create no end of problems for those in power. But, the dominant authorities do not leave it alone. They supervise it.

We have had in the seventies a variety of theories trying to understand education as part of the reproduction of society, which Henry Giroux has studied very well.[1] The fact is that the relationships between the subsystem of education and the global system of society are not mechanical relationships. They are historical relationships. They are dialectical and contradictory. It means then, that, from the point of view of the ruling class, of the people in power, the main task for systematic education is to reproduce the dominant ideology.

Dialectically, there is nevertheless another task to be accomplished. That is, the task of denouncing and working *against* the reproduction of the dominant ideology. Who has this second task of denouncing dominant ideology and its reproduction? The educator whose political dream is for liberation. The second task cannot be proposed by the dominant class, whose dream is for the reproduction of their power in society. Transformation has to be accomplished by those who dream about the reinvention of society, the re-creation or reconstruction of society. Then, those whose political dream is to reinvent society have to fill up the space of the schools, the institutional space, in order to unveil the reality which is being hidden by the dominant ideology, the dominant curriculum.

Of course, this unveiling is one of the main tasks of liberating education. The reproducing task of the dominant ideology implies making reality opaque, to prevent the people from gaining critical awareness, from "reading" critically their reality, from grasping the *raison d'être* of the facts they discover. To make reality opaque means to lead people to say that A is B, and B is N, to say that reality is a fixed commodity only to be described, instead of recognizing that each moment is made in history and can be changed in an historical process. An example of an obscuring myth is that unemployment in the U.S. is caused by "illegal aliens" who take jobs away from native workers, instead of seeing high unemployment as a policy of the establishment to keep wages low. This is obscuring reality. This is the task of the dominant ideology. Our task, the liberating task, at the institutional level of the schools, is to illuminate reality. Of course, it is not a neutral task, just as the other one is not neutral either.

To make reality opaque is not neutral. To make reality lucid, illuminated, is also not neutral. In order for us to do that, we have to occupy the space of schools with liberating politics. Nevertheless we cannot deny something very obvious. Those who make reality opaque through the dominant ideology, through spreading, multiplying, reproducing the dominant ideology, are swimming with the current! Those who demystify the reproducing task are swimming against the current! Swimming against the current means risking and assuming risks. Also, it means to expect constantly to be punished. I always say those who swim against the current are first being punished by the current and cannot expect to have a gift of weekends on tropical beaches!

And for me, finally, at least finally for this moment, in liberating education, the transforming teacher uses the education space without being naive. He or she knows that education is not the lever for the revolutionary transformation precisely because it should be! [laughter] This contradiction is at the heart of the problem. In order for education to be the tool for transformation it would be necessary for the ruling class in power to commit suicide! It would have to give up its dominant power in society, including its creation and supervision of the schools and colleges. We never had in history such a case and I don't believe that in this century they will give the example.

Ira Shor The authorities mandate a curriculum that they think will sustain the present structure of society. But school is not fully under their control. Education is not effectively reproducing the dominant ideology. It breeds student resistance—everything from political movements to vandalism. Teachers witness a lot of disorder in the classroom. On the other hand, school is not exactly out of control either. It is an area of political contention dominated by the authorities, where oppositional ideas and democratic culture can be organized by those who want to transform society, and where student alienation prevents the curriculum from working.

Freire Yes, that is an important addition. Before we leave this question, I want also to emphasize one important point you said before, about a frustration experienced by educators when they see that their teaching practice was not able to make the revolution they expected. In fact, they approached liberating education in an idealistic fashion. They expected from it what it cannot do, transform society by itself. In discovering finally its limits, they may start denying every effort, even important ones in the field of education, and fall into a negative criticism, sometimes almost a sick one, of those who continue to act as dialectical thinkers but not as liberatory educators. They continue to know intimately how society works, how power operates in society, but they are not able to use this understanding in the classroom. We need to know the limits and possibilities of teaching, reach to the limits, and extend ourselves beyond education to avoid this despair. . . .

Shor I want to ask how you would begin on Monday morning at a new school or college. What are the first things you would do as a liberating educator? Another issue is our right to begin transforming student consciousness. What gives liberating educators the right to change the consciousness of students? What ethics of transformation justify this pedagogy?

Freire About the right to begin the transformation of consciousness, I'll summarize what I said on manipulation, domination, and freedom, and then maybe add a few things. I said that the liberating educator can never manipulate the students and cannot leave the students alone either. The opposite of manipulation is not laissez-faire, not denying the teacher's directive responsibility for education. The liberating teacher does not manipulate and does not wash his or her hands of the students. He or she assumes a directive role necessary for educating. That directiveness is not a commanding position of "you must do this, or that," but is a posture of directing a serious study of some object in which students reflect on the intimacy of how an object exists. I call this position a radical democratic one because it attempts directiveness and freedom at the same time, without authoritarianism by the teacher and without license by the students.

This is not domination. Domination is when I say you *must* believe this because I say it. Manipulation is dominating the students. Manipulating culture makes myths about reality. It denies reality, falsifies reality. Manipulation is when I try to convince you that a table is a chair, when the curriculum makes reality opaque, when school and society present the system of monopoly capitalism as "free enterprise." In opposition, the liberating class illuminates reality. It unveils the raison d'être for any object of study. The liberating class does not accept the status quo and its myths of freedom. It challenges the students to unveil the actual manipulation and myths in society. In that unveiling, we change our understanding of reality, our perception.

Education always has a directive nature we can't deny. The teacher has a plan, a program, a goal for the study. But there is the directive *liberating* educator on the one hand, and the directive *dominating* educator on the other. The liberating educator is different from the dominating one because he or she moves more and more towards a moment in which an atmosphere of comradery is established in class. This does not mean that the teacher is equal to the students or becomes an equal to the students. No. The teacher begins different and ends different. The teacher gives grades and assigns papers to write. The students do not grade the teacher or give the teacher homework assignments! The teacher also must have a critical competence in her or his subject that is different from the students and which the students should insist on. But, here is the central issue: In the liberating classroom, these differences are not antagonistic ones, as they are in the authoritarian classroom. The liberating difference is a tension which the teacher tries to overcome by a democratic attitude to his or her directiveness.

The directive nature of a liberating course is not properly in the educator but in the practice of education itself, while the dominating educator keeps in his or her hands the objectives of education, the content of education, and the very power of directiveness in education. All these things are monopolized by the dominating educator, and something more, the very choice of the educatees about their education. Liberating educators do not keep the students controlled in their hands. I always try to relate to the students as cognitive subjects, as persons who are with me, engaged in a process of knowing something with me. The liberating educator is with the students instead of doing things for the students. In this mutual act of knowing, we have rationality and we have passion. And this is what I am. I am an impassioned educator, because I don't understand how to be alive without passion.

As teachers, we have something to offer, and we must be clear about our own offering, our competence and directiveness. But the offering is not a paternal one. It's not a gesture of angelic giving by the teacher. In the liberating perspective, we really have nothing to give. We give something to the students only when we exchange something with them. This is a dialectical relationship instead of a manipulative one. Do you see? This question of manipulation is very interesting to me, especially when I am asked about it in North America. In the culture here, in the daily life, there is great manipulation. There are many messages and directions for what you should be doing, what you should buy, what you should believe. Also, the culture here has many, many myths about freedom and happiness and about the rest of the world, which also you hear every day. "The American way of life," for example, is a political idea often presented as the only good one for the world. Another myth is that the special mission of America is to teach the whole world how to be free. I know that there are good aspects of life here and also good dimensions of American democracy. But, when such myths become global crusades, then they are instruments for manipulation. I think maybe people are so sensitive to the question of manipulation here because there is already so much of it.

From another aspect, there is also the fear of freedom, which Erich Fromm studied so well.[2] A liberating educator challenges people to know their actual freedom, their real power. As a result, people may feel manipulated when asked to reflect on such a difficult subject, because it is something they do not want to think about or they want to deny, their fear of becoming free, taking responsibility for their freedom.

Shor I agree with you about the fear of freedom and the sensitivity to manipulation here in the U.S. It may come from the pervasive domination in my culture, which constantly uses the words "freedom" and "liberty" in daily life. The mass media are everywhere and are tightly controlled by the dominant elite. Also, education is a mass experience now all the way through college. So, the official curriculum is one more mechanism for attempting domination on a grand scale.

Liberatory education challenges domination by illuminating reality for what it is, a culture where people have the power to confront manipulation. This critical pedagogy invites people to know what is hidden from us and to know how we cooperate in denying our own freedom. A liberatory class can also unveil the limits of domination in a society where the system presents itself as invulnerable. Many people, especially in an affluent society like the U.S., may refuse such an invitation and consider it manipulation merely to be challenged by such questions. . . .

Freire This is a great discovery, education is politics! After that, when a teacher discovers that he or she is a politician, too, the teacher has to ask, "What kind of politics am I doing in the classroom?" That is, "In favor of whom am I being a teacher?" By asking, "In favor of whom am I educating?" the teacher must also ask, "Against whom am I educating?" Of course, the teacher who asks in favor of whom I am educating and against whom, must also be teaching in favor of something and against something. This "something" is just the political project, the political profile of society, the political "dream." After that moment, the educator has to make his or her choice, to go farther into opposition politics and pedagogy.

The teacher works in favor of something and against something. Because of that, she or he will have another great question, "How to be consistent in my teaching practice with my political choice?" The educator might say, "Now I have discovered the reality of society and my choice is for a liberating education." I know that teaching is not the lever for changing or transforming society, but I know that social transformation is made by lots of small and great and big and humble tasks! I have one of these tasks. I am an agent with humility for the global task of transformation. Okay, I discover that, I proclaim that, I verbalize my choice. The question now is how to put my practice next to my speech. That is, how to be consistent in the classroom. For instance, I cannot proclaim my liberating dream and in the next day, in behalf of *rigor,* be authoritarian in my relationship to the students.

Shor Or give them the experience that learning is boring or to discuss ideas is to fall asleep in the classroom or to be passive in front of a talking teacher.

Freire Yes. Because of that, I also cannot be liberal, or even something more than liberal, liberalist! I cannot be spontaneist, a word we use now in Brazil. That is, I cannot leave the students by themselves because I am trying to be a liberating educator. Laissez-faire! I cannot fall into laissez-faire. On the other hand, I cannot be authoritarian. I have to be radically democratic and responsible and directive. *Not* directive of the *students,* but directive of the *process,* in which the students are with me. As director of the process, the liberating teacher is not doing something *to* the students but *with* the students.

I think, Ira, generally these changes happen in the history of many of us teachers. It does not mean that everyone must have the same experience. But, sometimes, it is a long process in which we learn a lot. Still, the more the educator becomes aware of these things, the more he or she learns from practice, and then he or she discovers that it is possible to bring into the classroom, into the context of the seminar, moments of the social practice in which he or she is. In the last analysis, education belongs to the social practice of society.

---

1. See Henry Giroux, *Theory and Resistance in Education: A Pedagogy for the Opposition* (South Hadley, Mass.: Bergin and Garvey, 1983).

2. See Erich Fromm's *Escape from Freedom* (New York, 1941), *Man For Himself* (New York, 1947), and *Beyond the Chains of Illusion: My Encounter with Marx and Freud* (New York, 1962).

POLITICS AND ELECTION

YOUR
DREAMS
By KATY

Dear Katy: I am 62 years of age. I have been having dreams about the President, the ex-President, the President-elect and the Supreme Court justices. I dreamed I had authority over them all and I commanded them to scrub the main street of our city. There were many people that were also telling them to keep on scrubbing, but I was the one who prescribed this punishment. I wonder why I have dreams like this.   JUDGE AND JURY

Dear J and J: I think this dream shows what you'd like your leaders to do for you—to clean up the cities, or to make things better "closer to home" (your city). Prescribing the punishment symbolizes your idea of the solution to many of our economic and social problems. The scrubbing action strongly suggests that you are more concerned with moral or spiritual leadership than the . . .   Political Kind,
KATY

Letters to KATY should include approximate age, sex, occupation and marital status. All names will be kept strictly confidential. Address KATY, The News, P.O. Box 2453, Grand Central Station, New York, N.Y. 10017.

POLITICS AND ELECTION

Participants in the roundtable discussion of June 4, 1988:

Richard Andrews, director of the Henry Art Gallery, University of Washington, and former director of the Visual Arts Program for the National Endowment for the Arts
Leon Golub, artist
Esther Parada, artist
Judge Bruce Wright, Supreme Court Justice, New York State
Group Material: Doug Ashford, Julie Ault, Felix Gonzalez-Torres

Richard Andrews My first response to your proposal to have a town meeting is to ask, "Why?" A town meeting is a moment when the citizens, who are empowered by the government, make a decision. It presupposes that those called are convening under some conventions, rules, or other operating principles. But the decision making, while not necessarily effortless, is not necessarily corrective, either. It is a mechanism to participate in, one way or another. I guess my biggest question about the town meeting you propose is what community will this be? Considering the audience of Dia, the community will most likely be one of artists, maybe even some artists involved in social action, plus some inactive socialists and active socialists. But if you really want to make it open to the general public, it seems to me that you can't. You don't make it possible for them to take action because it is in a museum situation, it's set up by artists in an art context. Even if you invite the public you don't empower them. You provide them with information but that's about it.

Julie Ault We hope the town meeting will provide some kind of empowerment. It's not that we're giving people power, but that a forum is provided where all of these people can get together—say we have a crisis in education or a crisis in the political sphere—they can identify issues, articulate ideas, perhaps form a coalition and do something. We don't know exactly what is going to happen, but we hope that something positive will come out of it.

Leon Golub I think the point is whose turf it's on. Dia Art Foundation turf is one thing, a church in Harlem is something else, it includes other people.

Ault   That's our challenge. The specialized audience is a limitation but at the same time we have to work really hard to use that context, and it's a community we are part of, one that we do not discount in favor of a fictional idea of "the people."

Andrews   I can understand. I could see it as a town meeting for the arts community. It's not an exclusionary principle because a town meeting like that is a little-used mechanism, except maybe during the sixties and with antiwar protests. But then you had a social galvanizing motion; it was a completely different time.

When I lived in Seattle, I went to tons of community meetings and neighborhood meetings because I was developing public art projects. It's a totally different thing to go into someone's living room where there are forty committed activists with full agendas. That is completely different. You have to go in and explain the art work's function and its social claim because the audience there has real power. You are a plaintiff, and you have to make your point and live with the decision. I am not arguing with your idea of staging a meeting here, I am just trying to clarify what it is, what is possible.

Bruce Wright   What you said about the site—Dia versus Harlem—was interesting. It wouldn't be easy to compare but one idea would be to hold a meeting in one situation and a similar meeting with a similar agenda in a different location and see whether the results were different.

Doug Ashford   Well, we recently had our roundtable on education here at Dia, and a week later I was at a meeting at the public high school where I teach. The same issues were approached in each but the identities of outsiders and insiders were obviously different in each case.

Felix Gonzalez-Torres   Our consciousness of Dia as an art institution leads to what I think is really the point. We are all faced with a dilemma: do we do art or do we get involved with the society at large? People say, "Why do you want us there? We don't know much about politics." But that's exactly why we want those people here. Things are always interrelated. I mean, something that affects the National Endowment for the Arts is political and may affect me or you in a certain way. Politics affects everyday life.

Andrews   Artists are no different than everybody else. Democratic principles are used by only .05 percent of the population; the other 99.95 percent of the population is either still figuring out how government works, or is naive. Most people don't realize how easy it is to move the government. It's the ignorance of the people that keeps the politicians in power.

I remember when I worked for a city arts agency, we used to lobby for our budget at city budget hearings. I remember one city council person coming up to me afterward and saying that after the police, the arts get more phone calls than any other issue. How many can this be? Well, the fact is, on something topical, something that is in the newspapers, they might expect fifty to a hundred calls. On something not in the paper if the city council person got five to ten letters they would stop dead in their tracks and call it a ground swell of public opinion. It is remarkable how much can be done effectively with just a few people paying attention. That is how political activists, really smart ones, work the system. You appear to have a large mass behind you but in fact you are just astute about how to use the democratic system.

Golub Twenty-five phone calls mean one thing, but the $10,000 contributor is the one that comes back with what he wants. It has to be a really huge groundswell to influence a politician. It has to be a real threat to his staying in power. If there is another candidate running and enough people are getting behind him, then they start paying attention. They don't pay attention otherwise. When it comes to something for which there are real forces contending and there is a great deal at stake, you need a lot to move politicians. Using money and pressure moves them faster than public opinion. That's the whole history of the federal government right now—influence peddling. And local government is even worse.

Andrews I still contend that you can do quite a bit. I respect your opinion but politicians are pretty much like everybody else. There is a relatively small number of politicians and a vast number of people in government doing things. Those people in government, if they choose not to do something, can slow the whole system down or speed it up. My response to you, Leon, is that your view doesn't allow for a position in the middle that says, "Figure out *how* to make the system work." You're just saying they're corrupt and it's not possible to take power as a citizen.

Golub I'm not saying that. But I am disagreeing with the idea that a few people can change things. At a certain level a lot can be changed but at other levels even if you have a ground swell you can't get these guys to move. A majority of the people in this country are in favor of abortion, but that doesn't show in the Congress. That is just one example.

Andrews You're exactly right. I was referring to local issues, either culturally or nonculturally based. Basically, the more local the issue, the closer the politician is to the populace, the more likely it is that a small number of people can influence him.

Catherine Saalfield and Zoe Leonard, video still from *Keep Your Laws Off My Body*, 1989.

Golub One thing we have to recognize is the contradictory nature of our democracy. We are in an extremely hierarchical society; language, authority, and power differences are clearly both demarcated and obscured. Ironically, this means that if you want to challenge something, often the lines of power are obscured, but when they want to do something, then the lines are very clear about how they go ahead and do it.

Wright That depends on where you are. Pitirim Sorokin speaks about the "organized minority." He gives as an example the United States Supreme Court, where five people can say what is proper for the entire country even if four others are in dissent. This is the situation we have right now with regard to the death penalty.

Gonzalez-Torres The Supreme Court is a really good example. Nine people get together and decide who you can love and who you can't love. For me that is really obscure, I can never grasp why something like that goes on. I'm referring to the 1986 Supreme Court ruling upholding Georgia's sodomy law allowing the state into people's bedrooms.

Wright It's not always the courts that finally decide things. I remember one instance in California where the State Supreme Court declared the desegregation laws unconstitutional. State senator Earl Desmond was asked if, given the Supreme Court's ruling, the state legislature would now repeal the desegregation laws. Desmond said, "Hell no, it may be a different Supreme Court in a couple of years." So it is the state legislature that finally decides things, it seems to me. The legislature simply undoes Supreme Court decisions they think are oppressive.

Gonzalez-Torres Who gave the power to those people to decide and who gave the power to museum people to put certain objects on the walls and not others?

Golub Law equals control and power. Judgment and decision making, despite "precedents," are self-constituted, self-arrogated. In other words, I give myself the right to do this. Now, how can others accept the fact that I am in this position? I am granted this position, chosen, "elected," or I force my way in, another form of election, that eventually becomes "precedent." How do communities constitute themselves? Who claims prerogatives of decision making? Who gives museums privilege? Who gives curators authority? They give each other rights. I appoint you, you then appoint "X," who then reaffirms my position.

Wright But apparently you can have some change occasionally. Look at what has been done at Stanford and the argument about the old virtues versus those that exist on, pardon the expression, the lower level. Timing is everything. And the amount of noise you make. For example, in 1941 or 1942, the Metropolitan Life Insurance Company decided it was going to create the Peter Cooper Village and Stuyvesant Town. And the chairman of the board announced that under no circumstances would Negroes live in either of those two places. So a group of us commenced a legal action, because even though the state and the city had condemned the chairman's position, it was clearly state action. The United States Supreme Court, however, was not prepared to recognize this segregation as state action and therefore unconstitutional. It was only after the loud noises of minorities and demonstrations and sit-ins and pray-ins and whatnot; it was only *after* that the Supreme Court began to recognize certain rights for black people in this country. It was a loud noise and it almost seemed for a time that the country was on a path toward self-destruction because of the violence and because of people like Bull Connor and so forth. There was a lot of noise, though, and it was startling. The change that started then lead some of us idealists to believe that it could happen elsewhere. We were quite wrong about that.

Ashford One of the things that keeps getting batted around is how people take on an identity of participation. That is one of the things for me anyway that is part of this whole crisis of democracy. I teach in Bedford-Stuyvesant,

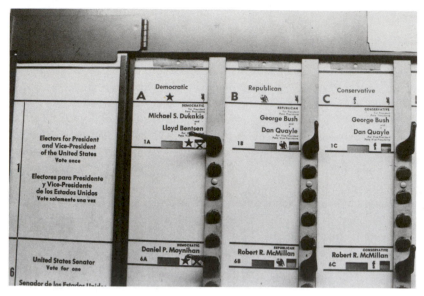

Voting machine, 1988 presidential election.

in a working-class black high school. There is an overwhelming attitude among the students that I'm idealistic because I'm white, and that Mr. Harris talks idealistically because he was with the Panthers, and that that's the sixties, and we don't know what it's about for them now. And what's very interesting to me is that they cite elections, which seem to be the very foundation of the democratic society, as that which will most obstruct political participation. The thing that limits their participation is elections.

Andrews The crisis of democracy in this country is the disbelief that democracy even exists, disbelief among a large portion of the population that there are any problems, and belief that they're not active participants in it. I think the students you are talking about probably don't believe in democracy. They may understand the concept and the history of the country but they don't believe they are actors in it. The difference between now and twenty years ago is a very real one. Then you had an activated population because of the Vietnam War, and artists could lead the charge. They didn't have, as you do now, a passive population, apathetic. When you have a town meeting you have to think about what you are trying to do. Are artists figuring out how to become more engaged? Or are you simply trying to make them into better citizens?

I guess the distinction I would make would be that in the sixties artists had the ability to be catalytic because of particular skills of communication. For a larger, suddenly aware population they could crystallize images and therefore make action possible. Right now there is no fixed focus for the kind of action we're talking about, except maybe around AIDS. The situation right now is this: if you really want to change things, you'd better be ready for the long haul, and you'd better be ready to go into these little communities. That is the way democracy works. A thousand little meetings in a thousand little living rooms building up to a hundred thousand meetings in state assemblies. You'd be surprised, you have five or ten people going to these neighborhood meetings over a fifteen-year period, one by one going through these issues; they pay attention and they make it work, they get the ear of the politician. They *are* the community representatives and if anybody wants to know the opinion of this section of the community, it's those five people they go to and that's the official version. Where do the congressmen go if they want to learn about the views of the wider population? They go to the county government. That includes, say, one person from that five-person community club who has been elected to go to the county system. What I'm saying is, in a situation like the one we have now, you really have to look at how one uses participation in a nonactive situation. You have to commit yourself to that process, to going to those meetings when the trash collection is discussed. It's not all about AIDS or the contras.

Golub   But you are talking in a reasonable, logical way. Now we have to look at the other side. What happens is those five people who have been going to those meetings for fifteen years start to think they know all the answers. They control the school board, they control some other aspect of everything. These are often people of good will—originally of good will and maybe also of continuing good will—who have become chained to the issues and solutions to which they have given their great effort. They often feel that the efforts they have made are not only not being rewarded but they have prepared for ten years and they don't like to be impugned in *their* issue. You continually have the problem of how to break open even that group of people. As it becomes stabilized, each group becomes a power broker and must be looked at from the outside with skepticism.

Andrews   If it is a democratic system then we are automatically empowered. The question is, how do you get much leverage? On the local level, five people, on the national level, 500,000 people. How many artists are there? According to the census there are 250,000 artists in this country. If you get half those people to do anything together on a national level, boycott dairy products or anything, somebody will pay attention to you.

Golub   I think that if people really learn that they *have* power then they are going to be a real threat, because there are more people out of power than in power. There are people dissatisfied at one level or another about all kinds of

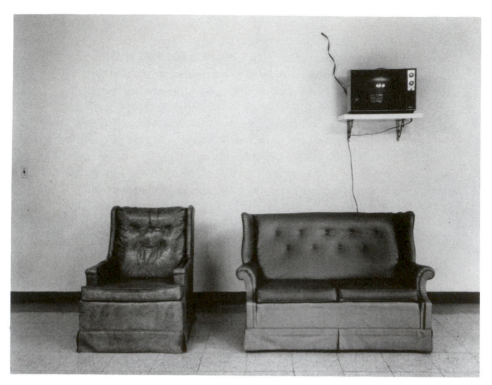

Lynne Cohen, *Retirement*.

issues. They have to be, in one sense, manipulated by the government, the information they receive has to be distorted to keep them a republic rather than a democracy. The notion of a republic is more bureaucratic than the notion of a democracy. Democracy means that the majority might actually change something.

Andrews The one area in which artists are able to really do something is image making. But the media has such a more sophisticated understanding of the role of myth in society and the role of heroes in society. Artists are certainly not oblivious to these techniques, but the imagery being used for political protests in this country by artists is usually inappropriate and does not really work. Just think of how the Reagan people dealt with photo opportunities—sticking Reagan in front of this or that backdrop. They knew exactly what they were doing, feeding a kind of subconscious mythological desire for heroes. It's really pretty rich imagery to plug into.

Esther Parada Students, teachers need to be aware of that and to introduce that into their curriculum. To some extent that happens, but not much.

Golub   One thing we have to be really conscious of in politics is that media has opened up all kinds of channels and they are emitting lots of different noises. Information flow is ruled by technology. Just look at the old-fashioned mimeograph machines; in some countries, they were locked up because the minute someone got hold of one you have too many copies. Now we have Xerox machines, fax machines, video cameras, and desktop publishing. These have opened up information to students or anyone else, the possibility of distributing information on the streets or anywhere. There are new ways of reaching audiences. We are talking about communication.

Parada   Another thing we should take into account is the problem of illiteracy and its relation to the electoral process. There are now about 30 million people in this country who are considered illiterate. Needless to say, this is a major obstacle to their participation in voting. They are literally intimidated by the process of voting, by the language of the ballot, and by some of the terminology that is used. Some programs are being developed to counteract that. We need to develop a theory of literacy which has to do simultaneously with literacy, education, *and* the political process. There is no such thing as a depoliticized education.

Ault   Last night I saw this town meeting special on television. It was on from twelve to three A.M., which is a really strange time slot for a live session. Anyway, John Johnson and Bill Beutel, two newscasters, organized it and set up several panels to discuss education, community activism, and politics. They invited primarily black, Hispanic, and Asian community leaders—politicians, borough presidents, and so forth. The overall topic was racism. The publisher of the *Amsterdam News,* Wilbert Tatum, described how the media asks, "Where are your black leaders?" Then they designate a black leader, say, Al Sharpton, and turn around and denounce him. They make sure these leaders are not really representative of the community, that they kind of embody the problems but don't really work with them.

It was such a shock to turn on the TV at twelve o'clock, expecting to see *The Honeymooners* and here was this live special *Town Meeting on Racism* with twenty-five articulate political and community leaders speaking frankly about the issues. The sad part is that it was on at twelve o'clock at night, which is ridiculous. Still, I'm sure it was very empowering for a lot of people to even see those issues discussed in the mass media.

Wright   You're right, it is important to start someplace. But activism can be very dangerous, too. I tried to be activist, for example, in expanding the role of the bench. I've been before disciplinary committees thirteen times in my eighteen years in this business. That's a lot. But you try to change what you see as evil and dangerous⸍to what you believe to be justice and you find out that judges are not supposed to do that. That's the theory. We are supposed to be absolutely above and out of politics, even though we come to the bench through politics. You're not supposed to say certain things. For example, in a lecture at Princeton I said that white policemen seem to have free license to shoot and kill blacks with impunity. Well, I don't know how someone got a copy of my speech, but before I knew it I was before the commission and they were asking, "Do you think it is proper for a judge to say those things?" It seems that free speech stops outside the courthouse door for a judge. Although my defense was, and always has been, that judges are supposed to try to elevate the law and educate the public to respect it by their example, that turned out not to be a very good defense. They censured me. That's bad for your record.

I have also criticized the manner of selection of judges, for example, I've been very outspoken about the selection of police and judges—those who control one's fate and indeed one's life. I think it's too late to send a policeman who has shot and killed somebody to a psychiatrist. I think it's too late to analyze a judge who knows nothing about the sociological background of the kinds of people he sits in judgment of in a city such as this. So, for instance, I have urged that all potential judges, in order to qualify for the bench, must show some knowledge of sociology, black history, Hispanic culture, and so forth—something of the lives of the people who will come before them. Most of the judges in this country are white, middle-class males.

Just before Alexis de Tocqueville completed *Democracy in America,* he took a tour of this country to see how things were doing in the 1830s, to see how democracy was doing. He came away with the mistaken belief that the nobility, or indeed the aristocracy, in this country reposed in the bench and the bar. He said that Americans sue at the drop of a hat. We still do. I think it is a good thing. It helped shape some of the aspects of democracy, those aspects that are real democracy. George Bernard Shaw said America was the only country in the history of the world to suffer a decline and a fall in its civilization without first becoming civilized. I think we're still in the process of trying to do that.

Parada Just to get back to the idea of the actual meeting, I assume you are tying in with people like Paper Tiger and Deep Dish, people like that—media activists. It seems to me that work is really important. Also, I would like to know more about what people are doing in computers, because that's what I have gotten more interested in lately. I'd like to see your organization help to establish some sort of clearinghouse, to make a connection between people who need to draw upon communication skills and people who have

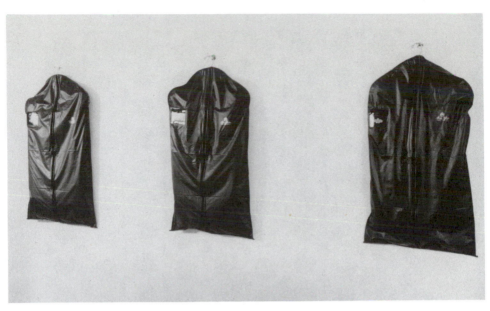

John Armleder, *346*, 1988.

them. I think there are people who are really happy to do that, they might do it as a donation. In advertising, these donations are what they call PSAs, public service announcements.

Golub The question is, do artists have a social point of view? If the answer is "yes," then they can do something collectively. The irony is that a social view may be at odds with the people in the community who support the arts.

Artists organize around issues. When I came to live in New York in 1964, there was a group called Artists and Writers Protest Against the War in Vietnam. That was in operation and I joined it. They organized about Vietnam. Twenty years later, Artists Call Against U.S. Intervention in Central America was organized. They organized around issues of potential intervention in Nicaragua. One of the problems with this whole town meeting thing, as I see it, is you just can't have a town meeting about having a town meeting. Artists become active when there is an issue that involves them crucially, and often political issues do, then you'll get their participation and then they'll start using their work as a weapon. Artists are not in the same business as documentary photographers who seek out struggle, civil war, events as they transpire. If you want to get artists involved, you have to organize them around issues, not around a general notion of organization.

All Americans tap into the modern media; it is what our culture is. But as far as artists participating in the media—I mean using the media against itself, trying to manipulate the media—I think you have to ask: Who benefits from it? In any kind of action, regardless if it is propaganda, interven-

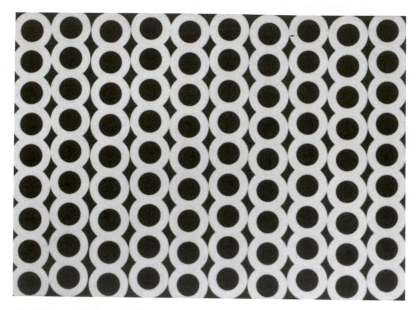

Curtis Brown, *We Came in Chains*, 1978.

tion, desire, anything else, you immediately get into the problem of neutrality. You know, "I'm neutral and you're not." You have to ask: Who benefits? You always find that there is somebody benefiting, whether it's cigarette advertising or anticigarette advertising. People benefit from gentrification or antigentrification. Who benefits from selling this kind of art as opposed to another kind of art? There is always a profit-and-loss statement involved with every kind of situation. Who benefits from changing education? Who benefits from adding 20,000 voters? And who does not benefit? Everything has its profit and loss, though often it is hidden. Profit and loss is entrenched in every situation. I think that is what we are talking about.

Mark P. Petracca

ELECTIONS OFFER ONLY AN
ILLUSION OF PARTICIPATION

Letter to the Editor
The New York Times
Monday, March 28, 1988

To the Editor:

For nearly three decades political scholars, analysts, and pundits have lambasted the American public for its poor performance at the polls. Graham Allison and Katie Smith (Op Ed, March 11) join the cry for Americans to move out of the stands as spectators and onto the playing field as political participants. Their charge is admirable, compelling, and dangerous, as it misses a number of significant issues raised by the phenomenon of non-voting behavior.

First, the authors are presumptively guilty of blaming the victim—in this case the American voter—for failure to vote. If Americans are staying away from the polls on Election Day, we must do something to alter this behavior. But who is really to blame? It is the new politics of political consultants, mass media, public relations, polling, targeted mailings, and political action committees, which encourages the average American to stay on the sidelines and watch the political contest.

In the early nineteenth century, Alexis de Tocqueville expressed his admiration for America's passion for associational life. Tocqueville believed that this passion would be the key ingredient in a vibrant and productive democracy. But how can modern American voters participate in the modern political campaign? The answer is that they cannot. Without the means to participate in the mechanisms that matter, the vote loses its essential meaning and value as an instrument of electoral governance.

We should not then be surprised that the rise of the new politics is closely associated with the collapse of electoral participation. Solutions such as those suggested by Mr. Allison and Ms. Smith make participation logistically easier and morally compelling. However, they will not make the vote meaningful again unless voters are given back the instruments of electoral empowerment.

The authors also imply that somehow we would be better off—as individuals and a society—if everyone who could vote did. Why? It is questionable that higher voter turnout in nearly every other Western democracy means better citizens or public policy. On the other hand, a larger electorate may only further legitimize the biases in the American political system, e.g., majority tyranny or the privileged position of business.

Further, I don't believe the problem with American democracy is about voting at all. Rather, it is about the absence of a participatory life and ethic for most Americans. In the aftermath of World War II, American democratic theory has placed far too much emphasis on the vote and the electoral system. Electoral politics is the politics of inclusion; elections incorporate and co-opt the citizenry in a stable and nondisruptive form of political participation.

Definitions of democracy and good governance that focus on electoral participation are a potent instrument for social control. Elections offer the illusion of participation in exchange for political quiescence. In sum, they limit and constrain our interactions with our government—substituting subordination for the promised liberation of participatory democracy.

Electoral involvement does not necessarily empower its participants; rather it tends to create power over them. Contrary to popular sentiment, I believe that a considerable number of Americans understand this. Perhaps instead of trying to compel their involvement as voters we would be well advised to heed their potent message about the apparent distribution of power in America.

Mark P. Petracca
Asst. Professor, Politics and Society
University of California
Irvine, California
March 17, 1988

AN INTERVIEW WITH
NOAM CHOMSKY

Bill Moyers Fifty-five percent of the people in the latest Gallup Poll express approval of President Reagan as he is preparing to leave office, so that you have polls showing opposition to his policies while he himself remains unusually popular in the public standing.

Noam Chomsky If you take a look at comparative poll results, he's not that unusually popular. The popularity of a president is usually predicted quite closely by people's sense of where the economy is going. When people sense that the economy is probably improving, they tend to approve of the president. When they sense that the economy is declining, they tend to disapprove of the president. Reagan himself has been reasonably popular, though not by and large beyond the norm for presidents. On the other hand, his policies have been unpopular, and sometimes this shows up quite dramatically. In the presidential election in 1984, there was a very intriguing exit poll which shows that voters disapproved of Reagan's policies by about three to two. The majority said they hoped his legislative programs would not be enacted. Now these were the people who had just voted for him by two to one. So what's happening?

Moyers That's a good question.

Chomsky It's pretty clear what's happening. Look at other studies of public opinion. Every year the Gallup Poll asks people, "Who do you think runs the government?" Consistently, about 50 percent say the government is run by a few big interests looking out for themselves. I suspect that the 50 percent who say that are roughly the 50 percent who don't vote, who tend to be the poor and the dispossessed. They don't participate in the political system.

Reagan is a very interesting political figure, a very natural phenomenon in a capitalist democracy. In a capitalist democracy, you have the problem that the general population participates in the decision making by participating in politics. The state is not capable of stopping them. You can't shut them out, you can't put them in jail, and you can't keep them away from the polls. It's striking that that has always been perceived as a problem to be overcome. It's called the "crisis of democracy"—too many people organizing themselves to enter the public arena. That's a crisis we have to overcome.

Moyers According to a certain view.

Chomsky Well, it's the view of a very wide spectrum. In fact, the crisis of democracy was articulated by the group around Jimmy Carter.

Moyers The Trilateral Commission—

Chomsky —and the report they put out called "The Crisis of Democracy." That report reflects attitudes that go way back. Even the mainstream democratic theorists have always understood that when the voice of the people is heard, you're in trouble, because these stupid and ignorant masses, as they're called, are going to make the wrong decisions. So, therefore, we have to have what Walter Lippmann, back in 1920 or so, called "manufacture of consent." We have to ensure that actual power is in the hands of what he called a specialized class—us smart guys, who are going to make the right decisions. We've got to keep the general population marginalized because they're always going to make mistakes. The Founding Fathers had very strong feelings in this respect. The Federalists, for example, were very much afraid of popular democracy.

Moyers That's why we have a representative form of government.

Chomsky The transition from the confederation to the constitutional system marginalized the public. Shays' Rebellion was probably the last reflection of the popular democracy of the earlier period.

Moyers You said Reagan is interesting as a political figure. Why?

Chomsky Because from a point of view that perceives democracy as a problem to be overcome, and sees the right solution as being farsighted leaders with a specialized class of social managers—from that point of view, you must find means of marginalizing the population.

Moyers Marginalizing?

Chomsky Reducing them to apathy and obedience, allowing them to participate in the political system, but as consumers, not as true participants. You allow them a method for ratifying decisions that are made by others, but you eliminate the methods by which they might first, inform themselves;

Demonstrators en route to United Nations headquarters, New York, during massive anti-Vietnam War rally on April 15, 1967.

second, organize; and third, act in such a way as to really control decision making. The idea is that our leaders control us, we don't control them. That is a very widespread view, from liberals to conservatives. And how do you achieve this? By turning elected offices into ceremonial positions. If you could get to the point where people would essentially vote for the Queen of England and take it seriously, then you would have gone a long way toward marginalizing the public. We've made a big step in that direction.

Moyers The president as ceremonial leader.

Chomsky Yes. That's why Reagan is so interesting. Although a lot of intellectuals put the best face they can on it, most of the population knows that Ronald Reagan had only the foggiest ideas of what the policies of his administration were. Nobody much cared. The Democrats were always surprised that he could get away with these bloopers and crazy statements and so on. The reason is that much of the population understood very well that they were supporting someone like the Queen of England or the flag. The Queen of England opens Parliament by reading a political program, but nobody asks whether she understands it or believes it.

Moyers So many books from within the Reagan administration—from the Stockman book to the Regan book to the new book that's on the news-stands—say that the president was detached from the decision-making process.

Chomsky More than detached. I think he doesn't know what it is.

Moyers He's performing well the ritualistic role.

Chomsky It's the flag. To the extent that you feel good about the way things are going, you'll say, "I like the flag, I like the Queen," and so on. To the extent that you don't like the way things are going, you'll say, "I'm un-happy about it," and so on. But this is quite dissociated from your positions as to what ought to be done.

We have an interesting political system in the United States, one that's different from those of the other industrial democracies. This is a very free country. By comparative standards, the state is very restricted in its capacity to coerce and control us. The police can't come in and stop us from talking, for example.

Moyers You're saying we are free as individuals—we can say anything we want to, for example.

Chomsky But we don't make use of those freedoms. Sophisticated mecha-nisms have been devised to prevent us from making use of those freedoms. In a society where the state does not have the power to coerce, other mecha-nisms must be found to ensure that the population doesn't get in the way—indoctrination, for example, or elimination of popular organizations like unions. To have ideas, to interchange those ideas with others, to turn these ideas into possible programs, and to press for those programs—all this takes access to information. It takes an independent media. It requires organiza-tions by which isolated people can group together. . . . Suppose I'm running for office, and I don't tell people what I think or what I'm going to do, I tell them what the pollsters have told me is going to get me elected. That's ex-pressing utter contempt for the electorate. That's saying, "Okay, you people are going to have the chance to push your buttons, but once you're done, I'll do exactly what I intend, which is not what I'm telling you."

If you express what you believe, you don't have to ask what the polls tell you.

Moyers If you conduct polls to tell you what people want, and they tell you, are you not listening to the voice of the people?

Chomsky   Only if that changes your mind. But of course the system is based on the assumption that it doesn't change your mind, it changes what you say. In other words, a political figure is not testing the waters and saying, okay, that's what I believe. If we had that kind of a political figure, we wouldn't bother voting for him. The political figure is not a barometer—he represents something, and he's supported by certain interests and has certain commitments. Now the political figure comes before us and tells us things which the pollsters have told him will increase his chances of gaining office. After the election, he will do what is demanded of him by those who provided him with resources. This has always been true, but what is interesting now is the extent to which it is recognized to be the democratic system. It is recognized that we don't care what we say. We don't express interests. What we do is reflect power. And so we have a candidate who's rehearsed in the answers that he's supposed to give. The debates, so-called, are basically stage-managed public relations operations.

Film still from Warner Brothers' *The Candidate*, 1972.

We see the effects of this in the remarkable decline of the level of what is said. This jingoist flag-waving has a tingle of 1930s populist fascism about it. We don't like to say it, but Hitler was a very popular leader. If he'd bothered to run an election, he probably would have won it. He used populist techniques—appealing to the population, but on the basis of chauvinistic and racist premises. Now we're beginning to see elements of that in the demeaning of the concept of patriotism by reducing it to coerced pledges of allegiance to the flag. That's astonishing. The fact that a political candidate can stand up in public and call someone a card-carrying member of the

ACLU—that means his advisers or the people who write his words for him are telling him support of the Constitution is subversive. The ACLU is an organization that supports constitutional rights. The phrase "card-carrying" is a way of implying, of course, that it's somehow subversive. All of these things reflect the general vacuity of the discussion. They are just parallel modes of marginalizing the public.

Moyers Of reducing the importance of the individual and the individual's participation in the political process.

Chomsky We're even proceeding beyond the point where people can ratify decisions made by others. We're simply being asked to elect ceremonial figures who will then be a surface for the interests behind the scenes that are conducting policy.

Moyers I once interviewed Edward Bernays, the pioneering figure in American business public relations. He talked about "the engineering of consent."

Chomsky Yes, he thought it was a wonderful thing. In fact, he described it as the essence of democracy.

Moyers The effort to persuade people to see things your way.

Chomsky He said the essence of democracy is that we have the freedom to persuade. But who has the freedom to persuade? Well, who runs the public relations industry? It's not the special interests—they're the targets of the public relations industry. The public relations industry is a major industry, closely linked to other corporations. Those are the people who have the power to persuade and who engineer the consent of others.

Moyers A vice president at AT&T in 1909 said that he thought the public mind was the chief danger to the economy. What did he mean by that?

Chomsky The general public might have funny ideas about corporate control. For example, people who really believe in democracy, people who take eighteenth-century values seriously, people who really might merit the term conservative are against concentration of power. The Enlightenment held that individuals should be free from the coercion of concentrated power. The kind of concentrated power they were thinking about was the church, the state, the feudal system, and so on. But in the subsequent period, a new form of power developed—namely, corporations—with highly concentrated power over decision making in economic life. We should not be forced simply to rent ourselves to the people who own the country and its institutions. Rather, we should play a role in determining what those institutions do. That's democracy.

Moyers That is the premise of your whole view, is it not? That in democracy the people should initiate—

Chomsky They should run their own organization, whether it's a community or a union.

Moyers Should corporations be run by their shareholders?

Chomsky No, they should be run by the employees. I don't think there should be shareholders. The very idea of shareholders reflects the conception of the wealthy getting more votes than the poor—a lot more votes, in fact. If we were to move toward democracy, even in the eighteenth-century sense, there would be no maldistribution of power in determining what's produced, what's distributed, and what's invested. That's a problem for the entire community. In fact, unless we move in that direction, human society probably isn't going to survive.

Moyers Why not?

Chomsky We now face the most awesome problems of human history— nuclear conflict and the destruction of our fragile environment. They're of a level of seriousness that they never were in the past.

Moyers By why do you think more democracy is the answer?

Chomsky More democracy is a value in itself. Democracy as a value doesn't have to be defended any more than freedom has to be defended. It's an essential feature of human nature that people should be free, should be able to participate, and should be uncoerced.

Moyers But why do you think if we go that route—

Chomsky —that's the only hope that other values will come to the fore. If the society is based on control by private wealth, it will reflect the values that it, in fact, does reflect now—greed and the desire to maximize personal gain at the expense of others. A small society based on that principle is ugly, but it can survive. A global society based on that principle is headed for massive destruction. We have to have a mode of social organization that reflects other values inherent in human nature. It's not the case that in the family every person tries to maximize personal gain at the expense of others. If they do, it's pathological. It's not the case that if you and I are walking down the street, and we see a child eating a piece of candy, and we see that nobody's around, and we happen to be hungry, that we steal the candy. Concern for other people's needs and concern for our fragile environment that must sustain future generations are part of human nature. But these elements are suppressed in a social system which is designed to maximize personal gain. We must try to overcome that suppression. That's, in fact, what democracy could bring about. It could lead to the expression of other human needs and values which tend to be suppressed under the institutional structure of a system of private power and profit.

Moyers   But by your own analysis, we're moving in the other direction.

Chomsky   Certainly the institutions are moving toward more centralization, more marginalization, the elimination of options, and so on. On the other hand, the population itself is increasingly dissident.

Moyers   What's the evidence for that other than the polls?

Chomsky   Something much more striking than the polls are the events of the 1980s. In the 1980s the government was driven underground. It was forced to undertake large-scale clandestine activities because the domestic population would not tolerate those activities overtly. The Reagan administration is the first administration to have created anything like the State Department of Public Diplomacy.

Moyers   I have to tell you, the Kennedy administration, the Johnson administration, and the Nixon administration all engaged in domestic propaganda.

Chomsky   Yes, but there's a substantial increase in scale under Reagan. The Reagan administration had a massive enterprise to control the public mind. In fact, when this was partially exposed during the Iran-contra hearings, one high administration official described it as the kind of operation that you carry out in enemy territory. That expresses the administration's attitude toward the population—the population is the enemy. You've got to control enemy territory, and by very extensive public diplomacy—meaning propaganda. Sure, propaganda has always been there, but there's a qualitative change in the resources and intelligence drawn upon to ensure that the enemy territory is controlled. When John F. Kennedy sent the American air force to start bombing in South Vietnam in 1962, he didn't have to keep it

Arnon Ben-David, from *The Pentagon,* 1987.

secret. It was on the front page of the *New York Times,* and nobody cared. When Johnson sent twenty thousand marines to the Dominican Republic to prevent a democratic revival there, it wasn't secret. When Johnson sent hundreds of thousands of troops to invade South Vietnam, it wasn't secret. When we subverted the only free election in Laos in 1959, it wasn't secret. Nobody ever cared about these things. The population was really marginalized. That changed as a result of the popular movements of the sixties which had a dramatic and lasting effect on the country.

Moyers If all this ferment is going on, if there is more dissidence now than you can remember, why do you go on to write that people feel isolated?

Chomsky Much of the general population recognizes that the organized institutions do not reflect their concerns and interests and needs. They do not feel that they participate meaningfully in the political system. They do not feel that the media are telling them the truth or even reflect their concerns. They go outside of the organized institutions to act. So on the one hand you have a lot of popular ferment and a lot of dissidence, sometimes very effective. On the other hand you have a remoteness of the general public from the functioning institutions.

Moyers We see more and more of our elected leaders and know less and less of what they're doing.

Chomsky The presidential elections are hardly ever taken seriously as involving a matter of choice. Congress, especially the House, is more responsive to public opinion than higher levels, but even here the rate of electoral victory by incumbents is in the high nineties. That's a way of saying that there aren't any elections.

Moyers You get those sorts of election results in communist and totalitarian states.

Chomsky It means that something else is happening, not choice. Options are not being presented. You have a complex situation in the United States. A cleavage is taking place between a rather substantial part of the population and elite elements.

Moyers But those elite elements are supported by a substantial part of the population. There are people who take the debates seriously, who go out and vote, who believe they're participating in a legitimate exercise of democracy.

Chomsky It's not a cleavage at the point of revolution. It's not as if you had an aristocracy facing a mass population. It's not Iran in 1978. It's split and complex and fluid—you can see tendencies toward popular marginalization from functioning institutions, and the abstraction of those institutions from public participation, or even from reflection of the public will.

Moyers Now put that in the vernacular. That means what?

Chomsky It means that the political system increasingly functions without public input. It means that to an increasing extent not only do people not participate in decision making, they don't even take the trouble of ratifying the decisions presented to them. They assume the decisions are going on independently of what they may do in the polling booth.

Moyers Ratification means—

Chomsky Ratification would mean a system in which there are two positions presented to me, the voter. I go into the polling booth, and I push one or another button, depending on which of those positions I want. Now, that's a very limited form of democracy. In a really meaningfully democracy, I'd play a role in forming those positions. Those positions would reflect my active, creative participation—not just me, but everyone, of course. That would be real democracy. We're very far from that.

But now we're even departing from the point where there is ratification. When you have stage-managed elections, with the public relations industry determining what words come out of people's mouths, even the element of ratification is disappearing. You don't expect the candidates to stand for anything, you simply expect them to say what the public relations expert tells them will get them past the next obstacle. The population expects Ronald Reagan to have memorized the lines.

Moyers I don't understand why the candidates for president don't take the campaign back from the media. Instead of having questions from journalists, they should want to sit like this and talk about abortion, foreign policy—

Chomsky That would allow the population the option of ratification at least. We could find out what this person really believes and decide whether we want that. These are among the concrete examples of how the institutions are less and less structures in which people meaningfully participate. . . . However, at the very same time people are complex creatures. If they can't organize and act and express their interests and their needs through formal institutions, they'll do it in other ways. To a large extent they are. So that's why I think you have this complex system. There's an increasing cleavage between articulate intellectual opinion and public opinion. The articulate intelligentsia have taken part in this so-called right turn of the 1970s and '80s. They've articulated and expressed it. But I don't think the population has. In fact, they less and less feel that the organized intellectuals are expressing what's on their minds, or helping them clarify what they think. Now that's hard to prove, but it's a sense I have about what's going on now.

Moyers What do we do about it? I don't want to leave people with a wholly negative analysis. You have said that we live entangled in webs of endless deceit, that we live in a highly indoctrinated society where elementary truths are easily buried.

Chomsky I do believe that.

Moyers What elementary truths are buried?

Chomsky The fact that we invaded South Vietnam. The fact that we are standing in the way, and have stood in the way for years, of significant moves toward arms negotiation. The fact that the military system is to a substantial extent a mechanism by which the general population is compelled to provide a subsidy to high-technology industry. Since they're not going to do it if you ask them to, you have to deceive them into doing it. There are many truths like that, and we don't face them.

Dan Rather, publicity photo.

Moyers How do we extricate ourselves from this web of endless deceit?

Chomsky An isolated individual can do it. Human beings have tremendous capacities. If they're willing to make the effort, if they're willing to look at themselves in the mirror and to think honestly, they can do it—with hard work.

Moyers One would at least have to have the money to subscribe to journals and newspapers.

Chomsky Unfortunately, that's true. You need resources. It's easy for me to say, because I've got the resources. But for most people, it's extremely hard.

That's why you need organization. If a real democracy is going to thrive, if the real values that are deeply embedded in human nature are going to be able to flourish, groups must form in which people can join together, share their concerns, discover what they think, what they believe, and what their values are. This can't be imposed on you from above. You have to discover it by experiment, effort, trial, application, and so on. And this has to be done with others. Central to human nature is a need to be engaged with others in cooperative efforts of solidarity and concern. That can only happen through group structures. I would like to see a society moving toward voluntary organization and eliminating as much as possible structures of hierarchy and domination, and the basis for them in ownership and control.

Moyers Do you think a citizen has to have far-reaching specialized knowledge to understand the realities of power and what's really going on?

Chomsky It's not absolutely trivial, but as compared to intellectually complex tasks, it's pretty slight. It's not like the sciences, where there are so many things you have to study and know something about. By and large, what happens in political life is relatively accessible. It doesn't take special training or unusual intelligence. What it really takes is honesty. If you're honest, you can see it.

Moyers Do you believe in common sense?

Chomsky Absolutely. I believe in Cartesian common sense. People have the capacity to see through the deceit in which they are ensnared, but they've got to make the effort. As you correctly pointed out, for an individual to make the effort is very hard.

Moyers It seems a little incongruous to hear a distinguished linguistics scholar from the ivory tower of Massachusetts Institute of Technology talk about common people with such appreciation and common sense.

Chomsky My own studies of language and human cognition demonstrate to me what remarkable creativity ordinary people have. The very fact that people talk to one another reflects deep-seated features of human creativity that separate human beings from any other biological system we know. When you begin to study the normal capacities of human beings, you get tremendous respect for them.

close up

Eric Pierpoint

REAL MEN

Human concepts of masculinity and femininity come under scrutiny by George (Eric Pierpoint), who is pregnant for the third time—but his first on Earth. Here, Sikes (Gary Graham) tells the Newcomer, "being a man" is something "you gotta prove."

Prove it? That's not easy for George, who has three more weeks of swollen ankles and emotional outbursts to contend with before he delivers. But he forsakes paternity leave to help Sikes investigate the distribution of male Newcomer hormones—the more powerful and more dangerous steroids of the '90s. They're being used by a bodybuilder (A.D. Muyich) whose quest for one definition of manhood could cost him another. (60 min.)

Additional Cast
Albert . . . . Jeff Marcus
Nick Coletta . . . . William Shockley
Cathy . . . . Terri Treas
Zimmer . . . . Robert Neary
Karina . . . . Debbie Barker

Page from *TV Guide,* February 19, 1990.

Barbara Ehrenreich

MEN I HAVE LIKED

Men have always played an important role in the American left. They enliven our gatherings, enrich our magazines with their considerable insights, and, in a few cases, even add a certain charm to otherwise quite businesslike meetings. Here, we will briefly consider two of them, each of whom I have long regarded with affection: Abbie Hoffman, who died on April 12 [1989], and Christopher Hitchens, who, despite his anti-choice column in the April 24 edition of *The Nation,* still seems to be enjoying good health.

Hitchens's column is the kind of thing that makes it difficult for a socialist-feminist to hold up her head among feminists who have not yet seen any advantage to be gained from collaborating with the other sex. Antileft feminists such as Robin Morgan and Andrea Dworkin must be feeling justified, once again, in their suspicion that the "male left" is a conspiracy to ensure the continuation of patriarchy into the postcapitalist phase of things. Other feminists are realizing, to their intense disappointment, that men who look unfavorably on such familiar human rights violations as slavery, internment, and torture do not necessarily have qualms about coercive pregnancy and childbearing.

Sadly, Hitchens is not alone, among male leftists, in his discomfort with the issue of abortion. Many men, of course, are quite clearheaded on the subject, and some 100,000 of them (by my estimation) joined the megamarch for abortion rights in Washington on April 9. But there is a sizeable and well-placed minority that is quite brave in confronting outbreaks of cruelty as they occur worldwide, but which, when hit with the subject of reproductive rights, grows testy, withdrawn, or preoccupied. My guess is that the problem stems from primal male fears of what might be called the *unfriendly vagina:* a specter which includes not only the *vagina dentata* of ancient male fantasy, but any female interior which fails to nurture every squirt of semen that comes its way. But enough speculation, let us briefly dispose of Hitchens's argument, in the hope that he will soon see his way to a more inclusive conception of human rights.

Hitchens's position is the well-worn "after the revolution, you won't need abortion" line, familiar to anyone who has tried to discuss reproductive rights with male adherents of the religious left. I also encountered a tentative version of this line in a recent conversation with Jason DeParle, who claims to be a liberal despite his position on the masthead of the *Washington*

Monthly, the large print, low-IQ alternative to *The New Republic.* In this view, abortion becomes a tragic artifact of capitalism, or at least of our current piratical version of capitalism, in which access to housing, food, health care, etc. is restricted to the generously paid and their dependents.

Proceeding from the assumption that the need for abortion will wither even more swiftly than the state, Hitchens offers to cut a deal, to which the parties are: "we," meaning "society" and Mr. Hitchens, and "you," meaning women. Abortion will be illegal, but "we" will give "you" free contraception (an as-yet undiscovered, utterly safe and foolproof variety, I trust), guaranteed nutrition and health care, plus a socialized "national adoption service."

Well, Chris, there are many attractive features to this deal. (I particularly like your promise to keep prayer out of the schools, for which I would do many things, just short of carrying an unwanted pregnancy to term.) But I cannot accept your offer, for the following reasons, each of which I hope you will carefully consider and endeavor to experience in your imagination:

Morning sickness, nausea and vomiting at other times of the day, varicose veins, hemorrhoids, nine months' abstinence from alcohol, cigarettes, aspirin, and antihistamines, labor, false labor, anemia, toxemia, postnatal depression, extreme fatigue, peculiar vicissitudes of appetite, difficulty moving, backaches, dental decay, stretch marks, occasional incontinence, the agony of episiotomy, insomnia, abcessed breasts . . .

Distasteful reading, I know, and I have not even mentioned the occasional postpartum hemorrhage, the strain on the heart and other organs, the *removal* of the episiotomy stitches, and much more. But my reason for mentioning these ghastly features of pregnancy and childbearing, which are apparently so little known among men, is to highlight the unnatural callousness of the "adoption, not abortion" position, even when the deal is sweetened, as in your case, with a nonracist, socialist adoption service.

It is true that I, like many other women, have endured many of the above-listed risks, discomforts, and major pains—plus others that modesty forbids me from detailing—in the service of *wanted* pregnancies. And I have done so even in the absence of the benefits that Hitchens generously offers as an inducement to childbearing. But the fact that I have endured them, and without any bribes from "you," i.e., "society," should in no way lighten your imaginary experience of pregnancy and childbirth. The pain, discomfort, and risk are no less in a wanted pregnancy; the difference is that they are *chosen.*

If this distinction escapes you, think of holding your hand over a flame, perhaps in order to reach something you want. It hurts, right?—and may lead to a serious burn, but you're strong and you can do it. Now, however, think of having someone, particularly someone you do not know or like—Anthony Scalia for example, or Jesse Helms—hold your hand over the flame *for you.*

Fortunately, Hitchens leaves a gaping loophole which women should be able to march through hundreds abreast. First, he chivalrously exempts from his abortion prohibition women whose pregnancy has resulted from rape or incest, though why the little products of rape, etc., are less deserving of life than those of more consensual approaches to reproduction, I do not know. But it is reassuring to see the exemption for mental health, since this means that affluent women will always be able to line up the requisite experts to prove that their mental health is endangered. Unless your postabortion utopia includes a drastic leveling of wealth and privilege, the elite will still enjoy the right to choose, and only the "masses" will be condemned to bear children against their will.

Let us now turn to the sadder, but somehow more socially redeeming, subject of Abbie Hoffman's suicide. The disturbing thing—at least after the shock of seeing the words "Abbie Hoffman" and "dead" in the same line of print—was the media's prurient fascination with the personal and emotional failings which could have led him to take his own life. There have been insinuations of an inability to "grow up," of a morbid fixation on the 1960s, of a failure to adjust to his decline from superstardom. In short, all the deadly clichés of the 1950s—"maturity," "adjustment," etc.—have been exhumed to bury the 1960s.

Reading the attempts to discredit Abbie's life with his death, I was reminded of an extraordinarily wise op-ed piece by William Styron, which appeared in the *New York Times* last December. The subject was Primo Levi, the Italian chemist, Auschwitz survivor, and author of several amazingly sweet-tempered books about the Holocaust and the Second World War. Levi committed suicide in 1987, prompting a reaction similar to what we are seeing in Abbie's case. One commentator even suggested that "the efficacy of all his words had somehow been cancelled by his death."

Styron, who has himself experienced depression severe enough to warrant hospitalization, is worth quoting at some length: "In depression, a kind of biochemical meltdown, it is the brain as well as the mind that becomes ill—as ill as any other besieged organ. The sick brain plays evil tricks on its inhabiting spirit . . . All capacity for pleasure disappears, and despair maintains a merciless daily drumming. The smallest commonplace of domestic life, so amiable to the healthy mind, lacerates like a blade.

"Thus, mysteriously, in ways difficult to accept by those who have never suffered it, depression comes to resemble physical anguish. Such anguish can become every bit as excruciating as the pain of a fractured limb, migraine or heart attack . . .

"In the popular mind, suicide is usually the work of a coward or sometimes, paradoxically, a deed of great courage, but it is neither; the torment that precipitates the act makes it often one of blind necessity."

The "disease model" may not fit every mental disorder, but I am willing to believe a sufferer who says that depression feels like a "biochemical meltdown," independent of objective circumstances. Certainly one can imagine circumstances that might have broken through Abbie's depression and saved his life: a vast renewal, for example, of the movement he spent his life building, encouraging, and cheering up. But failing that, Abbie was left facing a demon that very few of us, not even the bravest, could hope to vanquish.

As for the insinuations of immaturity, etc.: they do serious injustice to Hoffman's actual, post-1960s life. He had adjusted not only to substardom but, in his years underground, to total anonymity, and managed to build an entirely new identity—and name—for himself in midlife (something very few people could do, or are ever called upon to do). He was not fixated on the 1960s, but moved energetically on to the issues of the 1970s and 1980s. And, to my mind, he met the test of "maturity": He grasped the concept of his own mortality, and devoted his last years to working with and inspiring a new generation of activists.

Abbie's death means more work for the rest of us—agitating, organizing, protesting. Let us try to do it with the same grace and good humor that characterized his efforts right up to the end, and even in the face of what was surely unbearable pain.

Gary Indiana

BLOOD BROTHERS

The Steinberg verdict came down amid a flurry of other legal news. There was the sticky problem of jury selection in the Oliver North trial, and after that the guardianship of Nancy Klein. On Long Island, a technically adult teenager who was allegedly sexually abused by his father since early childhood, drew six to eighteen years hard time for molesting children. In California, following the machine-gunning of a playground full of schoolchildren, a popular movement to ban automatic weapons stirred the righteous frenzy of the National Rifle Association. In Florida, Ted Bundy's death sentence was carried out while a crowd of leering crackers outside the prison waved funny signs and swigged beer.

These cases swarmed with fuzzy, contradictory notions of criminality and punishment. The courtroom has always been a charged symbolic site; legal process and crime now dominate the popular imagination to an unprecedented extent. There are televised trials and televised manhunts, encouraging the fantasy of "solving" crime by forcing individual criminals through the mangle of publicity.

Politics and crime are strangely fused in American life. Our ideology insists on our underlying innocence, commitment to social justice and "freedom," noble intentions, and so on. We therefore have an unseemly predilection for the "bad apple in the barrel" theory: Nixon in the case of Vietnam, North and some other zealots in the matter of the contras. Because the palpable, systemic evils are always kept out of evidence, the political criminal is typically "brought to justice" on a set of trivial charges and acquitted for diminished responsibility.

Like Nixon's bombing of Cambodia, North's serious crimes are unindictable offenses, being basically identical to the will of the state. Evidence linking this national hero to the easy availability of crack in America's schoolyards—contra money having largely been raised by the smuggling of cocaine into Miami—has emigrated to the land of silence, where the *New York Times* sends unpalatable truths. So has the mountain of proof that our surrogates in El Salvador and Nicaragua take basically the same approach to guerrilla warfare that Ted Bundy took to dating.

Apart from the incongruously scrupulous dispatches of former *Times* reporter Raymond Bonner, the media of record regularly consign even the hardest atrocity documentation from Amnesty International, the Christic In-

stitute, and other human rights groups to the realm of allegation and rumor. The mainstream of public discourse has a special filter segregating state crime from private crime. Murder lives in a dark world, but private murder is offered for our delectation in explicit forensic detail, while state murder most often comes to us in the form of statistics, its victims and perpetrators neatly labeled to veil the gory particulars.

Bundy was characterized as "an enigma": how could anyone commit such hideous acts? Exactly the same acts, performed by the state and its emissaries, no longer appear inexplicable or depraved or even much to write home about. Stephen Kinzer and James LeMoyne of the *Times* have spent nearly a decade inventing excuses and euphemisms for right-wing serial murder in El Salvador and Nicaragua, distributing blame in a "balanced" manner among guilty and innocent, planting phantom insurgencies and spurious communists in the jungles of the American mind. The language of the state department, echoed by Kinzer and LeMoyne, domesticates much larger crimes than the prodigious killings of Bundy. Human rights "abuses" are cited and regretted, but always held to be on the decline. Salvadoran death squads are magically detached from their government sponsor. The patriarch must never be identified as a "murderer."

The ideological trickle-down can be seen in certain homicide cases, like those of Joel Steinberg and Robert Chambers. In each case, the uncontrolled rage of a physically powerful man resulted in the death of a defenseless female. Yet because both men at least marginally coincide with an accepted image of the empowered male—Steinberg an attorney, Chambers a handsome preppie, both white and middle-class—their culpability was softened, blame partially shifted to Hedda Nussbaum and Jennifer Levin, "murder" yielding to the more accidental-sounding "manslaughter." The Steinberg jury also had a problem with the concept of "depravity."

In this connection, the Bundy execution merely confirms the dark secret of capital punishment. The state doesn't really oppose cold-blooded (or hot-blooded) murder, serial killing, rape, or any other capital crime; it simply reserves the right to commit these crimes, invoking "the ultimate punishment" when a free-lancer usurps the state's violent privileges. The "enigma" of Bundy is an important myth, exemplar of an increasingly widespread kind of crime in which it is impossible to blame the victim. Bundy symbolizes the "bad apple" of civilian life, one-man death squad and loose cannon amok on the lawns of suburbia.

Serial killing in America has so far been committed almost exclusively by white males, and in every known case familial dysfunction or pathology has been linked to the serial killer's rage. Curiously, the mass media have

◀ Oliver North, Ted Bundy.

consistently refused to consider Bundy in this absolutely standard context. No one knows why Bundy killed so many women, although every other instance of serial killing by a free-lancer has its roots in extreme sexual or physical abuse in childhood, usually by a parent.

Moreover, since many forms of traumatic abuse have been passed from generation to generation as acceptable modes of discipline, "for the child's own good," social institutions such as schools and the military have often been deformed into "appropriate settings" for the release of psychotic anger stored up in childhood. From this perspective, a whole society's concept of what and whom and how to punish is sometimes the revenge of adults upon the helpless children they once were.

In *For Your Own Good*, Alice Miller examines the childhood of Adolf Hitler and the family in early twentieth-century Austrian society: "The family structure could well be characterized as the prototype of a totalitarian regime. Its sole, undisputed, often brutal ruler is the father. The wife and children are totally subservient to his will, his moods, and his whims; they must accept humiliation and injustice unquestioningly and gratefully. Obedience is their primary rule of conduct. The mother, to be sure, has her own sphere of authority in the household, where she rules over the children when the father is not at home; this means that she can to some extent take out on those weaker than herself the humiliation she has suffered. In the totalitarian state, a similar function is assigned to the security police." Hitler was beaten every day by his father from the age of four: "When he was eleven, Adolf was nearly beaten to death when he tried to free himself from an intolerable situation by running away."

This kind of study is usually regarded by authoritarian types as misleading. A psychiatric explanation of crime—a social explanation, rooting crime in the context of familial and social forces—robs us of the ability to distinguish ourselves from conveniently inexplicable "monsters." The media portrait of physically grotesque serial killers like Henry Lee Lucas, or nonmediagenic ones who murder boys, like John Gacy, usually include a horrifying sketch of the killer's family. In Bundy's case, a great deal of effort was made to stress how utterly normal and sane his childhood and family background were. Why?

Stephen G. Michaud and Hugh Aynesworth's book *The Only Living Witness* reports that Bundy was "a compulsive nailbiter and nosepicker, that he was only middling bright (I.Q. 124), that he was at best a fair student in college and a failure in law school, that he was essentially untraveled and poorly read, that he stuttered when nervous and had acquired only a surface sophistication." However, "The press stories about Ted have stressed his normalcy, his intellect, his attractiveness, his Republicanism." The same is true of Oliver North. "All-American," full of piety for God and country, a grinning Ken doll of right-wing ideology, North has the surface charm and quick intelligence of the classical sociopath, and, like Ted Bundy, fulfills a sadistic image of perfection. Outwardly handsome, inwardly inaccessible, North and Bundy are both men with a mission, propelled by sensitive, unknowable secrets.

North's fans admire precisely the same qualities for which Bundy was abhorred by residents of northern Florida. He offered no contrition, never admitted doing anything wrong, looked great in a courtroom, and came across as a contemptuous wiseass. Like Bundy, North knew things he would never tell, and much of his power emanated from his silence.

Bundy's execution drew a bead on the secrets of a hideous childhood. Whether or not it appeared hideous to the adults around him, something besides learning he was illegitimate opened a permanent fissure in Bundy's psyche. Some details are known, but the darkest ones have gone to the grave with him. He often claimed that pornography and alcohol triggered the killer inside him; like any practiced sociopath, Ted had an uncanny ability to tell people what they wanted to hear. Handsome and fresh-faced, Bundy looked like something ideal on the surface—in effect, a less exaggerated version of masculinity than Oliver North, a lover rather than a fighter. Like North, Bundy was the good middle-class son from central casting, a person with all the right "values" in his mouth and hence indistinguishable from normal people. It would have been intolerable to suggest that the family, cradle and crux of those values, was the nuclear torture chamber where Baby Bundy developed both the camouflage and the compulsion to kill.

On this point, something like collective hysterical denial is activated throughout American society. Eighteen-year-old Jesse Friedman, who never escaped his family home and was allegedly sexually violated by his father from the age of nine, was told by the judge who sentenced him for child sexual abuse, "The fact that you were a victim does not absolve you from responsibility." In prison, this excellent candidate for rehabilitation will have the chance to flower into a complete psychopath.

An incessant demagoguery concerning the sanctity of the family takes place in a social setting where the prevailing model of conflict resolution, reflected in virtually all "dramatic" television fiction, is the inductive leap from social dissonance to homicide. In the same time that protectionist rhetoric about the family has proliferated, a nervous awareness of child abuse has also spread. But concern remains fixated on the child-victim, whose later, utterly predictable explosions of violence elicit nothing but bewildered horror. The connection is never made that the creation of a family is not an automatic or desirable destiny of every "normal" person, that other kinds of lives could be equally or more fulfilling, or that unwanted babies grow up to become the bogeymen of "crime" because they were victims of crime from the moment of birth. Instead, American culture encourages the ugly wish that all its preborn fetuses will come to term, and all the males will grow up to be Oliver North.

Lead, Follow, or GET OUT of the WAY

Mass-produced desk-top sign.

Alexander Cockburn

THEM

The general and tendential laws of coverage of the machinists' strike against Eastern and of the struggle of the popular movement in El Salvador are remarkably similar.* Take the notion of "the public." In mainstream press reports of the strike something called "the public" is gravely inconvenienced. This public is interviewed at airports and tends to be traveling to Florida for the family's first vacation in twenty-one years on tickets purchased by the accumulated life savings of the grandmother—now in an emergency room fighting for life after being insulted by a picket; tended by relatives who, after six days without food or water in a waiting room at the Atlanta airport, "just want to go home."

This same public does not include families of machinists thrown out of work by Frank Lorenzo's asset-stripping strategies. When Lorenzo closed down Eastern's Kansas City hub operation back in September, some 4,000 workers were inconvenienced but somehow failed to make the "member of the public" status necessary to earn sympathetic coverage.

Now take this "public" to its incarnation as "the people of El Salvador." They live on a plane too ethereal for precise description. They "fear a return to the bad old days"; "some 70,000 of them have been claimed by a war seemingly without end"; they shun "extremes of left and right" and display "continuing enthusiasm for the right to vote." The only thing "the people of El Salvador" most emphatically fail to be are, precisely, people—in the form of army torturers, guerrillas, labor organizers, student leaders, members of different classes whose needs and aspirations are mutually antagonistic. "The people" do not belong to classes. Like "the public," they are victims seen mostly in long shot. "Some 40,000 of them died in the violence of the early 1980s," as opposed to some 40,000 of them were murdered by the army and the death squads of plainclothes Treasury Police, rural landowners, and businessmen, with many of their names appearing on lists circulated between police and security agencies not only in El Salvador but also in the United States.

---

* Some observers regard the operating procedures at work in the mainstream press to be virtually automatic, thus prompting the "spontaneous combustion of nonsense" theory of journalistic production. See here the extensive debate in specialist publications on whether professional journalists are mostly born fools (nature), or are made fools at journalism schools (nurture). Von Puffendorff's vast study of Pulitzer Prize recipients suggests a 78-22 split in favor of nurture.

TOWN MEETING!
POLITICS & ELECTION
ORGANIZED BY GROUP MATERIAL
Tuesday, October 18, 8 PM
DIA ART FOUNDATION • 155 Mercer St.
AGENDA

Meeting Co-Chairs: Lucy R. Lippard, writer and activist
Jerry Kearns, artist

PAST: Introduction by Lucy R. Lippard and Jerry Kearns, a recent history of cultural responses to political crises.

PRESENT: Open to the floor. Discussion on the following:

What are the major aspects of the current political crises?

How are you responding to these crises individually and collectively?

Are these various methods and strategies successful?

FUTURE: Are there events approaching us that will demand cultural action?

What are the possibilities for action on a local and national level?

Please come prepared to speak on these issues. The Town Meeting on Politics & Election will be recorded, transcribed and incorporated into a publication organized by Group Material for the Dia Art Foundation.

This agenda is based on a panel discussion held in June 1988: Richard Andrews, former Director of Visual Arts, NEA, Washington D.C.; Leon Golub, artist; Esther Parada, artist; Judge Bruce Wright, Justice of the Supreme Court, State of New York.

This project is supported in part by public funds from the National Endowment for the Arts, a federal agency, and the New York State Council on the Arts. Admission is free. For more information call the Dia Art Foundation, (212) 431-9232.

POLITICS AND ELECTION

Chairperson, Jerry Kearns Last week when Lucy Lippard and I began planning tonight's meeting, she said we should be careful to keep this history part short. She didn't want you to think this was the "Lucy and Jerry Show." After all, this is a town meeting. I said, "Okay." Then she said that since she's the oldest she should do a verbal overview of the last twenty years of the art scene's left wing. I said, "Okay." Then she said that since I am an artist and thus suspected of forming overviews I should say something more personal. I said, "Lucy, this is supposed to be a town meeting. People will think I am telling my life story as a maybe not-too-clever career move." "No," she said, "don't worry about that. Just keep it short."

Chapter One: "The Red Herring." It was a sunny, windy Saturday afternoon, fall 1976. I was walking around Soho looking at various greats, near-greats, and not-so-greats, when a small pink leaflet caught my eye. In boldface caps it beckoned all cultural workers (which I guessed meant artists) to attend a Sunday night meeting to discuss how generally fucked up life was becoming and what we cultural workers could do about it. That sounded like fun to me. I went. The sponsor was a group called Artists Meeting for Cultural Change, AMCC. That Sunday night we sat for nearly three-and-a-half hours in a big circle, maybe sixty people, all on steel folding chairs, in the original Artists Space on Wooster Street, above what's now Paula Cooper's gallery. It was very uncomfortable. Sometimes it was boring. It was also immediately clear that most of the people knew each other and that there was a distinct pecking order among them. After we went around the circle telling our names a lovely young woman in an overlong army coat read a complex report detailing the history of the Rockefeller family. Near the end she told us that these same bastards were right that minute uptown at the Whitney trying to have their way with art history. The Whitney had agreed to exhibit their collection under the title "200 Years of American Art." This woman won the circle's hearts and minds. Almost immediately we agreed to go up to the Whitney and kick some ruling-class butt.

Hearing all of this I figured that I had come to the right place. But as things went on, I, as usual, fell in with a bad crowd. Many meetings later, after endless debates, battles, and tirades, the AMCC split apart. There were multiple reasons why, but later I figured it really was because the group had more voters than butt kickers. Plus, just then a small faction was reading a paperback issue of the Soviet Revolution. A light went on. They saw it clearly. The AMCC was no doubt being crippled by a classic replay of the Bolshevik/Menshevik struggles. The only choice left was to purge, split the group, break away from the counterrevolutionaries. Like I said, I went with the Bolsheviks. We were twenty-two strong. We went to the street. We were really gonna get down with the workers. Fuck that bourgeois art world! For about six months we fought about how to do that. Each month the group would get a little smaller—sure sign that we were cutting more dead wood. We fought to the last man. We never did decide where the workers were holed up, or how to approach them, or when, or even who they were. Finally, we got down to about five people and we were sitting in a loft on East Houston Street, mad as hell at each other.

Chapter Two: "The Edge." For about two years from 1977 to 1978, I and several of the remaining Bolsheviks, now known as the Red Herring Collective, were also members of the Anti-Imperialist Cultural Union. The AICU was founded by poet Amiri Baraka and a group of black revolutionaries from Newark. They were veterans of the urban warfare of the late sixties and had evolved by the late seventies from black nationalism to fledgling Maoists. Ours was an intense union. We had angry black revolutionary Maoists from Newark and angry white Bolsheviks from Soho. It made for a heady mix.

One of my first assignments was gluing up street leaflets announcing a puppet show and a political forum on Angola. The forum featured Amiri Baraka debating a young Neorican communist of a different bent. The leaflet was bright yellow with black ink; the graphic was a photo of severed heads held high on bayonets by a group of revolutionaries. It was just the kind of image guaranteed to draw a big crowd. The event was held in a church basement in the Lower East Side. And I was the voice of the Brezhnev puppet. For me the AICU was a voice crying out at a painful edge of U.S. culture. We were, and we made full-tilt struggle culture. We accepted confrontation as the only way out of a repressive system.

In 1978, about the time some AICU members were holding meetings to discuss why other people weren't attending meetings anymore, it happened. Over in Brooklyn, twenty-five cops beat community activist Arthur Miller to death on a Bed-Stuy street. There were dozens of eyewitnesses. Miller's death was clearly a killing, a police murder, another in a long history. Almost immediately the newly formed Black United Front, BUF, called for a march on the 79th Precinct. In the sweltering heat of a July Saturday, 9,000 citizens knocked on the door and asked to talk to the chief. He wasn't home.

The following Tuesday night, I went to Brooklyn's House of the Lord Church on Atlantic Avenue for the BUF's first town meeting. The House of the Lord's public meeting room holds about 250 when jammed. It was jammed in 1978. There were rows of old wooden benches, several folding tables, and a Coke machine. Also two wall murals, one depicting the life and death of Malcolm X, the other an image of a black Christ descending from heaven with a Black Liberation flag in his hand to talk with assembled heroes: Martin Luther King, Malcolm, Rosa Parks, Nat Turner, and Sojourner Truth. I went back there for weekly meetings for nearly two-and-a-half years.

At first I just donated prints of my photographs. Eventually I collaborated with various BUF members on numerous projects, slide shows, leaflets, posters, calendars, banners, books. It was a nuts-and-bolts experience at making urban-protest culture. Police brutality was a constant. I often assisted the Peace and Justice Committee who worked full-time with victims of cop violence. I photographed many young men and some women who had been beaten by the local cops. Several times I appeared with the photos as evidence in court hearings against the police. In 1978 and 1979, the BUF led three major marches, each averaging about 10,000 people, across the Brooklyn Bridge. We were seeking justice for Arthur Miller. We went to the City Hall. The mayor wasn't home. We went to Wall Street and finally to the United Nations. As usual, the police eventually got off. Just like they did with the killings of Michael Stewart, Eleanor Bumpurs, Clifford Glove, each dead, each an innocent victim of police violence.

In 1980 I read a political article that Lucy Lippard wrote in the now-defunct 7 Days magazine. A later version of this article was called "Hot Potatoes." In it she said that the art world was hot on new underground art and that this stuff was tough, rough, and political. I couldn't believe it. I said that's for me. So I called her up, invited her for a Chinese lunch, and we've been good friends ever since.

Chairperson, Lucy Lippard Ironically, Jerry, I still keep hearing that political art is hot. But in fact, cultural organizing is now at a ten-year low. These things tend to go in cycles. They are affected by, and they reflect, the particular political crisis of the time—and there sure as hell is a political crisis now! There is a repulsively clear crisis of electoral politics, and a crisis in political participation as well.

Anyway, Jerry and I were asked to chair this meeting because we have both been around a long time and we can dispel the notion that artists have been sitting on their asses for the last twenty years. Twenty years ago, almost to the day, I belatedly joined the antiwar movement. Three of us did the opening show at Paula Cooper's new gallery in brand-new Soho to benefit student mobilization against the war in Vietnam. The Art Workers Coalition got started soon afterward, and we did another show at Paula's. The AWC lasted until 1971 or 1972, after becoming a real thorn in the flesh of local institutions and powers that be. One concession we got was free admission one night or one day a week at most museums. But we didn't get artists on the boards of trustees at any of the art museums, which was another one of our platforms. That might have changed a few things for the next decade. The AWC also made a lot of us realize that the art world was not so separate from the machinations of what we called the military-industrial complex as we had thought.

Rumor has it that the seventies were real calm, the "Me Decade." But as Jerry said, right after the AWC went under, or a couple of years later in 1975, the AMCC began, largely in response to the ridiculous exhibition proposed by the federal government to mark the Bicentennial. The idea of having a revolution commemorated by the Rockefellers! By the end of the seventies, there were Group Material, Fashion Moda, Colab, PAD/D, and others. Pretty soon "The Real Estate Show" gave birth to ABC No Rio, and really an awful lot was going on in those years. All this happened before the Reagan administration came in. That certainly was a kick in the gut.

For me and for a lot of other women, the seventies and the eighties were the women's movement. The art part of it began in 1969, an outgrowth of the Art Workers Coalition; a parallel development occurred simultaneously on the west coast with WAR (Women Artists and Revolution). Soon after, the Ad-Hoc Women's Artists Committee was formed. Catchy title, eh? We didn't think that we would last more than a couple of months. We went on for years. And we founded WEB, which *was* a catchy title; that was West/East Bag, a liaison group. We did a lot of wild demos around town on art and nonart issues. We left polemical tampaxes in the Whitney washrooms. We faked a press release saying that the Whitney Annual was half women and half people of color. Then the FBI came after us. In the late seventies we started *Heresies,* the feminist publication on art and politics, and we decided that the time had come to be generous, so we decided to give the rest of the left the benefit of feminist wisdom. We started PAD/D, Political Art Documentation/Distribution, which for eight years has done political and public art projects on intervention, gentrification, Reaganism, racism, war, and so forth. We published a magazine, *Upfront,* did forums and performances once a month, and in 1984 organized "Artists Call Against U.S. Intervention in Central America," a national campaign in thirty cities across the U.S. and Canada. In its main sweep through New York City in January 1984, "Artists Call" had thirty-one shows simultaneously in museums and galleries in the city. We also had a performance festival, a music festival, poetry readings, a procession for peace, and endless other stuff. Art Against Apartheid, had, and still has, a similar national presence. In the meantime a lot of energy was put into demonstration art, media analysis, and film, video, and performance projects.

Each one of these groups was sparked by a political crisis that pulled

Bruce Beattie, 1988.

artists kicking and screaming out of their studios and into the streets, still screaming and kicking. Since there have been some continuing presences in these groups we haven't had to reinvent the wheel each time, but the impetus for each new cycle has come from the younger generation. Group Material isn't exactly geriatric yet, but they have been at it for nearly a decade. And small groups in the last couple of years have really been most effective. I think we are all curious to see what comes next. That is why we have divided tonight's agenda into three parts: past, the history you are getting now; present, which *is* now; and future, which is the hope that all of you represent.

Kearns Group Material has asked us to convene this meeting to give you a platform to discuss and define the nature of the current political crisis. The idea is that by listening to each other we can deepen our understanding of what is going on. Why is there such a discrepancy between the lived reality of our experience and the representation of national perceptions of it? How many homeless children will it take to expose the hypocrisy? Clearly the central role now afforded the control of images—for instance, the incredible power of television—casts responsibility on those who work with images. Among others, that's us. Like it or not, society has shifted from a culture dominated by the verbal to one dominated by the visual. Media technology is controlled and manipulated by an elite; and this power structure, in turn, demands more responsibility of people who work within that technological sphere—in this case, visual artists. Circumstances demand that we voice a critique of the culture. This meeting is part of that process.

Republican National Convention, 1984.

Lippard The first questions are: What is the nature of the current political crisis? And, how are you responding, individually or collectively?

Arnie Sacher I'm Arnie Sacher and I am a writer. I don't have much in the way of answers, but I have a couple of questions. What frightens me about the Bush campaign is that it illuminates or crystallizes a certain tendency that I have seen developing in the progressive and radical communities over the years. That tendency on the left is to oscillate between two extremes: on the one hand, to see the general public as foolish, ignorant, racist, sexist; but on the other hand, to say, "The people are about to rise up and become part of a struggle for social change, if we only find the right words and the right techniques." What actually gives me some pause as I listen to the language and the tone of the Bush campaign—and I think rhetoric is something you've got to take very, very seriously—is that it shows that there is, in this culture, a tremendous amount of guilt and a tremendous amount of fear. So what I am urging for the moment, even beyond declamations and beyond saying how good we are or how we are going to organize, is to figure out some way of attending to that psychic reality, because I think it constitutes a profound and elusive crisis.

And I also want to talk about a strange thing in our own movement, modern liberalism and radicalism. The other day I read a piece in the *New York Times* by Anthony Lewis, one of the most critical people writing in the mainstream press. Lewis said that Bush and Dukakis and to a degree all politicians are not dealing with the real issues. Now, what are the real issues? First, that Japan produces more VCRs and high definition TV sets than we do? Second, that schools are not the key to productivity? But I think there is another thing that needs to be considered. We need to ask ourselves not only what are the crises in the culture, but also what is the future of that culture: what dreams, what visions, what feelings of life are we bringing to it. Are we only reactive? Do we need only respond by saying we want good schools, we want this, we want that? Are we part of the ongoing discussion, or do we have an imagination and serious ways to break the crisis?

Alexis Danzig My name is Alexis Danzig. I'm a member of the Women's Caucus at ACT UP [AIDS Coalition To Unleash Power], a member of the Majority Action Committee, and arrest no. 146. I just came back from the Food and Drug Administration where ACT UP had a pretty interesting action last Tuesday. I don't know if anybody caught it on TV, because it wasn't covered very well in New York City, but we got great coverage in Rockville, Maryland, and in Washington, D.C., and the areas around there. The action was successful because there was such a strong presence of visual art, one of the best ways we have found to get out our facts. We put up posters and banners—you have probably seen them around town—and, for this particular event, we brought out, as a media stunt, a bunch of grave-stones inscribed with reasons why people had died and reasons why the FDA was implicated. We presented a list of demands. For example, people of color count for only 17 percent of the total enrollment in the only twenty-nine protocols, while 54 percent of PWAs [People With AIDS] are people of color according to the Centers for Disease Control. Also, the CDC has no category for lesbians or bisexual women with AIDS, making those women's lives totally invisible. I don't need to go through the whole list, there are about twelve more items, but what we are doing with activism and art work is highlighting and getting out information that the government is sitting on and that no one gets to hear unless they come to our meetings. So, I'd like to invite all of you to our Monday night meetings. We have a Women's Caucus and a Majority Action Committee, which deals with issues of AIDS in minority communities, where the majority of people with AIDS are at this point.

Jack Ben-Levi My name is Jack Ben-Levi, and I am also with ACT UP. Our next action is going to be this Thursday at 5:30 at 51st and Lexington. George Bush will be addressing some Republicans at the Waldorf Hotel. Our intention is to completely surround the building.

But to add to what Alexis just said about the FDA action: as she said, we did not get very much coverage of our action in the New York press.

And I think the reason for that is that the "ideologically correct" *New York Times* has put a blanket on our activities. So we have to take control over disseminating the information ourselves. In this particular case we distributed a lot of information to smaller communities through local papers. But for the most part, we have had to disseminate it ourselves through fact sheets and other means. One good example is the ACT UP exhibition, "Let the Record Show," that was displayed in the window of the New Museum about a year ago. A lot of people who would never set foot in a museum saw that just walking down Broadway. I'm just mentioning that as another tactic that has to be adopted to be able to reach many people.

Ed Eisenberg My name is Ed Eisenberg. I was formerly with PAD/D, and now I am active with the Coalition for a Nuclear-Free Harbor. Do you realize they are building a naval base in the middle of our harbor? Even though community groups around the country are struggling to remove military bases, in New York, where we're getting one, there is very little outrage. Yet, the ships docking at this base will be carrying nuclear weapons. Needless to say, with weapons coming in and out of our city constantly, there is a tremendous risk of accident. So I've been trying to develop a project for next spring that would involve covering the city with a grid of street stencils. The stencils would serve as distance markers, noting how far downwind of the proposed nuclear base any given site might be. For instance, we would be about 7.5 miles away here. I'd like to make less politically active people aware of the threat that this base presents. If anybody would be interested in working on this you can speak to me after this meeting.

Bill Batson Right now I work with the Coalition for the Homeless. The most current cultural activity that I was involved in was a group called Artists for Jackson. We worked in Jesse Jackson's campaign in New York City.

I would like to reiterate two things that were touched on by other speakers, two things that I think are very important. First, as artists we have issues that we want to express; we have our jobs and our careers and our ways of working, these things we deal with constantly. But the second thing is, there are some issues that are so urgent and so compelling that I think you almost have to stop doing art altogether until the struggle is over. You come out of your studio or you come out of your apartment and there is somebody lying on your doorstep. You can make art about it, you can try to express it, but when it comes down to it, you almost have to pick them up physically. My point is that even as you do that work, your art training and the resources that you have suggest themselves. So the arts community can play a valuable role in social change on many levels.

Americans May Not
Be Loved Around The World,
But Our Fashions Are.

While our country has become a world power in fashion, only one store in New York carries the All-American look. From Calvin Klein underwear to Basco sport coats to Timberland shoes. We may be hated, but we look cool.

97 Third Avenue, at 12th Street, New York. (212) 473-7320

Hudsons New York, advertisement, 1987.

We are becoming a visual society. People are looking at all these political commercials this year, and that is all the information that they are getting about the candidates. Why? Because that's where all the money is being spent. I was working on a voter registration campaign called "Keep Hope Alive." We were on the street and in the neighborhoods; our goal was to have physical contact. Even if you just put a button on somebody, they have physical contact with a campaign worker, they have an image and some of the ideas. Hopefully, it is not just a media cult, just Michael Dukakis or George Bush. Hopefully, people's choices, even in such a simple thing as wearing a campaign button, have to do with issues and what they believe this person represents. So, there are a lot of issues having to do with representation that artists have a vested interest in. If, as artists, we ignore such issues as poverty, drugs, civil rights, Central America, then we are just painting against the clock.

Sam Wiener Hi, my name is Sam Wiener. I'm here to seek help for a very practical proposal. I am here to seek help for some sort of street action that will take place on Wednesday, November 2—that's one week before the election, two weeks from tomorrow. What we have to do is get into the streets and do something that will provide the media with a picture byte, something that the TV will pick up and put on the evening news, something that will make some difference hopefully. At four o'clock, when the matinees let out, fifteen of the Broadway shows are going to have groups of actors and actresses converge on the little triangle right above the Times Building in Times Square. There will be a stage. We've got permission from the city. The theater people are committed. So what I want to do now is to get a large number of artists together to do something really spectacular as a backdrop for this theater event—it's going to be song-and-dance numbers—I don't know how political the performance will be but it will get the press there, it will get the TV cameras there. I would like to see something done that will have a visual impact that can't be neglected by these TV people. What we want to do is get together and really churn up something spectacular for this thing, like the thing that took place in Times Square two or three year ago. It was a mock trial. It was spectacular!

Lippard Yes, there were huge puppets of Jeanne Kirkpatrick and Reagan and others. It was about four or five years ago.

Wiener It was wonderful. Now, we don't have much time, but I would hope that we could do something approaching that kind of spectacle. This election is being fought on TV, let's not make any mistake about it. What we need to do is create images that they simply have to put on their news broadcast.

Hunter Reynolds Hello, my name is Hunter Reynolds. I'm an artist and I am the art preparator for Paula Cooper Gallery. I would like to add that on Tuesday, October 25, we are having a press conference at the gallery. This is designed specifically for artists to voice their support of Dukakis's arts platform. Anne Hawley, who will probably be the head of the NEA if Dukakis is elected, will speak about the specifics of his platform. There will be other speakers as well, and we have confirmation that the TV news and press will be there. So try to come by.

Lisa Knaur My name is Lisa Knaur. I am a filmmaker and a writer. I'm also on the board of the National Organization of Cultural Workers, called the Alliance for Cultural Democracy. It's been around for about twelve years. It has a national membership of cultural organizers, community-based artists, educators, arts administrators, and political activists from around the country. What it stands for briefly is the idea that culture is an inalienable right. We believe that you can't talk about democracy in this society in the political or economic sense without talking about cultural democracy. We believe that all people have the right to culture, to experience it and to participate in its production and its criticism, and its circulation. We believe that all different communities, all different peoples in this country need to have the right to their own forms of cultural expression, and the right to the means of that cultural expression.

The one specific project that I'd like to mention is something that has been worked on for the last couple of years in ACD: a declaration of cultural human rights. This is intended to do two things: one, to critique what exists; and two, to put forward a vision, a program, a set of policies that we think can help transform this culture and guarantee cultural rights for all people. We've written various drafts of the declaration of human rights. If people are interested in looking at it, giving feedback, or being involved in trying to make this something, please talk to me. Hopefully this can be more than just another manifesto that gets discussed among artists and the left. We hope to use it as a lobbying tool and as an educational tool, particularly in relation to institutions that control the means of cultural, economic, and political expression.

Irving Wexler My name is Irving Wexler, and I'm a member of what is left of PAD/D. I'm looking at the curious discrepancy between the fact that progressive left-wing culture in the U.S. is in a huff and the fact that there exist everywhere around the country enormous pockets of unconscious resistance. What are the major aspects of this curious political crisis? Clearly, there is some kind of a connection between the crisis in politics and the crisis in culture. And I just want to remind you that the current crisis in culture also has a history. When I was a kid in the 1930s, there were many progressive artists' groups, loose-knit organizations that preceded the ones that Jerry and Lucy spoke about. That was perhaps the first great progressive cultural movement of the United States. It came out of the New Deal; there was a coalition among artists in America for the first time. But following that coalition — exemplified by the WPA art projects — Americans shied away from such collective cultural movements. There was a strong left cultural movement in the fifties, but in some ways it was almost without meaning. It was

Lance Carlson, *Women's Boots, Courtesy Bloomingdale's,* 1988.

divorced from real political issues, operating in what Gramsci called a "pathological vacuum." These artists' collectives of the 1950s did not emerge from arts movements as in the thirties, but rather from an almost inchoate need by artists to protest or to make of their creative works social statements. Today, I feel like we are seeing another downward movement in progressive cultural activity. But this time it is even stronger than in the fifties.

Unidentified Speaker   I don't know if I'm speaking to the past or the future, I'm just going to say what my opinion is. It seems to me that the central problem in American politics is not social struggle or class struggle, but a desperate struggle for power by many different ethnic groups. One of the philosophers who was instrumental in forming the legal spirit of the United States suggested in his writing that democracy was probably impossible in a very populous society, say, more than 50 million people. From this I conclude that the United States is not a democratic nation but an empire. It is comprised, as all empires have been, of numerous smaller nations and ethnic groups. In this sense, then, the situation that you describe as a political crisis in the United States is really one symptom of an empire in the process of decay.

Andrea Kanterwitz I have been an activist and doing political art for a number of years. I spent this past summer in Jay, Maine, painting a mural for the strike there—it's been going on for a year-and-a-half! Amazingly, the town's people had come together behind the strike, the whole community was united. It was the most well-organized effort that I have ever seen. Unfortunately, they lost the strike. It was really depressing. But I talked to a friend of mine who had been up there and he said that people were really determined not to let go of what they had learned in the strike, and a lot of the union members are now running for elective office. They are involved in what is happening in the whole state of Maine. They are really determined not to let go of their political power even though they have suffered a really serious setback. And I think we should all try to learn from that attitude.

The other part of that story is that as economic times get worse in this country, there will be more Jays. People will simply learn from their own experiences. And they will get fed up and look for other solutions. This summer, many of the workers who went out and campaigned for Jesse Jackson all over the state of Maine had voted for Reagan in 1984. But because of what they went through, actually having to learn a hard lesson from their own experience, they really changed a lot and learned a lot politically.

Batson The esteem of our communities is sometimes fragile. You ask people to vote and then your candidate gets annihilated. You don't want people to be discouraged. You have to give them something *beyond* the election, and that's what Jesse Jackson has given people. He was quite clear about one purpose, though it never made it to the media. He has noted repeatedly that there is a census coming up. We have to make sure that every individual in this city and in our country is counted so that we can get money for programs that are important. Jackson talks a lot about reapportionment. For instance, if Washington, D.C., were made a state it would have two senators and a governor, all of whom would probably be black because over 90 percent of the population in the District of Columbia is black. There are a lot of similar things going on in this city, less obvious political moves, that people are starting to be organized about. I don't think we have time for pessimism, cynicism, or apathy.

The last thing I'd like to say is that you have to think carefully about what a vote for George Bush means. We need to win this state. There is no scenario whatsoever for Michael Dukakis to win the White House without winning New York state. But a Bush vote is also a signal: if people vote for George Bush in this city it means that they are satisfied with homelessness, they are satisfied with racism, they are satisfied with crack addiction, and they are satisfied with a substandard educational system. So it's very important that we make sure that people get to the polls and vote.

Unidentified Speaker I think that was a very passionate speech on voting. I just have a few follow-up remarks. First, I think that the real poll we should take is how many people think that any major change in this country can ever occur from voting? That is a very different question from whether we should vote or not. Second, I think that the purpose of voting is to bring everybody into the system, to make them participate. In that sense, Jesse Jackson's campaign is a perfect example of bringing people into the system and giving them something to believe in. I just wonder if they ever get anything they really want. And I think everybody in this room needs to ask themselves that question sometimes.

One of the major quarrels I have with Jesse Jackson is over the war on drugs. I think the war on drugs masks a huge hidden agenda. What is really going on with the war on drugs? For one thing, massive militarization of our southern border. We've got the military all involved down there, the perfect recipe for intervention in South America. But in addition, this so-called war on drugs has facilitated a weakening of First and Fourth Amendment rights, illegal search and seizure, court cases that have ruled that suspects can be picked up on the basis of a "drug pusher profile" (which can be as vague as wearing new blue jeans), changing the rules of evidence, and so forth. I don't know about you, but I think this is pretty insidious stuff. So I think we really need to look at the agenda of the war on drugs. Some of the legal situations that it has produced are, in my mind, really questionable.

Sacher Sometimes talking twice is overkill, but I am moved to take the risk tonight because I have noticed two very distinct threads running through the discussion this evening. First, I want to say that to speak honestly about stuff like Jesse Jackson or the Middle East, about being Jewish, about being black, about the complexities of politics—this is frankly, rather difficult in a room like this. I think we want to avoid a certain coerciveness or a sense of frenzy, the kind we know from the 1930s. If we are going to be independent politically, we have to have the space and time to do more thinking and less declaiming. The second thing I want to say is this: in this room I probably feel closer to people and feel more sympathy with my views than I would anywhere else. But on another level, I feel oppressed. The oppression comes from something like this: when I was in camp as a kid I could never concentrate on the group activities. They were always kind of pushing me into them. I feel that way now. Of course, I want to participate in many of these activities; indeed, they are urgent. But I'm also an anarchist and I think we need to dream and reflect a bit. A lot of times when I sit alone looking at the sun, when I see someone who is attractive to me, when I am in an odd mood, how I relate this feeling to the world, to the culture,

to the kind of life I want to see, is very, very important, yet I am ambiva-
lent. On the one hand, you don't want to be resigned, you don't want to be
passive, you want to get up and do something. On the other hand, you want
to pull out of the hysterical culture that is always *making* you do something.
My friend Igal Rodenko in the War Resisters League says, "You got to, got
to!" We are part of a big public relations war: they've got an image, so
we've got to fight them with an image. So it's a very strange position I'm in,
I feel a solidarity and affection, yet I feel also an odd sense of repression, of
being pushed into action too hard and of being forced to raise heavy moral
issues with too much declamation and not enough reflection.

Mitchel Cohen Hi, my name is Mitchel Cohen. I am primarily an activist.
And I help edit a magazine called *Red-Balloon.* I just got back from Washington last night, from a highly successful demonstration at the Pentagon.
There was a lot of militant activity there. We physically shut down the south
parking lot. There were also many practical ideas that came out of that process. What I want to suggest here is that there has to be a way of seeing our
political work itself as an art form. At Monday's demonstration at the Pentagon, the woman who was chairing the legal part of the rally said, "And
now we'll have some culture." Then someone from El Salvador was dragged
up on stage to play the guitar for a few minutes. Everyone applauded nicely,
then he sat down. The suggestion is that culture and art are just part of a
spectacle that we use to keep people interested in the boring politics, the
"real" political work. No one can see the whole thing as an artistic project.
In the future, I'd like to see us conceive of the political work we do as an art
project, as a work that involves people directly in transforming our lives and
that directly affects our social situation. One quick example: about a year-
and-a-half ago, I was involved with a group called Brooklyn Heights Against
Apartheid. We did seven actions at Kennedy airport against South African
Airways. We were trying to shut down the airline. Rather than appealing to
those in power to do it for us, pass legislation, do this and that, we tried to
organize people to go out and shut it down ourselves. It involved a lot of
artists; we created performance art, conceptual art, poster art, stuff that
physically got in the way and fucked up and sabotaged that airline. In the
future I would be interested in a similar sort of action against the *New York
Times.* They have been kind of exempt from criticism because of this
freedom-of-speech concept that we hold so dear. But if people would like to
involve themselves in a project like that, I would be interested.

Wiener As we're nearing the end of the evening, I would like to say that we
do have reason for hope, in spite of what some people have said. I think the

sentiment here is that gradual changes are better than gradual regression, which is what we will get if we vote the wrong way, or if we don't vote. So I'm here to urge you to choose the lesser of the evils.

I grew up in the South when we still had segregated toilets and two different drinking fountains in our courthouse. That has changed, even if all the civil rights battles have not been won. After that we went through the Joe McCarthy era. I was in college when an edict came down saying there could be no more political meetings on campus. That has changed, even if political repression is on the rise again. Later, I was involved with protesting atmospheric testing, when they were blowing up atomic bombs in the air. That has changed, too. We protested and we got somewhere with it. And we stopped Vietnam, didn't we? Bit by bit I think we have stopped aid to the contras, etc., etc. So it's not hopeless. It's down, but it's not hopeless.

Lippard I think the fact that you are all here tonight is in itself a hopeful sign. And the fact that so many of you stayed obviously indicates that you are all hopeful. And I am too, believe me. As Bill Batson was saying, we shouldn't let go of what we have learned here tonight. And as someone else said, we shouldn't go home discouraged, that is for sure. I think it is important that we all continue to participate in these town meetings. The next one is on cultural participation. That means cultural representation as well. It's bringing a much broader base of people into whatever actions we do. So that makes me think of what Bernice Reagon, who is a cultural anthropologist as well as a singer in Sweet Honey and the Rock, said about coalition. She said, "If you are in a coalition and you are real comfortable in it, then that coalition isn't big enough."

Don Moffett, *Meet Me at the Vortex of Our Differences*, 1989.

CULTURAL PARTICIPATION

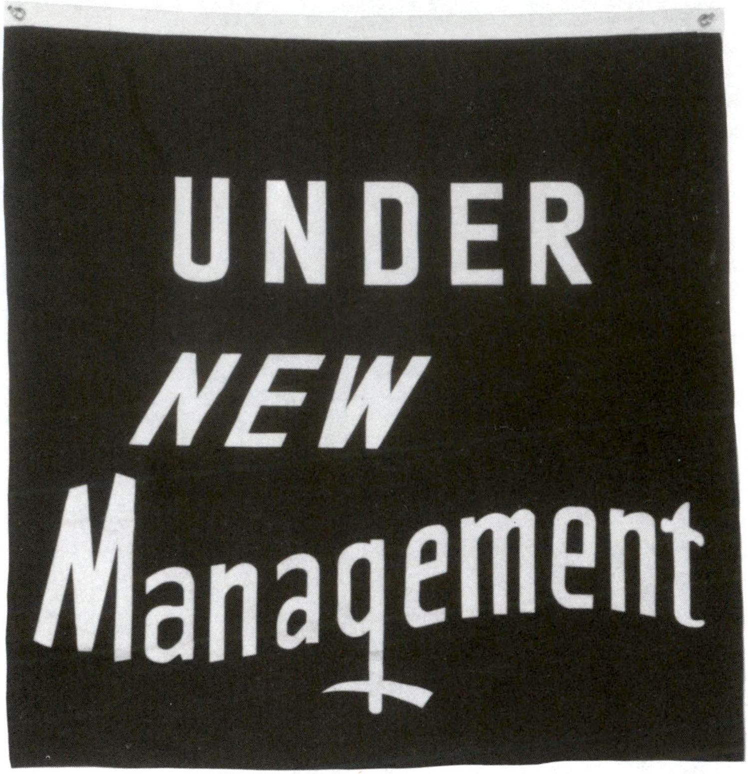
UNDER
NEW
Management

CULTURAL PARTICIPATION

Participants in the roundtable discussion of June 11, 1988:

David Avalos, cofounder of the Border Arts Workshops, and artist; formerly in residence at the Centro Cultural de la Raza, 1978-1988
Martha Gever, editor of *The Independent*
Lucy Lippard, artist and cultural activist
Randall Morris, director of Cavin Morris Gallery
Robert Farris Thompson, professor of art history, African Studies, Yale University
Deborah Wye, curator, department of prints, Museum of Modern Art, New York
Group Material: Doug Ashford, Julie Ault, Felix Gonzalez-Torres

Doug Ashford   When we were putting this roundtable together, one of the things that we talked about was how there seems to have been a recent resurgence of participatory practices by artists, art making that confounds what we understand as conventional forms of art and media. Since some people here are involved in those practices or are knowledgeable about the institutions that promote or inhibit them, perhaps we could address that subject. Cultural participation has been transformed in the last five years or so—the ground has changed dramatically. So how can we now see our own practices in terms of participation?

David Avalos   I think that in terms of cultural participation we have to pay more attention to the mass media. But it's a two-edged sword. On the one hand, we can't kid ourselves any longer that the public's attention is on museums or other nonprofit spaces. It's not. It's on the media: TV, newspapers, magazines, music, films, video. So if everybody's attention is on the media, then you have to find ways to get into the media—and not just in the art sections of newspapers and magazines. You need to come to grips with issues that charge a whole community, not just issues about whether or not broken plates are where it's at this month.
   On the other hand, this also indicates that we need to understand how drastically our sense of what is public has changed. We see public space as something that you pass through, not as a place to congregate. In Southern

California especially, it's something you go through to get from point A to point B in your car. There are exceptions: Chicano low riders get into their cars and get out on the streets to socialize, to see and be seen.

Simultaneous with this disappearance of actual physical space as a location for social interaction, we've had the emergence of the mass media as a new sort of public space. Yet virtually all of it is privately owned and privately consumed with no connection between the two. When we watch TV, when we're sitting in our underwear in the living room or when we read the newspaper sitting in the bathroom or whatever, we have this idea that we're engaging in some sort of public information exchange. But that's ridiculous. You can't talk back to the newspaper editorial, or the TV set.

Is space evaporating in front of our eyes? Is public space for the debate of democratic ideas disappearing? And if it is, then how do we go about inventing space? Organizations don't fail to have space for blacks or Chicanos or Indians or women because someone just forgot about them; they're designed not to have it. You don't have undocumented workers in the U.S. because someone decreed at the governmental level that there's space for undocumented workers. The workers insisted on making that space. And the people who exploit their labor insisted on making that space. Artists have to be the same way. We have to insist on creating space within the society for the discussion of the ideas that we're interested in, and in this way work toward the possibility of a democratic society.

Martha Gever I'd like to say a few things about mass media as public space. First of all, the mass media is an industry, an enormous and extremely lucrative industry that is increasingly becoming the property of transnational corporations. We are watching Rupert Murdoch, for instance, put up satellite stations in Europe, while at the same time he continues to expand his media empire here and in Australia. So, the mass media is a highly problematic area, and one that has to be analyzed quite rigorously by people who want to use it. It's very easy for artists to become, in a way, the research and development arm of the mass media. The media is, after all, quite good at finding out what is groovy and new and entertaining, and then reproducing it.

One of the things I'm working on with other people around the country is a campaign to try and force a greater democratization of public television. By definition public television is supposed to be public and not commercial. But in this country over the years it has become more and more a vehicle for upscale advertising. In the late seventies, when smart advertisers were looking for upper-middle-class buyers, they began to use public TV, because it was much cheaper than mainstream television. Now public TV has become basically the property of the corporate sponsors and the subscribers the sta-

Elizabeth Sisco, Louis Hock, and David Avalos, *Welcome to America's Finest Tourist Plantation*, 1988. Poster that appeared on the back of public buses in San Diego during the city's hosting of Super Bowl XXII.

tions solicit. Subscription drives are geared toward, essentially, again, an upper-middle-class audience—and that's who they program for. So, even in the area of mass media, which is designated as public space, the space reserved for a democratic communication, in fact, it's very difficult to convince the people who control it to open it up. They're very reluctant to give up their power. And their power is incredible, just enormous. Broadcasting is one of the most powerful tools that anybody can have.

Avalos But it's important that people are beginning to understand that they should have some say about what's coming into their homes. Museums and nonprofit spaces are supposedly accountable to the public because they receive tax dollars. Although they're not necessarily accessible to the public, they're accountable to them because taxes are supposed to be used to serve all the people. Commercial or corporate enterprises are not accountable to the public, except insofar as they exist to make a profit from the people. Buses receive a lot of state and federal dollars, though, and that's why they should be a little bit more accommodating and accessible.

There's an ad at the gas station where I get gas. Have you noticed those little billboards that are appearing everywhere now? There's a little billboard on top of the pump and it says, "We Fuel Your Freedom." And it shows an enormous ball and a chain, and the chain is broken because the car is accelerating. Now this is a classic symbol of political liberation: the broken chain. And here it is being presented to the American public as a sign for the message: "Consumption is the road to freedom of choice." The essential characteristics of a democratic society are now the turf of advertisers.

Program chart is on A-136
Pay-TV movie details begin on A-10

Wednesday

Sept. 24, 1986   **8 PM**

(31) VIDEO MUSIC BOX; 60 min.
(41) MONTE CALVARIO—Novela; 60 min.
(47) LA DUENA—Novela; 60 min.
(50) ANCIENT LIVES (CC)—Documentary; 60 min.
(55) MOVIE—Drama (BW); 2 hrs.
"Suez." (1938) Slow but handsomely produced account of the building of the Suez Canal, with the usual historical distortions. Tyrone Power, Loretta Young, Annabella.
(61) MOVIE—Adventure; 2 hrs.
"Treasure Island." (1950) Robert Newton has

a field day as Long John Silver in this Disney adaptation of Robert Louis Stevenson's classic about 18th-century piracy and buried gold. Jim: Bobby Driscoll. Dr. Livesey: Denis O'Dea. Merry: Ralph Truman.
(68) NEW YORK TONITE; 2 hrs.
(A&E) AIR POWER—Documentary (BW)
(CBN) BRING 'EM BACK ALIVE; 60 min.
(CNN) NEWS—Farmer/Curie/Shaw; 60 min.
(HBO) MOVIE—Crime Drama; 1 hr., 40 min.
"Best Revenge."
(LIF) BERRENGER'S—Drama; 60 min.

PREMIERE   **9:00PM** (abc) (7) (8)

Page in *TV Guide*, September 24, 1986.

Gever During the Reagan years, the debate about deregulation of broadcasting (which has been effectively accomplished, although very recent developments may push us back even more) has been around freedom of speech. The private media industry has said, "We represent freedom, and any attempt to regulate us is counter to freedom." Cable television—one of the models for direct cultural participation—began to allow collaborative or democratic efforts by groups and individuals throughout the country using public access channels. While those channels are mandated by most municipalities granting franchises to cable companies, now many of those companies are challenging public access on the basis of the First Amendment. The notion of the public interest, to which the broadcast and cable industries pay lip service, is being redefined in terms of consumer markets—the marketplace model.

Lucy Lippard I think culture—especially the media—has to be open to variety and differences. I'm not going to get into the immense complexities of each community and their politics, backgrounds, and internal problems, but certainly if there's any place that they can meet, it's around culture. Cultural differences—or the boundaries between groups—are only a state of mind; we're all in it together on one level or another, or on different levels, simultaneously.

Avalos At the Centro, where I work, one of the principles is that we refuse to be seen as gatekeepers to the past. That would freeze us in a position that would not allow us to participate in the public forums that are getting at what a democratic society is all about. But unfortunately, that's usually how ethnic artists and ethnic organizations are portrayed, as totally caught up in the past.

The Centro Cultural de la Raza was started in 1970 as an aspect of the Chicano civil rights movement. The founders saw the Centro as a place where they could determine their own cultural future and define themselves as artists. From the beginning there was an understanding of the very political nature of art itself—in other words, not being political art, but art politics. As artists, Chicanos have a completely different tradition, and different motivations. Since the Conquest, the native people of North and South America have understood exactly the political nature of culture and art. They've understood exactly how it has been put at the service of political power, at the service of colonialism, at the service of imperialism.

By the time I started working full-time for Centro in the late seventies, the main idea was that art is just one aspect of creativity. As artists we were part of a whole community—and when I say community, I mean the Chicano community—along with clergy people, educators, grandmothers, unwed mothers, what have you. We were all in the process of creating our own futures, defining what it was we were all about.

We don't see art as simply a reflection of society. We see art as a vehicle for making society, for creating the future, for activating people. We don't see artists as entertainers or decorators. We see artists as, for the most part, educators. Most of the artists I know have had the benefit of a college education; they're intellectuals to a certain extent, and they're also community activists. We don't see artists as frivolous or unessential. We insist on seeing artists as a voice in the shaping of society—a role that people usually aren't willing to concede to artists. So, a lot of the work of the Centro Cultural comes out of this awareness of social contradictions, an awareness developed in the context of civil rights activism.

One of the revelations of the Chicano movement is that it only occupied center stage in the U.S. political arena by virtue of the mass media's coverage of it. Prior to 1965, people like Rodolfo "Corky" Gonzalez in Denver, one of the leaders of the movement, used to refer to us as the "invisible minority." Nobody even knew we existed. That's the way the media deals with groups that they see as powerless, or that they want to keep powerless. They prefer indifference; that's very powerful, you know, disdain and indifference. But when the movement came along, they had to begin covering us. Then in the late seventies, you began to see cover stories in the major weeklies like *Time* and *Newsweek* in which people talk about the demographics of our community and how, with newfound self-determination and self-definition, our community had emerged as a political entity. Then the emphasis shifted from *us* defining ourselves as people demanding participation in a democratic society, to *their* perception of us as an audience, as a market. They said, in effect, "You've made it. You've arrived. You, too, can purchase a BMW. You, too, can drink Coors beer. You, too, can vote for a presidential candidate." And, of course, all three things are marketed exactly the same way. So, at the Centro we have no illusions. There's a real clear understanding that the center of consciousness in this society is not the art world, but is advertising, marketing, public relations—that's where the value systems of this country are encapsulated.

This creates a real challenge, then, for the kind of cultural work you're doing. From the beginning there have been these strange flip-flops within the Chicano movement. Initially, people were making public art on walls, in barrios, in community locations, for two reasons. One, because alternative spaces and museums were not interested in Chicano artists. And, two, because even if they had been we, the artists, felt that the people we were making the work for—our relatives, our neighbors, and so forth—don't go to those places. So we said, "Let's paint on walls in our communities, let's paint our history."

What you're finding nowadays, twenty years later, is that it's very hard to get anyone excited about mural projects. Most of the Chicano artists that started out painting murals years ago are now just as happy to have their work shown in commercial galleries or museums. And they have every right to make a living at what they enjoy doing. I don't take the position that there's anything wrong with being able to make a living at making art. But at a time when we should be in the public arena more than ever before, we aren't.

By definition, gatekeepers are there to attract the resources and to sanctify a sexist, racist, oppressive society, and all the efforts to get them to be something other than that are bound to fail. It's like going into a go-go bar and talking one of the topless dancers into delivering a feminist pitch. Of course, the guys who hang out there are the ones who need to hear it the most, but people just don't go into go-go bars to have their minds expanded in that way. There has to be a sense of where people are at when you approach them.

So in the arena of public art, everywhere across the country, people are saying, "Wait a minute. That's our money. You can have it in the museums, but we don't want it here, in *our* space." So you have this head-on collision between what the public wants and art that is based on the modernist ideal. The curators and artists say, "What's wrong with these people? They should be happy to have an Ellsworth Kelly here in San Diego." And the people just say, "Forget it. We don't want it." That's one of the arenas where this whole cultural participation thing has to be hashed out.

Museums are democratic institutions. They are funded by the taxes of everyone, and in principle at least, they're supposed to be working for everyone. I think that we—Chicanos—need to be there, and we need to have a voice in the way museums select and present work. In the long run, I think museums have to be redefined and restructured, but for now I think we need to be in museums simply because there is no place that we should be eliminated from. I think that the other tactic—embarrassing them and showing how inadequate they are in presenting the creative power of all people in American society—is something that should be done, too. These are supposedly the professionals; these are the ones that have all the resources and all the power.

Ashford   Right from the start, no matter what the nature of the work is, the institution has an enormous weight of advantage. I feel that one of the things Group Material can do is try to work on both sides of a fence, or a wall, between the artists and the institutions.

Avalos That's one power the museums don't have, they can't work on both sides of the fence.

Ashford Maybe they can. I think Deborah really crossed the fence with the "Committed to Print" show at the Museum of Modern Art.

Avalos But the fact that there's a black Supreme Court justice doesn't mean that the justice system in this country isn't racist.

Lippard When Group Material did "Americana" at the Whitney in 1984, all those artists who would never have been in the Whitney Biennial were in it, through being in Group Material's show within a show. That was an important model. But I think what people are wary about, in dealing with museums, is co-optation. In the community I work with, a lot of people finally looked at things a little more realistically and said to themselves either you stay out of museums on an absolute principle—which is one thing, if you just don't want to be part of that particular system—or you try to be in both places at one time, be effective both inside and outside. Jerry Kearns has been instrumental in getting this across. He has said, "They aren't just their museums. They're ours, too. The whole place is ours, and we shouldn't always be putting ourselves outside of everything. We should just barge in there and say, 'Fuck you, I belong here, too,' and then see what little part we can take away." Nobody has any great illusions about total conquest or anything, but our voices should be heard in the "centers."

Gever I think at a certain level, this question has to be politicized. I don't think that you can see it as a neutral act. And I would also like to say that there are certain works that the institutions, not just the museums but larger cultural institutions, are *not* willing to co-opt at this point. Work around gay issues, for instance, is not very easily co-opted. I am familiar with this issue because some of the filmmakers and videomakers I encounter through my job at the Association of Independent Video and Filmmakers (a membership organization with over 4,500 members) *want* to be co-opted. I'm not saying all, but some of them. And, there are a lot of young people just out of art school whose dream is to be coopted. Of course, they want to do their own films. But there's material that the institutions—the gatekeepers—won't touch. And I think it's very important keep that quite up front, because it has to be dealt with. The Museum of Modern Art is not going to open its arms to overtly political work.

Lippard Like feminist art—the old-fashioned radical kind of feminist art has never made it into museums.

Deborah Wye I don't think that the dominant cultural institutions should be so easily discounted. But how to deal with them is another problem. It's very difficult. Access alone is sometimes prohibitive. Now it will cost, I think, six dollars to get into MoMA. I know I wouldn't go very often if I didn't have a museum pass. Or just a catalogue today costs twenty dollars. These are concrete problems that limit the audience to a particular class, for the most part. But I do think that it's important to try to expand the museum audience. When I did the "Committed to Print" exhibition, for instance, I asked the visitor service representative how many people had come to see it. She said the attendance was approximately 200,000 for that one exhibition. I'm happy that I was able to get 200,000 people to look at that work. Now that's not as many as watch television. It's not the mass media. But it's a start. So there's a whole other question: what is the role of the museum, if so few people go to it?

Well, one thing I think we have to remember is that the people who do go to museums are often the same ones who are making decisions about what is seen in the media. So the people who run the museums actually make important decisions that have a wide influence on the rest of our culture.

Ashford How were you able to do "Committed to Print" at MoMA?

Wye Well, I'm a print curator, and I just kept coming across prints of social and political subject matter in all the work from the sixties to the present done by American artists. So I thought the show was inevitable, and I thought everyone else would think it was inevitable, too. Also I was seeing certain prints being made that seemed to be about important things, and I was trying to collect them for our museum, just in my regular business of going about acquisitions. In trying to come up with an exhibition idea, I looked back over the things that I had been recommending for acquisition for the last couple of years and it seemed like something was really happening. Then, of course, I discovered the whole graphic tradition of social and political commentary since the beginning of prints, something that, as a modern print curator, I really wasn't particularly involved with.

I don't want to be too defensive about museums. I just want to try from inside to make them different. We had a roundtable discussion at the museum a few months ago, and all the younger people were talking about exhibitions of contextual aspects and trying to do exhibitions in different ways, with new methodologies, more critical approaches, and things like that. So I'm just putting in a pitch for the museum not to be dismissed entirely. It serves an audience that is worth trying to reach, and worth trying to change.

YOU'RE SEEING LESS THAN HALF THE PICTURE

WITHOUT THE VISION OF WOMEN ARTISTS AND ARTISTS OF COLOR.

Please send $ and comments to:
Box 1056 Cooper Sta. NY, NY 10276 **GUERRILLA GIRLS** CONSCIENCE OF THE ART WORLD

Guerrilla Girls, street poster, 1989.

Lippard Why do museums feel so threatened whenever activist artists or feminists or artists of color picket, or make demands? Apparently we're stronger than we realize when we get together.

Wye It isn't so much that they're afraid or even against them, they often haven't even heard about these artists. Someone could be very well known in a minority culture and absolutely unknown to these curators who read all the mainstream art magazines, go to all the galleries, and feel like they spend a lot of time learning about art. They just haven't heard of these minority people.

Lippard Tell me about it! I mean I've been writing about some of these people for years and so have others, often in the mainstream magazines, and *that* doesn't make any difference. But I'm not going to get off on that. I'm just curious. Why do you think that the dominant culture is so hostile to this kind of thing?

Wye I haven't noticed outright hostility. They could be interested, but they don't even know how to relate to it.

Lippard That's a form of racist, ethnocentric hostility, politely expressed. They just don't live in the same world.

Wye That's it. They don't live in the same world. If I bring in for acquisition an object by a nonmainstream artist, I can't even recommend a price for it because it's not even sold in the markets the other curators know. They can't test the price because these artists don't show in the galleries they go to. It's a world of the unknown. That's what I see, rather than hostility.

Lippard One does get a little paranoid about it, though, because the fact is these artists are unknown *on purpose*. The information, the art, is there to be known. The institutions are well equipped to know it. MoMA's library has lots of material on it. Yet this goes on, and it has gone on in very different ways for years. I've been around for thirty years, watching, and the fact remains that the distance between dominant culture and "minority" cultures has not closed that much.

Wye Why do *you* think they're hostile?

Lippard There's a basic class analysis.

Avalos Okay, but the artists I know, who have come out of the Hispanic community that I work with—no matter what their class—my experience is that these people are dying to get into museums.

Felix Gonzalez-Torres Are they?

Lippard Sure, why shouldn't they be?

Avalos I don't know of anyone who has stood up and declared that they're not going to have anything to do with museums. I think that Debbie's experience with the print show bears that out. Nobody refused to participate. Nobody said, "Hey, I'm above that, or I'm beyond that, or I'm too hip for that."

Gonzalez-Torres I disagree when you say that artists are dying to get into the museums. I really question how effective that is.

Avalos I'm not saying that museums are that effective. I'm not addressing the issue of effectiveness at all. What I'm saying is that the vast majority of artists are dying to get into museums. I don't know any who would refuse to show in a museum.

Lippard Well, I know people who have said no to shows, who told the curators to go fuck themselves, but they're few and far between.

Avalos Because of the particular circumstances of the show?

Lippard Because of politics and general principles, not the principle "I will never be in a museum," but a principle about what the show is, who the people who are doing it are, who's paying for it, what the ideology behind it is, and how art and artists are going to be *used* in it.

While we're on the subject of the dominant institution, I'd love to hear what people have to say about the Latino shows that are big at the moment. There's "Hispanic Art in the U.S." at the Corcoran, and there was "MIRA!" sponsored by Canadian Club or Seagrams, and another by Coors. The collusion of alcohol and Hispanic art shows is interesting.

Avalos That really bothers me, the idea of turning over financial support for the arts to commercial interests, to corporations who use it to expand their markets. The idea of Coors sponsoring the so-called Hispanic show is abhorrent. But this isn't just the fault of the ideological taskmasters—the museum and the NEA—it's also the fault of artists themselves, who don't try to organize.

Robert Farris Thompson One thing we should realize is that the black situation in the visual arts now is so powerful that many don't need us. They're doing it without us. Also, we should address the situation of the visionary painters and sculptors in their seventies, eighties, and nineties—groups beyond race and class. I refer to black men and women who are over seventy who respond to a spiritual imperative when they become painters. This leads me to talk about black "yard-shows," so-called environments (a phrase the museums use). This art form is a challenge, by the sheer audacity of turning lawns into yard-shows. Who gives a damn about 57th Street or Soho; black visionaries have their own art projections, some yard-shows seem ritually enacted. There may be two ceramic vessels at the door to guard against evil-intending visitors. Lots of circular elements, perhaps to wheel you away if you're evil, or wheel you in if you're kindly. Tires, hubcaps, pinwheels, stones, pipes, mirrors, sheathing the property with messages and flash.

Plus, I'll throw out some names: Rachael Presha, "The Purple Lady" of Suffolk, Virginia, for instance, who painted trees in her yard purple, telephone poles purple, her shoes purple, a baby carriage purple, and so forth. To know her is to accept purpleness. She's saying, very freely and very obsessively, something about color that's also very witty.

Mary T. Smith, of Mississippi, who likes to dress in checks and stripes,

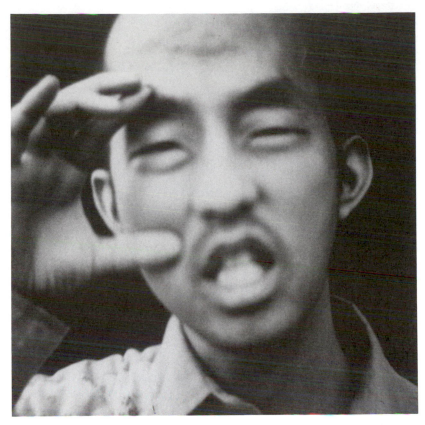

Peter Reiss, *Brian Mats Umoto*, 1986.

picks a particular kind of corrugated roofing material to paint on, which sort of transmits her clothing tastes into her medium. Then she puts images into the corrugation and places the whole thing in her yard.

Or take Jean Lacy, a black woman artist of Dallas. She paints, for instance, miniaturized tenement walls, and inserts in the windows Egyptian silhouettes. She's telling us that we are children of the Sudan, thus bringing the insights of a parallel black classical tradition right into the inner city.

Or John Biggers, a black painter of Houston, Texas, who takes shotgun houses, a major black contribution to the architecture of this country, and paints them to read like private temples of black cultural continuance.

Or, Renée Stout, an African-American artist in Washington, D.C., who invents a glittering kind of cabalistic script. She's sometimes writing messages that start with diamondlike ciphers and end with, sometimes, numerals; and it has to do with love and self-protection.

A lot of these "admonitions," in painting and sculpture, that emerge in black America, are spiritual. But how can we come to grips with spiritually intense art unless we not only know our artists, but know them at levels of long-built trust and friendship? But people say, "How can you be objective about Romare Bearden if you were friends with Romare Bearden?" or something like that.

Taking a page from Djuna Barnes—that passage in *Nightwood* where a woman knows her lover is coming into the room by the particular chime of cosmetics on the dresser; the intensity of love gives you the ultimate objectivity, because you're attuned to real structuring, as opposed to trying to figure out with outsider-arrogance—literally proud that you don't know the women and men whose works and values you dare to assess.

I would say, therefore, that you don't abdicate your critical edge when you write from levels of trust and affection, where artists open up because they know you take them seriously. And I could care less what, say, Hilton Kramer thinks about this issue of objectivity versus transmission of the spiritual insights of an artist.

Lippard Well, at one point dissident artists felt that we could create our own separate community and screw the rest. We could participate in a community united by common beliefs, which would exist beyond the art world. I mean, after all, the art world is a tiny, incestuous, and often disregarded community. If all cultural workers were to form a national community, it might be larger than the so-called art world, which has a certain amount of money and power behind it, but is in fact relatively small. Most people, including wealthy people and educated people, have no idea it even exists. They never go to museums, most of them, or galleries, or read the magazines.

Avalos That's true, and the gatekeepers only deal with the minority of image makers. One of the things that I want to talk about is community and creating. Communities are creative. They are not free-floating bodies that just exist out there. There has to be a sense of creating a place as well as creating a community for your work. But, listen, Randall was telling me something very instructive about Martin Ramirez, an Hispanic artist he's been doing a lot of research on. Ramirez was the focal point of the essay Octavio Paz wrote for the catalogue of the Houston-Corcoran show on contemporary Hispanic art.

Randall Morris First, let me say that I feel like I'm coming from a bizarre place, since I'm the only dealer on the panel. But then if it were a panel of dealers, I'd be the least typical of that group, too. I deal with artists who basically have no representation, who are frowned on by a mainstream because they are self-taught and have not gone through the "traditional" channels.

David, you said that you didn't know any artists who didn't care whether or not they were in a museum, but most of the artists I deal with could care less. The work winds up in museums, sometimes, but it really doesn't change what is going on in their lives. For them art making is not a job, it's who they are; the art is who they are. There is *no* separation between art and life.

There are aspects of our work that I want to mention, then I will get back to Ramirez. First, there is this concept of a mainstream art, but if you analyze the word "mainstream" you realize it is one of the most meaningless and destructive words that has ever been invented. You can call an artist an "outsider," meaning he's outside of the mainstream, but if you dismiss the idea of the mainstream entirely, you realize that the "outsider" is really outside of nothing. I find it a really basic point that "mainstream" is a construct to nullify the radical.

Second, when I began to study these individuals who pursued art in their own ways, I began finding out how individuals cope with this society on every level. Now I am particularly fascinated with the ethical aspects of it. What I'm starting to realize over time is that there is a universality to these artists we're calling "outsider" or "self-taught" artists. And they're influenced by each other's lives because they live on the same planet. White Southern artists are influenced by black Southern artists who are on a self-taught level, for example. You can call them idiosyncratic, or you can call them outside the mainstream, but they don't see it that way, just like the people Bob was talking about. They're carrying the basic moral structure of their people, the past, present, and future of who they are around with them, and it enters each work of art that they make.

Finally, what I came to see was that most of the art in the world is interwoven, and that trained artists are actually in the minority—really the narrowest representation of how this world makes art and how it makes music and how it lives basically. So, at the gallery we have begun to compile information on untrained artists. This archive may be one of the first. In my field, the dealers with integrity are at the forefront of research, because they're the ones who actually go out there and do the field work. What I'm getting at is that I feel there is a contextualization that's missing from the presentation of a lot of contemporary art. In the past, museums and dealers have treated the public as being too ignorant to deal with the meanings that pertain to an art work. The public should make its own decisions about how much it wants to know about a work. That's been going on in African art for a long time; dealers, collectors, even viewers have had to do their own research. If I see a piece I like, I do homework. It doesn't kill the power or the mystery of a piece for me to know where it came from, who did it, and how it was used.

Which brings me to Martin Ramirez, who is considered to be one of the greatest self-taught artists in this country. He was in the Hispanic show. And all of a sudden I have people coming into the gallery and seeing the pieces and saying, "Oh, he was in the Corcoran's Hispanic show." Yet his work has been shown for over ten years now. And you have these reviews coming out by people like Donald Kuspit, who say that because Ramirez was in a mental institution and because he used a "hermetic" language, it was not universal—it was the language of the insane. But no one ever bothered to learn Ramirez's language, which was *Mexican*, basically. In doing our culture-clash research we've gotten very much into syncretism which is the blending and melding of religions and lifeways. In the case of Mexico we've also been studying the dance masks very seriously. If you look at the masks, and by extension, the beauty of the culture's long memory, then you begin to see Ramirez's work. But no one ever did that before. No one ever took Ramirez's work back to Mexico, no one ever gave it a Mexican context. And it's so important to his drawings, and everything he did. There's not one element in any of Ramirez's drawings that is not a Mexican element. Or another example: Ramirez was supposed to be illiterate, yet there are words all through his paintings. There's one word that shows up in one of his major works: it's "delite." It's been accepted by every critic who has written about it as "delight," but in Spanish "delite" means "sinner." He was in an institution for thirty years and died in that institution, yet there is no indication that anyone ever spoke to him in Spanish. I believe that what they called autistic mumbling was praying; there are religious images throughout his work. I believe that he was a religious visionary in the context of his mother culture and that America read him as a lunatic. This is a California hospital pre-*One Flew Over the Cuckoo's Nest*. I'm just using him as an example because one could find a thousand stories like that in the field. What I'm saying is contextualization doesn't hurt the art, willful de-contextualization does.

Lippard Exactly. For years it has pissed me off that so many artists can't be bothered to explain their work, like they're so insecure or brainwashed that they think that if somebody *knows* something about what they're trying to say, it will detract from it. I've been looking at art for thirty-odd years and I still can't tell by osmosis what a lot of artists are trying to do or say. If I'm given more information, it helps me to see more, and then we have an exchange that is much more informed and caring *and objective*. Titles and captions don't kill visual power, they augment it.

Wye At the Modern, we had this debate about *Guernica* and whether the label should describe the historical circumstances of the bombing. We actually went around the table and said whether we thought it should or shouldn't. Some people thought it would take away some of the mystery or the universality of the art.

Lippard That's a perfect example. Isn't that incredible? The mystery or universality of something is done in because you *know* something about it? The historical context gives *Guernica* substance.

Gever Isn't that one of the primary tenets of modernism, though, that art should be isolated from its context? Perhaps if it were folk art or political art or some other so-called minor form it might need a context, but not Picasso.

Avalos The thing is, when they call something political art they do it for one of two reasons: either to denigrate that art or to hide the fact that all art is political. In the end I think it is education that is most important. Education may be the last public space where there are signs of hope. But even there you find corporate involvement. I read in a recent article about a corporation in Texas that built a school for the children of its employees. They made a deal with the local school district that the corporation would supply all the building materials and equipment if the school district would supply the teachers. This is something we have to keep in mind.

Mass media has not brought us together. Mass media and mass marketing have fragmented us into about thirty to forty different demographic niches. So we all get the same newspaper, but some of us are going to spend our time in the sports section, some of us are going to read the art pages, some are going to listen to the editorials, others are going to look at the fashion section. Still, that one document is going to reach any number of demographic niches. And I think that we have to look at our public institutions as just that: public. They have to deal with all of society, across the board. Having said that, the lack of examples where this has been accomplished is another thing altogether.

Lippard But such broad-based cultural participation is happening more frequently now, which makes me optimistic. When we were organizing in the sixties, we were looking back to the thirties and early forties, before World War II, to find models for cultural activism that had disappeared during the McCarthy period. And we were appalled to find ourselves saying exactly the same things, having the same goals, that people had been citing thirty years ago. It was depressing because, of course, so little had changed, because so little was remembered and carried on. People have even forgotten their recent history. Young artists don't know what the Art Workers Coalition was demanding of the New York museums—things like a free day, nonwhite and women's representation, condemnation of the Vietnam War, decentralization into neighborhood centers, etc. All this sounds mysterious to people now, even though it was only twenty years ago. The Bicentennial protests in 1976, same problem. But it seems to me that this is one place the dominant institutions can damn well do their job. They could at least *document* the alternatives as well as the mainstream, tell the truth about the participation in social movements of mainstream artists, to educate students and the public about the cultural diversity that exists.

"WHEN I WAS A YOUNG SOLDIER

FOR THE REVOLUTION":

COMING TO VOICE

Angela Davis spoke these words. They moved me. I say them here and hope to say them in many places. This is how deeply they touched me—evoking memories of innocence, of initial passionate commitment to political struggle. They were spoken in a talk she gave at a conference focusing on "Poetry and Politics: Afro-American Poetry Today." I began writing poetry when I was young, ten years old. Poetry came into my life, the sense of poetry, with reading scripture with those awkward and funny little rhymes we would memorize and recite on Easter Sunday. Then it came into my life at Booker T. Washington grade school where I learned that poetry was no silent subject. That moment of learning was pure enchantment, for we learned by listening and reciting, that words put together just so, said just so, could have the same impact on our psyches as song, could lift and exalt our spirits, enabling us to feel tremendous joy, or carrying us down into that most immediate and violent sense of loss and grief.

Like many African-Americans, I became a writer through making poems. Poetry was one literary expression that was absolutely respected in our working-class household. Nights when the lights would go out, when storms were raging, we would sit in the dim candlelight of our living room and have a talent show. I would recite poems: Wordsworth, James Weldon Johnson, Langston Hughes, Elizabeth Barrett Browning, Emily Dickinson, Gwendolyn Brooks. Poetry by white writers was always there in schools and on family bookshelves in anthologies of "great" works sold to us by door-to-door salesmen, book peddlers, who came spreading their wares as though we were a dark desert people and they weary travelers bringing us light from a faraway place. Poetry by black writers had to be searched for, a poem copied from books no one would let you borrow for fear of loss, or taken from books found by puzzled white Southern librarians eager to see that you "read right." I was in high school before I discovered James Weldon Johnson's collection of *American Negro Poetry*. It had never been checked out of the library even though it had been on the shelves for some time. I would keep this book as long as I could, working to memorize every poem so I would know them all by heart.

For me, poetry was the place for the secret voice, for all that could not be directly stated or named, for all that would not be denied expression. Poetry was privileged speech—simple at times, but never ordinary. The magic of poetry was transformation; it was words changing shape, meaning, and form. Poetry was not mere recording of the way we Southern black folks talked to one another, even though our language was poetic. It was transcendent speech. It was meant to transform consciousness, to carry the mind and heart to a new dimension. These were my primitive thoughts on poetry as I experienced and knew it growing up.

When I became a student in college creative writing classes, I learned a notion of "voice" as embodying the distinctive expression of an individual writer. Our efforts to become poets were to be realized in this coming into awareness and expression of one's voice. In all my writing classes, I was the only black student. Whenever I read a poem written in the particular dialect of Southern black speech, the teacher and fellow students would praise me for using my "true," authentic voice, and encouraged me to develop this "voice," to write more of these poems. From the onset this troubled me. Such comments seemed to mask racial biases about what my authentic voice would or should be.

In part, attending all-black segregated schools with black teachers meant that I had come to understand black poets as being capable of speaking in many voices, that the Dunbar of a poem written in dialect was no more or less authentic than the Dunbar writing a sonnet. Yet it was listening to black musicians like Duke Ellington, Louis Armstrong, and later John Coltrane that impressed upon our consciousness a sense of versatility—they played all kinds of music, had multiple voices. So it was with poetry. The black poet, as exemplified by Gwendolyn Brooks and later Amiri Baraka, had many voices—with no single voice being identified as more or less authentic. The insistence on finding one voice, one definitive style of writing and reading one's poetry, fit all too neatly with a static notion of self and identity that was pervasive in university settings. It seemed that many black students found our situations problematic precisely because our sense of self, and by definition our voice, was not unilateral, monologist, or static but rather multidimensional. We were as at home in dialect as we were in standard English. Individuals who speak languages other than English, who speak patois as well as standard English, find it a necessary aspect of self-affirmation not to feel compelled to choose one voice over another, not to claim one as more authentic, but rather to construct social realities that celebrate, acknowledge, and affirm differences, variety. In *Borderlands: La Frontera,* Gloria Anzaldúa writes of the need to claim all the tongues in which we speak, to make speech of the many languages that give expression to the unique cultural reality of a people:

For a people who are neither Spanish nor live in a country in which Spanish is the first language; for a people who live in a country in which English is the reigning tongue but who are not Anglo; for a people who cannot entirely identify with either standard (formal, Castilian) Spanish nor standard English, what recourse is left to them but to create their own language? A language which they can connect their identity to, one capable of communicating the realities and values true to themselves. . . .

In recent years, any writing about feminism has overshadowed writing as a poet. Yet there are spaces where thoughts and concerns converge. One such space has been the feminist focus on coming to voice—on moving from silence into speech as revolutionary gesture. Once again, the idea of finding one's voice or having a voice assumes a primacy in talk, discourse, writing, and action. As metaphor for self-transformation, it has been especially relevant for groups of women who have previously never had a public voice, women who are speaking and writing for the first time, including many women of color. Feminist focus on finding a voice may seem clichéd at times, especially when the insistence is that women share a common speech or that all women have something meaningful to say at all times. However, for women within oppressed groups who have contained so many feelings— despair, rage, anguish—who do not speak, as poet Audre Lorde writes, "for fear our words will not be heard nor welcomed," coming to voice is an act of resistance. Speaking becomes both a way to engage in active self-transformation and a rite of passage where one moves from being object to being subject. Only as subjects can we speak. As objects we remain voiceless—our beings defined and interpreted by others. It is this liberating speech that Mariana Romo-Carmona writes about in her introduction to *Compañeras: Latina Lesbians:*

Each time a woman begins to speak, a liberating process begins, one that is unavoidable and has powerful implications. In these pages we see repeated the process of self-discovery, of affirmation in coming out of the closet, the search for a definition of our identity within the family and our community, the search for answers, for meaning in our personal struggles, and the commitment to a political struggle to end all forms of oppression. The stages of increasing awareness become clear when we begin to recount the story of our lives to someone else, someone who has experienced the same changes. When we write or speak about these changes we establish our experiences as valid and real, we begin to analyze, and that analysis gives us the necessary perspective to place our lives in a context where we know what to do next.

Awareness of the need to speak, to give voice to the varied dimensions of our lives, is one way women of color begin the process of education for critical consciousness.

Need for such speech is often validated in writings by people engaged in liberation struggles in the Third World, in the literatures of people struggling globally from oppression and domination. El Salvadoran writer Manlio Argueta structures his powerful novel, *One Day of Life,* around the insistence on the development of political awareness, the sharing of knowledge that makes the revolutionary thinker and activist. It is the character José who is most committed to sharing his awareness with family and community, and most importantly with Lupé, his friend and wife, to whom he says:

. . . that's why the problems can't be solved by a single person, but only by all of us working together, the humble, the clearheaded ones. And this is very important; you can be humble and live in darkness. Well, the thing is not a matter of being or not being humble. The problem lies in our awareness. The awareness we will have. Then life will become as clear as spring water.

I first read this novel in a course I taught on Third World literature and it was clear then that speaking freely, openly has different meaning for people from exploited and oppressed groups.

Nonliterary works by writers opposing domination also speak to the primacy of coming to voice, of speaking for the oppressed. In keeping with this emphasis on speech, Alicia Partnoy proclaims, in her brave work, *The Little School: Tales of Disappearance and Survival in Argentina,* "They cut off my voice so I grew two voices, into different tongues my songs I pour." Here speech has a dual implication. There is the silence of the oppressed who have never learned to speak and there is the voice of those who have been forcefully silenced because they have dared to speak and by doing so resist. Egyptian writer Nawal El Sa'adawi protests against such silences in her *Memoirs from the Women's Prison.* She dedicated her book "To all who have hated oppression to the point of death, who have loved freedom to the point of imprisonment, and have rejected falsehood to the point of revolution." Or the resistance to being silenced Theresa Hak Kyung Cha describes in *Dictee:*

Mother, you are a child still. At eighteen. More of a child since you are always ill. They have sheltered you from the others. It is not your own. Even if it is not you know you must. You are bi-lingual. You are tri-lingual. The tongue that is forbidden is your own mother tongue. You speak in the dark, in the secret. The one that is yours. Your own . . . Mother tongue is your refuge. It is being home. Being who you are. Truly. To speak makes you sad. To utter each word is a privilege you risk by death.

In fiction as well as in confessional writing, those who understand the power of voice as gesture of rebellion and resistance urge the exploited, the oppressed to speak.

To speak as an act of resistance is quite different than ordinary talk, or the personal confession that has no relation to coming into political awareness, to developing critical consciousness. This is a difference we must talk about in the United States, for here the idea of finding a voice risks being trivialized or romanticized in the rhetoric of those who advocate a shallow feminist politic that privileges acts of speaking over the content of speech. Such rhetoric often turns the voices and beings of nonwhite women into commodity, spectacle. In a white-supremacist, capitalist, patriarchal state where the mechanisms of co-optation are so advanced, much that is potentially radical is undermined, turned into commodity, fashionable speech as in "black women writers are in right now." Often the questions of who is listening and what is being heard are not answered. When reggae music became popular in the United States, I often pondered whether the privileged white people who listened were learning from this music to resist, to rebel against white supremacy and white imperialism. What did they hear when Bob Marley said, "We refuse to be what you wanted us to be"—did they think about colonization, about internalized racism? One night at a Jimmy Cliff concert attended predominantly by young white people, Cliff began a call-and-response refrain where we the listeners were to say "Africa for Africans." There was suddenly a hush in the room, as though the listeners finally heard the rebellion against white supremacy, against imperialism in the lyrics. They were silent, unable apparently to share in this gesture affirming black solidarity. Who is listening and what do they hear?

Appropriation of the marginal voice threatens the very core of self-determination and free self-expression for exploited and oppressed peoples. If the identified audience, those spoken to, is determined solely by ruling groups who control production and distribution, then it is easy for the marginal voice striving for a hearing to allow what is said to be overdetermined by the needs of that majority group who appear to be listening, to be tuned in. It becomes easy to speak about what that group wants to hear, to describe and define experience in a language compatible with existing images and ways of knowing, constructed within social frameworks that reinforce domination. Within any situation of colonization, of domination, the oppressed, the exploited develop various styles of relating, talking one way to one other, talking another way to those who have power to oppress and dominate, talking in a way that allows one to be understood by someone who does not know your way of speaking, your language. The struggle to end domination, the individual struggle to resist colonization, to move from object to subject, is expressed in the effort to establish the liberatory voice—

that way of speaking that is no longer determined by one's status as object—as oppressed being. That way of speaking is characterized by opposition, by resistance. It demands that paradigms shift—that we learn to talk—to listen—to hear in a new way.

To make the liberated voice, one must confront the issue of audience—we must know to whom we speak. When I began writing my first book, *Ain't I A Woman: black women and feminism,* the initial completed manuscript was excessively long and very repetitious. Reading it critically, I saw that I was trying not only to address each different potential audience—black men, white women, white men, etc.—but that my words were written to explain, to placate, to appease. They contained the fear of speaking that often characterizes the way those in a lower position within a hierarchy address those in a higher position of authority. Those passages where I was speaking most directly to black women contained the voice I felt to be most truly mine—it was then that my voice was daring, courageous. When I thought about audience—the way in which the language we choose to use declares who it is we place at the center of our discourse—I confronted my fear of placing myself and other black women at the speaking center. Writing this book was for me a radical gesture. It not only brought me face-to-face with this question of power; it forced me to resolve this question, to act, to find my voice, to become that subject who could place herself and those like her at the center of feminist discourse. I was transformed in consciousness and being.

When the book was first published, white women readers would often say to me, "I don't feel this book is really talking to me." Often these readers would interpret the direct, blunt speech as signifying anger and I would have to speak against this interpretation and insist upon the difference between direct speech and hostility. At a discussion once where a question about audience was raised, I responded by saying that while I would like readers to be diverse, the audience I most wanted to address was black women, that I wanted to place us at the center. I was asked by a white woman, "How can you do that in a cultural context where black women are not primary book buyers and white women are the principal buyers of feminist books?" It seemed that she was suggesting that audience should be determined by who buys certain books. It had never occurred to me that white women would not buy a book if they did not see themselves at the center because, more than any group of people I could identify, white people have traveled the globe consuming cultural artifacts that did not place them at the center. My placement of black women at the center was not an action to exclude others but rather an invitation, a challenge to those who would hear us speak, to shift paradigms rather than appropriate, to have all readers listen to the voice of a black woman speaking a subject and not as underprivileged

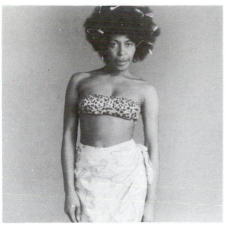

Peaches

Elaine

Tanikka

Liz

No, really. I am shocked. I mean the images of Black women are just down right strange. In some cases the images are so monstrously ugly that they scared me! Indeed, if I were as ugly as American culture has made me out to be, I'd hide my head like an ostrich in the sand, burying it so long, when I pulled it out, I'd have the look of a thousand-year-old egg. All marble and marve. In some cases, like that pickaninny or beautiful African queen mess, these images are so unlike me—my sisters or any other women I know—I didn't know it was supposed to be me. No, really. In history, in media, in photography, in literature, the construction of Black women as the embodiment of difference is so deep, so wide, so vast, so completely absolved of reality that I didn't know it was me being made fun of, somebody had to tell me. Images so strangely funny one had to laugh. Laugh hard, long, loud. Had to. No, really!

To lift the voice in laughter is saying something. I don't always know exactly what, but saying something nonetheless. We don't laugh to keep from crying, we laugh to keep from slapping the inventor of these crazy-ass-images upside his head, 'cause you can bet they're made by men. And though not completely voiceless in her construction—even the hands of women are dirty—these images like a noose about the neck, dangle from thin threads of desire wrapped around fingers owned by men; some White, some Black. No, really!!

Carrie Mae Weems, *Untitled*, 1988.

other. I wrote *Ain't I A Woman* not to inform white women about black women but rather as an expression of my longing to know more and think deeply about our experience.

In celebrating our coming to voice, Third World women, African-American women must work against speaking as "other," speaking to difference as it is constructed in the white-supremacist imagination. It is therefore crucial that we search our hearts and our words to see if our true aim is liberation, to make sure they do not suppress, trap, or confine. Significantly, knowing who is listening provides an indication of how our voices are heard. My words are heard differently by the oppressive powerful. They are heard in a different way by black women who, like me, are struggling to recover ourselves from the ravages of colonization. To know our audience, to know who listens, we must be in dialogue. We must be speaking with and not just speaking to. In hearing responses, we come to understand whether our words act to resist, to transform, to move. In a consumer culture where we are all led to believe that the value of our voice is not determined by the extent to which it challenges, or makes critical reflection possible, but rather by whether or not it (and sometimes even we) is liked, it is difficult to keep a liberatory message. It is difficult to maintain a sense of direction, a strategy for liberated speaking, if we do not constantly challenge these standards of valuation. When I first began to talk publicly about my work, I would be disappointed when audiences were provoked and challenged but seemed to disapprove. Not only was my desire for approval naive (I have since come to understand that it is silly to think that one can challenge and also have approval), it was dangerous precisely because such a longing can undermine radical commitment, compelling a change in voice so as to gain regard.

Speaking out is not a simple gesture of freedom in a culture of domination. We are often deceived (yes, even those of us who have experienced domination) by the illusion of free speech, falsely believing that we can say whatever we wish in an atmosphere of openness. There would be no need to even speak of the oppressed and exploited coming to voice, articulating and redefining reality, if there were not oppressive mechanisms of silencing, suppressing, and censoring. Thinking we speak in a climate where freedom is valued, we are often shocked to find ourselves assaulted, our words devalued. It should be understood that the liberatory voice will necessarily confront, disturb, demand that listeners even alter ways of hearing and being. I remember talking with Angela Davis a few years ago about the death threats that she often received before speaking. Our conversations had a profound effect on my consciousness, on me as a listener; it changed my understanding of what it means to speak from a radical position in this society. When one threatens—one is at risk.

Often I am amazed as a teacher in the classroom at the extent to which students are afraid to speak. A young black woman student wrote these words to me:

My voice is not fit to be heard by 120 people. To produce such a voice, my temperature increases and my hands shake. My voice is calm and quiet and soothing; it is not a means of announcing the many secrets my friends have told me—it quiets the rush of the running stream that is their life, slowing to make a mirror to reflect their worries, so that they can be examined and problems be rectified. I am not relieved by voicing my opinions. Placing my opinion up to be judged by the public is a form of opening myself to criticism and pain. Those who do not share my eyes cannot see where to tread lightly on me.

I am afraid. I am, and will always be afraid. My fear is that I will not be understood. I try to learn the vocabulary of my friends to ensure my communication on their terms. There is no singular vocabulary of 120 people. I will be misunderstood; I will not be respected as a speaker; they will name me Stupid in their minds; they will disregard me. I am afraid.

Encouraging students to speak, I tell them to imagine what it must mean to live in a culture where to speak one risks brutal punishment—imprisonment, torture, death. I ask them to think about what it means that they lack the courage to speak in a culture where there are few if any consequences. Can their fear be understood solely as shyness or is it an expression of deeply embedded, socially constructed restrictions against speech in a culture of domination, a fear of owning one's words, of taking a stand? Audre Lorde's poem, "Litany for Survival," addresses our fear of speech and urges us to overcome it:

and when we speak we are afraid
our words will not be heard
nor welcomed
but when we are silent
we are still afraid
So it is better to speak
remembering
we were never meant to survive.

To understand that finding a voice is an essential part of liberation struggle—for the oppressed, the exploited a necessary starting place—a move in the direction of freedom, is important for those who stand in solidarity with us. That talk which identifies us as uncommitted, as lacking in critical consciousness, which signifies a condition of oppression and exploitation, is utterly transformed as we engage in critical reflection and as we act to resist domination. We are prepared to struggle for freedom only when this ground-work has been laid.

When we dare to speak in a liberatory voice, we threaten even those who may initially claim to want our words. In the act of overcoming our fear of speech, of being seen as threatening, in the process of learning to speak as subjects, we participate in the global struggle to end domination. When we end our silence, when we speak in a liberated voice, our words connect with anyone, anywhere who lives in silence. Feminist focus on women finding a voice, on the silence of black women, of women of color, has led to increased interest in our words. This is an important historical moment. We are both speaking of our own volition out of our commitment to justice, to revolutionary struggle to end domination, and simultaneously called to speak, "invited" to share our words. It is important that we speak. What we speak about is more important. It is our responsibility collectively and individually to distinguish between mere speaking that is about self-aggrandizement, exploitation of the exotic "other," and that coming to voice which is a gesture of resistance, an affirmation of struggle.

Deirdre English

THE FEAR THAT FEMINISM WILL
FREE MEN FIRST

For feminists, the most difficult aspect of the 1980s backlash against
women's abortion rights, and other emancipatory new rights and attitudes
related to sex, is the fact that a large part of the antichoice ("pro-life")
movement is made up of women. What we have for the past ten years grown
accustomed to calling the "women's movement" claimed to represent the collective good of all women: the opposition was expected to be male. But now
we are faced with an opposing women's movement, and one that also claims
to stand for the best interests of all women. It is as confusing, as frustrating,
as if, at the height of the civil rights movement, a large percentage of blacks
had suddenly organized to say: "Wait a minute. We don't want equal rights.
We like things just the way they are."

The very existence of such a movement represents a deep crisis in the
community of women, and a profound challenge to the analytical and syn-
thetical powers of feminist theory. Before proceeding, an old feminist touch-
stone is a good reminder: though we may be in conflict with them, other
women rarely prove to be our real enemies. Even in opposing the politics of
the antifeminist woman, we must begin by recognizing and honoring her experiences, her prospects, her hopes and fears.

To do that, it is essential to separate the motivations of those men who
organize against women's rights and the women who do so, even when they
are found holding the same credo in the same organizations. For while men
in the antiabortion movement stand to increase the measure of male control
over women, the women can gain nothing but greater sexual submission.
Now that is a suspicious thing in itself, because any people asking only to
give in to a more powerful group must be well convinced that their survival
is at stake. After all, the antifeminist woman is neither stupid nor incompe-
tent, whatever she may wish her male leaders to believe. Legitimately
enough, she has her own self-interest in mind, in a world in which she did
not create the options.

The Other Woman

Clearly, the antichoice activist is not primarily concerned with refusing an
abortion for herself: that she has the power to do so no matter what the laws

are. (By contrast, women in the pro-choice movement are almost invariably women who feel, at some level, a personal need for abortion rights.) But no one is taking away another person's right to bear children, no feminist is circumscribing individual ethical or religious beliefs that would prohibit abortion. What is solely at question to the antichoice activist is the *other* woman's right to make this decision herself; her objective is to refuse social legitimation for abortion decisions that are not her own.

The antiabortionists are, as they have been accused, seeking to impose their morality on society. But that is part of the very definition of moralism: a *moralist* is "one concerned with regulating the morals of others." The antiabortion movement is a perfect example of a moralistic movement, and it demonstrates some interesting things about the functions of moral systems.

In opposing the Right-to-Lifers, pro-choice advocates most frequently argue that a woman has an absolute right to control her own body. The insistence on individual rights is at the foundation of the feminist position. A woman's right to control her own body encompasses endless new meanings in feminism: from the right to refuse sex (as in marital rape) to the right to a freely chosen sexuality; from the right to be protected from sexual violence to the right to plan one's own reproductivity. The complete realization of those rights alone would mark a new era for women. For now, the recognition of woman's body as the terra firma of female liberation must be counted as one of the great political accomplishments of our day. But it is far from enough.

After all, this is a society: we are interdependent; individual actions have repercussions. The struggle is not and can never be only over the actual act of abortion. The struggle is necessarily over a larger sexual morality — and moral systems do have a bearing on virtually everybody's behavior. The antiabortion people have tried to insist on single-issue politics partly because it is much easier for them to attack the keystone of abortion than to defend the system of morality that is tied to compulsory motherhood. It falls to us to identify the moral system they are upholding and, at the same time, to define our own.

The antifeminist woman is right about one crucial thing: the other woman's right to have an abortion does affect her. It does something very simple and, to many women, very upsetting: it takes away their ability *not* to choose. Where abortion is available, the birth of every baby becomes a willed choice, a purposeful act. And that new factor destroys the set of basic assumptions on which many traditional marriages have been based. It breaks the rules and wrecks the game.

Nancy Spero, *Untitled, 1986.* Censored spectacolor light board project for Times Square, New York City, sponsored by the Public Art Fund.

The Sex Contract

Remember the rules of the old game? They began with this: men did not get to have sex with women (at least not women of their own class or higher) unless they married them. Then men were morally obligated to provide for the children they had helped to conceive. In other words, sex was supposed to incur a major responsibility for men—as it did for women. Only thirty years ago, the average marrying age in the United States was twenty for women and twenty-two for men, and hundreds of thousands of brides have been pregnant on their wedding day.

Men always complained about this sexual bargain. "Nature kidded us," said a young Irish Catholic father of two in a short story by Frank O'Connor. "We had our freedom and we didn't value it. Now our lives are run for us by women." But men's regrets, however deeply felt, were still the complaints of the relatively more powerful party. It was women who, for physical and financial reasons, really *needed* marriage.

In a society that effectively condoned widespread male sexual violence and severely restricted economic opportunities for women outside of marriage, the deck was heavily stacked. If men did not "value their freedom," women had little freedom to value. The one short-lived power women had was withholding sex; and even that was only good until marriage—possibly periodically thereafter, with the more tolerant husbands. But in general, women had to earn their keep not only with sex, but with submissiveness, and acceptance of the male not as an equal partner but as a superior. Seen in these terms, the marriage contract seems a little more like extortion under the threat of abandonment.

But to point this out is not the way to play the game. The essential thing about the system—like moral systems in general—is that everyone must play by the same rules. In the past, the community of women has often been hard on those who "give away" for free—or for money—what the rest trade for love and marriage. Then came birth control, the sexual revolution, and legalized abortion.

The Escape Clause

It was the availability of relatively reliable contraception that provided the first escape clause to the old marital Russian roulette, for both men and women. The "99 percent effective" pill sparked the sexual revolution in the 1960s and 1970s and permitted women for the first time in history to decisively separate intercourse from reproduction. (Only after that historic schism could the modern woman's new fascination with discovering her own sexuality begin to emerge.)

For the most part, women of all classes and religions enthusiastically welcomed the advent of reliable contraception. True, it did have the effect of releasing men from some responsibility for the sexual acts, but the gains for women seemed much greater. Sexual liberation and birth control brought women new-found sexual pleasure, began to erode the double standard, allowed women to plan their pregnancies—and therefore participate in the work world on new terms—and in general seemed to tend to equalize the sexes. Other things, unfortunately, did not change so fast. Especially not the economy.

Catch 22

Most women who want to have children still cannot make it, financially, without a man. In an era in which an increasingly large number of people are spending significant parts of their lives outside of the marriage coupling, the socioeconomic differences between men and women become increasingly, painfully obvious. According to 1978 Bureau of Labor statistics, only some 7 percent of women make more than $15,000 per year, while more than 46 percent of men do. Marriage is still the major means of economic stability—even survival—for women.

In this sense, men have reaped more than their share of benefits from women's liberation. If women hold jobs, no matter how poorly paid, men may more easily renounce any responsibility for the economic support of women and children. Thus woman's meager new economic dependence, and her greater sexual freedom outside the bounds of marriage, have allowed men to garner great new freedoms. Because there is no "trick of nature" to make the link between sex and fatherhood, and little social stigma on he who loves and leaves, a woman faces the abdication of any male responsibility for pregnancy—let alone for any ensuing children. If a woman gets pregnant, the man who twenty years ago might have married her may feel today that he is gallant if he splits the cost of an abortion. The man who might have remained in a dead-end marriage out of a sense of duty finds increasingly that he faces no great social disapproval if he walks out on his family, even while his kids are still in diapers.

Divorce leaves women putting a higher percentage of both their incomes and their time into child care. According to the U.S. Census, the number of one-parent families headed by divorced women jumped about 200 percent in one decade—from 956,000 in 1970 to 2.7 million in 1981. During the same period, the number of single-parent families headed by men actually declined. (Nationally, there are more youthful products of divorce cared for by relatives other than a parent than by their fathers alone.)

It is also worth noting the difference in the economic impact of divorce on fathers versus mothers. Roughly 40 percent of absent fathers contribute *no* money for child support after divorce, and the other 60 percent average a contribution of less than $2,000 per year. A recent study of 3,000 divorces showed, shockingly, that men improved their standard of living an average of 42 percent in the first year following divorce, while women with children saw their living standard decline by 73 percent. Under these circumstances, the fear has risen that feminism will free men first—and might never get around to freeing women.

All this is not to imply that either men or women *should* stay in loveless, unhappy marriages out of some sense of duty. Rather, both sexes need the right to change their circumstances. So far, our progress, like all progress, has been ragged: men, more independent to begin with, have been able to profit from women's new independence sometimes more fully than women themselves.

It seems revealing that the antifeminist backlash, as well as the antisexual-liberation backlash, took so long to develop the momentum that it has today. It is the period of unremitting economic decline that has brought it on, the nightfall of economic prospects for women. It is as though the country reserved judgment during ten or fifteen years of experimentation with sexual politics, as long as economic conditions permitted it. In a climate of affluence, women had more hope of successfully freeing themselves from male-dominant relationships. But today, a greater number of working women are perceiving that the feminist revolution may not rapidly succeed in actually equalizing the material opportunities of the sexes. When working-class men no longer hold their own against unemployment, union management rollbacks, or even inflation, what hope is there for women to close the economic gap between the male and female worker?

Giving up marriage and children for an interesting career may be one thing (although this is an either/or choice that men rarely face), but it may not be a decent trade for a dead-end job in the pink-collar ghetto. If men can no longer support families on a single paycheck, most women certainly cannot. The media presents us with the image of successful management-level women, but in fact even these women are almost always contained in middle-management positions, at under $20,000 a year. For the less-than-fervent feminist who is not prepared to pay any price at all for independence, the future looks bleak.

Fear and Reaction

It begins to seem clearer that the antifeminist woman, like other women, is grappling with the terms of her survival. She is responding to social circumstances—a worsening economy, a lack of support and commitment from men—that feminists did not create and from which feminists also suffer the consequences. The conditions she faces face all women.

The differences lie in our strategies for dealing with all this. The antifeminist woman's strategy is defensive: reactionary in the sense of reacting to change, with the desire to return to the supposedly simple solutions of the past. Like other patriotic or fundamentalist solutions, like going to war or being "born again," the longed-for return to the old feminine style seems to promise an end to complexity, compromise, and ambivalence. For many of the advocates of the antichoice movement, the ideal is ready-made and well polished. It is the American family of the 1950s: dad in the den with his pipe, mom in her sunny kitchen with cafe curtains, the girls dressed in pink and the boys in blue. It could be called nostalgic utopianism—the glorification of a lost past rather than an undiscovered future. What has not been accepted is that the road to that ideal is as impossible to find—and to many people, as little desired—as the road back to childhood.

To feminists, the only response to the dilemma of the present lies in pressing onward. We must continue to show how a complete feminist sexual and reproductive politics could lead to the transformation of all society, without curtailing the freedom of any individual. True reproductive freedom, for example, would inevitably require fair opportunities for financial equality, so that women could bear children without facing either dependency or impoverishment. There would be practical child-care support for working parents of both sexes and an equal affirmation by men of their responsibility for parenthood. Yet, the individual's right to choose whether to bear a child would remain at the heart of the feminist position.

Today, the individual decision to have an abortion remains a sobering one; it puts a woman face-to-face with her dreams and her prospects and with the frequently startling fact that she is choosing not to be a passive victim, but rather an active shaper of her existence. The difficulties she will encounter as she continues to try to create her own destiny will repeatedly call for that same strength of will. In demonstrating it, she is already helping to bring about a new order of sexual equality, a world more worthy of the next generation. Few who have clearly seen the vision of that new world will want to turn back.

Delegates at National Women's Conference, November 19, 1977, cheering a resolution supporting the Equal Rights Amendment.

Polly Thistlethwaite

REPRESENTATION, LIBERATION, AND THE QUEER PRESS

I came out in a library. It was in the "new" public library building, which was really the done-over old Sears store in my Midwestern town. The new library's whole queer section consisted of fifteen, maybe twenty books on two bottom shelves of a back wall range in a dark basement corner, no lie. I think the entire bookstack arrangement centered around those Dewey decimal queer 306.7s being tucked into the building's most out-of-the-way place. Anyhow, in there I found *Sappho Was a Right-On Woman*, *The Stone Wall*, and *Our Right to Love* nestled in with some socio-psycho trash like *Sexual Deviance* and *The Homosexual in America*. Of course I was afraid to check these books out, especially those Arno reprint series books with the burnt orange covers saying HOMOSEXUALITY all over them, so on Saturdays I would inconspicuously snatch them up along with bluff material from the nearby feminist 301s, and, flushed, take them to a table across the room to read. This was the bravest thing I'd ever done. If somebody who knew me came by, I could quick switch the books so it looked like I was reading Betty Friedan.

Lesbian and gay people lay special claim to the power of the printed word. It's through the printed word, consumed privately, anonymously, that we often first call ourselves queer, where we first find others who think what we think, do what we do, write what we feel. Coming out stories are thick with accounts of self-discovery through novels, dictionaries, magazines, libraries. The mass-mediated word, key to democracy and empire building both, also finds, unites, and empowers queer communities across regional, class, ethnic, and generational boundaries. All this is kept in check, of course, by censorship and a legion of insidious oppressive political and cultural constraints.

The lesbian and gay press has shaped and reflected the rise of gay and lesbian liberation. The proliferation of gay and lesbian newspapers, newsletters, and magazines in the U.S. has allowed us to weave a well-informed network of previously isolated individuals and insulated communities. In 1924, Chicago's Society for Human Rights published two issues of the journal *Friendship and Freedom* before organizers were arrested and brought to trial on obscenity charges. No copies of the journal are known to exist; only photographs of the covers remain. Lisa Ben's *Vice Versa* appeared in 1947 and 1948, the earliest known lesbian periodical in the U.S. It was a carbon-copied newsletter passed hand to hand among a West Coast circle of friends—you know, the softball team and the secretarial pool, girls like that.

The national "homophile" organizations of the 1950s and 1960s (The Daughters of Bilitis, the Mattachine Society, and One) built themselves by defying the law against putting queer stuff in the mail. *One, Inc. v. Olesen* (355 U.S. 371, January 13, 1958) established that homophile publications were, yes, "more than cheap pornography," therefore eligible to be distributed by our postal service. The paperback porn industry began to boom postwar too, with drugstore lesbo pulp novels selling like hotcakes to dykes craving popular images of themselves. Other fringy mainstream but not specifically queer publications like physique magazines, science fiction club newsletters, grocery store scandal sheets, and eventually the *Village Voice* published queer-seeking-queer personals, like this one from the June 1, 1965 Wide World Confidential pullout section of the tabloid *Keyhole:* "MODERN MICHIGAN MODEL . . . with understanding husband seeks uninhibited fun-loving females and couples . . ."

In the spring 1979 Lesbian Herstory Archives newsletter, Joan Nestle writes, "The roots of the Archives lie in the silenced voices, the love letters destroyed, the pronouns changed, the diaries carefully edited, the pictures never taken, the euphemized distortions that patriarchy would let pass." Self-representation is essential for liberation. We must represent ourselves to ourselves and others on our own terms. Historically, we've been the social, medical, religious, psychological, legal "other," "freak," "deviant" according to the reporter, anthropologist, physician, theologian, analyst, politician, artist. In large part, the gay, lesbian, and feminist publications of the late 1960s and 1970s, *The Advocate, Come Out!, Gay Community News, Lesbian Tide,* and *off our backs,* began as publications from activist organizations or collectives, steeped in radical politics. Community-sustained lesbian and gay archives cropped up across the country during the seventies and eighties, as did lesbian and gay presses and bookstores. Though not unfettered by notions of assimilation, success, and respectability, the rise of lesbian and gay publishers, distributors, and archives has allowed queers control of the way we represent ourselves to each other, fostering the rise of our liberation movement. The printed word, rendered by us for each other, allows the queer nation to build, bolster, and unify.

Lisa Duggan

SEX PANICS

What is to be done? This summer's escalating attacks on the autonomy of
the National Endowment for the Arts have sent artists, arts administrators,
and arts advocates reeling. The scramble is on to mount an effective line of
defense. But the methods of attack have made defense uncommonly
difficult—they are one part apparently rational circumspection about the use
of taxpayers' dollars to support "offensive" art, and one part irrational panic
and hate-filled attack on "deviant" sexuality.

The arts community has responded directly to the "rational" part, but
has generally avoided the underlying, and far more destructive, panic and
hate. Arts supporters have been on familiar ground when confronted with
arguments about the need to restrict funding for unpopular art. Everyone
knows what to say: art isn't supposed to be tamely popular, it *should*
provoke, question, enlighten; the public purse is best served by the peer review process, which places evaluation of art where it belongs, in the hands
of artists, not crudely partisan politicians. But nearly everyone goes strangely
mute when faced with completely unhinged hysterics over images of interra-
cial homoeroticism, sadomasochism, and nude children.

This muteness is expected; it is enforced by the logic of a sex panic. Sex
panics, witch-hunts, and red scares are staples of American history. While
often promoted by relatively powerless but vocal minorities hostile to cultural difference, they have been enthusiastically taken up by powerful groups
in an effort to impose a rigid orthodoxy on the majority. In this context,
"moral reforms" and the like have been the public-relations mask for what is
in fact an abnegation of any responsibility to confront and address very real
problems, i.e., poverty, militarism, sexism, racism. Often in these PR campaigns, words assume the reverse of their common meaning: liberation becomes chaos, desire becomes deviance, and dissent becomes the work of the
devil.

In the grip of a sex panic, if you are accused of sexual "deviance," your
defensive strategies are limited to either confession and repentance or denials
of personal "guilt," both of which only reinforce the legitimacy of the attack
("I am not now, nor have I ever been . . ."). If you refuse to deny or apolo-
gize, you are isolated and calumnies are heaped upon you. No one will defend your actions, only your right to due process and a good lawyer.

In the case of Congress and the NEA, sex-panic attacks on photographer Robert Mapplethorpe had the predictable effect. The Corcoran canceled its scheduled exhibition of his photographs (denial), arts supporters in the House accepted a symbolic NEA funding cut as "punishment" for its support for the Mapplethorpe exhibition (apology), and members of the Senate voted overwhelmingly to restrict funding for sexualized imagery (the sex panic grows unchallenged). Volumes have been spoken about the value of the peer review process, about the importance of the abstract right to artistic freedom. But very few arts supporters have been willing to say much to defend sexual images per se, and this muteness about bodies and sexuality implicitly concedes that the particular images at issue are indefensible.

Initially, the art world was collectively flabbergasted at attacks on the NEA. After all, most Americans at least give lip service to the idea that the arts should be free from government restrictions. But this cultural consensus is relatively recent and, as we all have now been reminded, relatively fragile, especially with regard to sexual content.

From the nineteenth to the mid-twentieth century, conflicts over the regulation of sexual behavior and sexual representations intensified in legislatures and courtrooms. Social- and sexual-purity crusaders managed to pass layer after layer of repressive legislation penalizing prostitution, homosexuality, and pornography, and severely restricting child and adolescent sexuality. (For instance, juvenile detention homes established during the early twentieth century were used to incarcerate teenage girls almost exclusively for sexual activity.) They were opposed with increasing effectiveness over time by civil libertarians and other advocates of cultural openness and sexual freedom. In the post-World War II period, a partial truce was achieved in the continuing conflicts through a slowly developed, contradictory, and hypocritical compromise consensus. In the arena of sexual behavior, antiprostitution and sodomy laws would remain on the books, but they would be only selectively enforced. (For example, prostitutes are usually arrested, not johns; and conservative politicians have been known to fuel their reelection campaigns by periodic sweeps of prostitute hangouts and gay bars, which are normally left alone, moral crusades aimed at clearing the streets of "undesirables." In Indianapolis, for instance, during an election year in the early eighties, police used hidden video cameras to monitor gay public spaces and made arrests based on the "evidence" collected.) In the arena of sexual representation, "obscenity" laws would be enforced, but works of "serious" artistic or literary merit would be exempted.

This precarious consensus has been periodically disrupted by both repressive panics (the persecution of gay people in the military and the government, the passage of "sexual psychopath" laws in the 1950s) and moves toward greater openness (the repeal of some sodomy laws, the formation of prostitutes' rights groups in the sixties and seventies). But the consensus remained substantially intact right up to the 1980s, when conflict broke out all over the place. Early eighties right-wing hysteria over pornography was fanned, ironically, by a feminist antipornography crusade (which transmuted the necessary critique of sexism in pornography into a campaign for the legal suppression of sexual imagery). But such efforts at censorship energized civil libertarian and feminist oppositions, which managed to defuse the repressive agenda of the Attorney General's Commission on Pornography in the mid-eighties. Antigay hysteria fanned by fear of AIDS resulted in an indefensible indifference to human suffering during the latter part of the decade, but also fueled a revitalized activism among gay people and advocates of humane health care.

The result of all the renewed conflict is that the postwar consensus is closer than ever before to a complete breakdown. And so the moral conservatives have felt free to do what the art world thought they wouldn't dare. They have directed their antiporn, antigay fervor at the "high," the "respectable" arts—the stuff shown in museums rather than adult bookstores. They don't have the power successfully to advocate the outright banning of art work or the prosecution of artists, but they have hit upon a strategy used with some success by antiabortion activists: the defunding of materials they object to, and the intimidation of arts institutions into self-censorship to protect their bottom lines. Their tactic is to inaugurate a sex panic, and arts advocates are learning quickly how the logic plays itself out. The restrictions don't even have to pass into law to have the desired effect—the Corcoran cancelation was a *preemptive* measure.

Of course, it is not purely accidental that the conservatives hit upon Robert Mapplethorpe as a primary target for a sex panic. Mapplethorpe's work exposes the contradiction and hypocrisy at the heart of the postwar consensus. His images cross the designated boundaries, appropriating images from the stigmatized zone of "pornography" and carting them across the lines into the free zone of "art." Mapplethorpe's strategy was radically to disrupt the belief that images of some bodies and practices are fit only for squalid, hidden, or persecuted surroundings.

Mapplethorpe is certainly not the only artist to have created sexually explicit imagery, or appropriated "pornographic" conventions. But he has moved much further than most others into the mainstream institutions of culture, partly because his images are of such high formal quality and conventional presentation, and partly because he was a well-connected white male. He got far enough into the mainstream to cause conservatives to fear that he was posthumously succeeding in a strategy of legitimation of the practices he represented. Or, as Walter Annenberg put it in the *New York Times*, "[He] went too far, trying to justify his own inclinations." He went

far enough, anyway, to elicit the sort of hysterical attacks that had been con-
fined, earlier in the decade, to less artistically respectable representations. Judith Reisman, a former feminist but now right-wing antiporn campaigner
associated with the American Family Association, put it all rather starkly in
the *Washington Times*. She describes Mapplethorpe's photographs of nude
and partially nude children, not engaged in any sexual activity (for example,
Honey, 1976), as "child pornography" and "photographic assault and rape."
She claims that his representation of his own rectum with bullwhip inserted
"encourages" the "sadistic acts, which, on the evidence, facilitate AIDS."

Reisman's charges neatly illustrate the favored tactics of 1980s antiporn
attacks. Consensual sadomasochism is equated with violence, anal eroticism
is damned as the cause of AIDS, and any depiction of the bodies of children
is blasted as child abuse. Public outrage at real violence, real suffering, and
widespread abuse is diverted away from substantive analysis and action into
a censorship campaign.

The charge of child pornography has been the most successful of all
these tactics. The widely respected sex education book *Show Me* was suppressed under child pornography laws by the early eighties. In 1988, Virginia artist Alice Sims was arrested and her children removed to a foster
home—police considered her personal snapshots of her naked daughter,
studies for a series of drawings called "Water Babies," to be evidence of
child abuse. And when Broadway actress Colleen Dewhurst testified in opposition to censorship before the Meese Commission on Pornography, she
was asked if she or her theater organization therefore supported child
pornography.

Attacks like these cannot be fended off by reasoned appeals to the First
Amendment or the NEA's peer review process. Moral conservatives will push
their opportunity to erode the postwar consensus on the regulation of sexuality in a rightward direction, extending content restrictions on images
from the adult bookstores into the museums. If they can frighten arts supporters into silence about sex, they will be encouraged to continue. To secure
creative freedom against the onslaught, arts activists must seize the opportunity to push back in the other direction. The time has come to argue
forcefully for the complete deregulation of consensual sexuality and its representations. Nothing less will move us forward.

Television still from *Star Search* with Ed McMahon. ▶

TOWN MEETING!
CULTURAL PARTICIPATION
ORGANIZED BY GROUP MATERIAL
Tuesday, November 22, 8 pm
DIA ART FOUNDATION • 155 Mercer St.
AGENDA

Meeting Chairperson: David Avalos, Artist, San Diego

I.   Welcome and introductory remarks by David Avalos

II. <u>Open to the floor</u>: Discussion on the following questions --

A. What are some aspects of the present crisis of cultural participation?

B. Culture for whom? Who is given access and who is denied access to the institutions of representation? In what ways do cultural institutions serve and in what ways do they fail their communities and public?

C. How does consumerism affect our participatory power? How do various marketplaces and institutions define communities and dictate sociality?

D. What are some non-mainstream, alternative, and/or oppositional practices? What are the problems and solutions presented by these practices?

E. What are our options? How can we begin to build cultural democracy?

This agenda is based on a panel discussion held in June 1988: David Avalos, Martha Gever, Lucy Lippard, Randall Morris, Robert Farris Thompson, Deborah Wye.

CULTURAL PARTICIPATION

Chairperson, David Avalos   Now, since this is a town meeting in the New England tradition, perhaps we should start with a quotation from a New Englander, Ralph Waldo Emerson. He said, "A friend is one before whom I may think aloud." I think the purpose of tonight's meeting is just that—to think aloud. It's not to demonstrate to each other how erudite we are, or how tough we are, or any of that. The purpose is to kick the can around for an hour or two, or however long it goes. And if we leave here with an idea, with an encouragement to continue the work that gets at making communities, I think that I and everyone in Group Material will be very satisfied.

What is meant by cultural participation? By "cultural participation" we mean how society, our culture, is created in a day-to-day way versus how the cultural gatekeepers are presenting us to ourselves. That's how I define it. But I'd like to hear your ideas about what is meant by cultural participation.

Mary Steele   There is something I feel very strongly about. Todd Gitlin said in the *New York Times Book Review* on November 6 that postmodern culture is a process of recycling. Everything is juxtaposable to everything else because nothing matters. Postmodern writing confesses or celebrates helplessness. Make the most of stagnation, it says, give up gracefully. The same weekend, on *The World of Ideas,* Bill Moyers asked Noam Chomsky a question about the twenty-first century. Chomsky said that unless we address the global problems confronting us now, we won't get very far into the twenty-first century. Now supposedly, postmodernism is a way of feeling that one has control of the situation. If you can't beat the enemy, join him. If you address only superficialities, pretty soon you can forget the realities underneath. In this sense, Bush's campaign was the perfect postmodern campaign. We can do better than this.

Saving our planet is a life-and-death matter for everyone. And I believe artists can play a persuasive role in making people see this. Rather than limply mirroring the cynicism and materialism of our times, we should make art as central to everyone's lives as it has been in past cultures and as it is now in cultures removed from the industrialized world. A series of shows on a theme like "nature and humanity" by artists all over the country could be presented under the auspices of some ecology group like the Nature Conservancy and funded by some large corporation that needs to improve its standing with the public. This is idealistic, but we have got to do something. We can't just sit around and limply let this effete point of view drown us.

Unidentified Speaker If, by culture, you mean what we do day by day, then it is redundant to talk about cultural participation. We do that by simply being here. I think television has destroyed diversity in culture. It spreads one way of thinking to the whole country and suddenly you don't have to be active because TV brings it all to you. That makes cultural participation seem meaningless. No one has to produce anything.

Avalos Well, there are people out there producing things. And as far as the question about our everyday lives, that is a question of for what purpose and in whose service we do our work. Cultural participation is about whether or not we are really able to participate in democracy and form our own cultural definition in a way that allows us some sense of control and self-determination.

Unidentified Speaker But to me "culture" is not a positive or a negative term. Technically it means the shape that our society is taking.

Avalos Who is giving it that shape?

Unidentified Speaker We are. But we can't say we are participating if we are not participating because we are 238 million people and we make up the culture and we create it; it's not something that is created by a few people and given to others. It's just something that is America. That is what culture means: how people act.

Avalos Your point is well taken, but it's not a question of participation or nonparticipation. It's a question of the quality of that participation and the nature of that participation in relation to self-determination.

Geno Rodriguez I want to respond to the young man who spoke earlier. I think you're on the right track. I see art as a result of culture, but culture is the result of a people's health, education, and social well-being. Culture is a way of being in which we all have equal opportunity to participate. We all go to schools, we all go to work, we all do other things. The difference is that some people in the process of participation are exploited or oppressed while others profit. But both people participate equally. It has nothing to do with black, brown, yellow, or white. It has to do with some Americans being enfranchised and some being disenfranchised.

Avalos   I think it gets back to a question of the quality of that participation. Is there a sense that there is a crisis of cultural participation? I feel there is. Maybe we could talk about that.

Lucy Lippard   I would like to return to the very valid question you brought up, which is, what are we talking about when we say "culture"? Obviously different cultures do things differently; that's not something we've brought up. And, culture for whom? Everybody has culture, but a lot of people do not get *at* culture, or do not get culture laid out for them. So we should redefine culture before we go on or we are going to get muddled. How was it meant?

Avalos   So you want to redefine culture?

Lippard   Yeah, just like that. When I say "culture" I mean this whole fabric of one's life, things that have to do with where one lives, what one has inherited, and just plain economic facts of life. But we are not talking about "art" in a lot of these questions. We'd better get that straight before we go on or we are just going to be talking across each other.

Avalos   Well, let me ask this: Does the divorce of art from people's everyday lives constitute a crisis as far as you are concerned?

Martha Rosler   I'm not sure whether we are trying to address solutions or we're trying to develop a theoretical perspective. But to put it simply, I think we have a war between mass culture and fine art. Artists may feel somewhat impotent in relation to mass culture, but mass culture is our culture, it is "people's culture." It is not generated by people, however. People are in a very real sense the objects or the creatures of mass culture. Which is not to say that people don't also have a culture of everyday life. It's simply that the culture of everyday life is not represented in what we take to be our official culture, which is television and *People* magazine and the *National Enquirer*. I think that the fact that we developed a dandyistic art like pop art has to do with artists feeling an extraordinary impotence in the face of a culture of mass representation, which does not represent the mass, but rather the thing.

I don't know if it is helpful to redefine a crisis in these terms, but I see two levels of crisis. One is that artists feel a tremendous sense of disempowerment and disconnection from people in general because they have been in effect superseded by a mass culture, a culture that appears to be a culture of society as a whole but which, in fact, is only a culture that is *directed at* the society as a whole. The other crisis for artists is that we find ourselves

Charles Schultz, *Peanuts*, 1982.

empowered only within our own sphere, what Allan Kaprow called "the church of art," or within our own recently wonderful marketplace, a place where we know we are valuable because we can make a tremendous amount of money if we play the game right.

Paul Werner I'd like to disagree with what Martha Rosler just said. I think that we are disempowered by both mass culture *and* high culture. Therefore, it is not a very wise approach to play one against the other. Rather, we need to see how they *both* disempower us. Try painting a politically progressive work and taking it to the *New York Times* or CBS. You will get no response.

Saul Mantz To me, the fact that you define mass culture by the way you will be greeted by the *New York Times* or CBS is a problem. Culture is not defined by the media or by those who have money, but by the people; it gets its legitimacy from the fact that people are doing it, and believe in it.

Avalos One of the problems that artists face is how to focus attention. The mass media is an incredible attention-focusing device. By keeping that attention, the media makes it very difficult for others to get messages and images across and to engage in dialogue. That relates to the war between a fine art and mass culture that Martha mentioned because that war has already been won by mass culture. Part of the anxiety we share as artists is that we are playing catch-up.

One possible way of looking at culture is to look at it as a system of values. In looking at the mass media, the question is what effect is it having on value systems and identities? Because of TV and advertising we don't think of ourselves in terms of what we produce and how we participate in society in an active way; we think of ourselves in terms of what we consume, and this consumption makes us passive. I think the recent election makes us aware of that.

Rodriguez Something that bothers me is that as a people with a sense of crisis, we nevertheless constantly refer to our "powerlessness" and to "them" and "us." That is a problem. One part of the problem is that we keep saying, "you," we blame mass media, for instance, but we never point the finger at ourselves and say "me." *I* watch TV, *I* buy products, *I* am responsible. So long as we keep talking about "them" and "us," we are saying we have no control or that we cannot assume control. As long as you think that you can't do something you are not going to do it. As long as there is somebody to blame you will never take responsibility for yourself.

Karen Ramspacher I'm a member of ACT UP, the AIDS Coalition To Unleash Power. They do something, they act up. And we all can. Through consumerism we have power. If you think that a company is backing something that is not right, don't buy their products. Or demonstrate. Or call them, say what you think. It makes a difference.

Avalos The question of making a difference leads me to Item B on the agenda: "Culture for whom? Who is given access and who is denied access to the institutions of representation? In what ways do cultural institutions serve, in what ways do they fail their communities and public?" I know that people must have a lot to say about this.

Judy Wienman My name is Judy Wienman. I would assume that everybody agrees that culturally, ethnically, economically, people don't have equal access to the art world. We are not participating equally. So what can artists do if they want to have shows in galleries run by a system that is mostly upper-class white Americans? We must come up with completely radical ideas for sharing money and recognition. Also, I'd like to work in an art community that is completely integrated racially and sexually—which it isn't.

Adam Simon My name is Adam Simon, and I'd like to address the last comments. I'm part of a group called 4 Walls, and we just did a week of one-evening exhibition events, symposiums, and shows that were up for just one evening. The first one was on election day. It wasn't well publicized, but we advertised that we would put up the work of the first one hundred artists who called. This notice went out to the entire White Columns mailing list, which I think is about 2,500 people. In any case, this was a one-night open show on election day. Two things happened. First, we didn't even get a hundred people; we got seventy-five. I think that tells you something about the way people think about alternative venues. Most artists are not interested at this point. They are only interested in careers and galleries. But the second thing is the show was really interesting. Most of the work was directed to the election or American culture in relation to the election. So that was hopeful.

Avalos Something is happening in terms of artists' struggles for cultural participation that is way ahead of the sort of "cookbook" approaches in the major institutions. You know what I mean, they say, "It's Cinco de Mayo, let's have an Hispanic art show. Or, "February is coming around, I wonder if there are any black artists available for black history month." There have to be organizations that go beyond this kind of situation.

Rodriguez As far as the exhibition of all-Hispanic shows, all-black shows, or all-whatever shows, there are two or three different ways of looking at that. One thing is if there were not black, brown, and yellow institutions there would be few places where artists of color could exhibit. That is one of the reasons why those institutions have to be maintained. Unfortunately, that also forces what I call "cultural apartheid," the separate-but-equal development of groups within our one culture. At a meeting at MoMA recently there was talk about decentralizing institutions of art, and they said, "Well, they would have their museum up in Harlem and their museum up in wherever." That is not decentralization, that is ghettoization. I'd like to see a branch of the Whitney up in the South Bronx!

I was involved in the initial planning of the Corcoran's Hispanic show, and I think it was a colossal insult to select a non-Hispanic curator. Also, that show received $150,000 from ARCO and $150,000 from the Rockefeller Foundation—just for planning! It's no coincidence that ARCO just finished an in-house study on Hispanics in America and what they take their future economic and political strength to be. So these are just a few of the types of racism in the art world. Whether it's the Corcoran's "We can do it

◀ Publicity photo for *Dawn of the Dead*, directed by George Romero, 1978.

our way," or it's "Stay back on your farm and we'll give you some money but don't bother us in our white prestigious institutions," or it's simply the general lack of understanding of the different cultural backgrounds of America and Americans, these are all problems that stem from who's got power and how that power is shared. And that's the bottom line.

Avalos How do people feel about applying affirmative action to the boards of trustees and to the administrative staffs of cultural institutions as one remedy?

Alice Yang My name is Alice Yang, and I am Asian-American and I work at a cultural institution in New York. I think the problem with applying affirmative action is that even though I see myself primarily as Chinese, I was also privy to a very good East Coast education. In the art community I have been identified largely by my racial background. But I also think I was brought in very easily because of my educational background. So I want to point to the issue of class in this whole equation. I want to raise this as a point of self-criticism or self-questioning, because in many projects I am involved with I am made to identify with my so-called culture or my community. In fact, I feel quite divorced from that community. I would be curious to hear what other people of color have to say about that.

Betti-Sue Hertz In the equation of fine art and mass culture, what was missing was popular culture, and I think that some of the things we are talking about are issues of ethnicity, localism, and regionalism. I am associated with Fred Wilson's gallery, Longwood Arts, and I also work at the Bronx Council on the Arts. One of the things that I think about a lot at the gallery is: Where is this institution? The fact that Longwood is situated in the South Bronx has given it a certain perspective, particularly in regard to who its audience is. And this is another issue we have not really discussed: what an audience is. The community at Longwood is not just an artists' community, but it is also made up of people who live in the area and people who work in the building, because it's a multiservice building. MoMA is probably also responding to its immediate community, one of the most affluent neighborhoods in America. If you are situated in the middle of the South Bronx in an old schoolhouse with social-service programs, then your shows and your artists' participation start to mingle with that reality.

In terms of action, I am part of a group of women and we have curated a show called "Literacy on the Table: Cultural Fluency and the Act of Reading." There are many issues involved with that show, but in terms of audience, we are looking to get an audience from the literacy community, as well as the artistic community and the communities who usually participate in the exhibition space. I think that kind of thinking will help us to expand into other classes. You can be black, Hispanic, or Asian, but if your exhibition has an elitist class identification, then you can be assured of nonparticipation by your audience.

Honore Rosal I want to get back to the question you asked before about whether or not affirmative action is a useful way of diversifying museum boards. I think that connects directly with your other question about ethnic shows like the one of Latin American art at the Bronx Museum or the Corcoran show. As far as I'm concerned, it's not useful to place a woman, a black, a white, a Hispanic, or whatever person on a board and say that is enough. The museum's function as an institution is still so segregated from any kind of community that you or I know, the influence of one woman, one black, or one Hispanic board member is going to be minimal. Similarly, having a show of Latin American artists somewhere over here in Brooklyn doesn't affect the art community as a whole.

Avalos We are talking about art being divorced from the general public, yet we are also talking about a situation where public tax dollars are supporting cultural gatekeeping institutions. One of the things that has to happen in this case is a connection that perhaps didn't exist before. You see it especially in the very volatile issue of tax-dollar funding for public art. Right now there is a very lively debate all across the country about what voice communities will have in the choice of and in the placement of public art. There are people who are taking different approaches other than the plop approach of perpetrating work upon an unsuspecting public. I think that as difficult as those questions are to resolve and with the setbacks artists have taken in various places, at least there is a forum and a context for discussion. That is what caused me to raise the question, how do you bring this process of art making into a community context so that you can discuss it and people are not separated but completely embraced? We need to understand that and act upon it.

Mitchel Cohen A lot of discussion on the crisis in the art world and in culture is reminiscent of arguments and discussions about the crisis within Marxism. Just as many Marxists have gone into academia, many artists strive to get into museums and galleries, and to me that is what the crisis is all about. This situation may not be the cause of the crisis, but it reproduces this disempowerment that many of us feel in our lives.

I envision a whole different strategy: seeing supermarkets, subways, factories, and hospitals as potential cultural institutions. As artists, we should be trying to relink people's everyday lives with the artistic part of themselves which has been severed by society. And one way of doing that, no matter how utopian it may sound, is to pressure unions and other workers' and community-based organizations to demand, as part of their contract negotiations, space inside factories for the workers to put forth the artistic side of themselves.

Avalos As artists we often talk about going to various other groups—communities, labor unions, and so on—and insisting on a place on their agenda, but the unions rarely come to artists and community groups and ask for collaboration. I think that is very telling.

Cohen That's not quite what I was saying. I was saying we have to end the separation between artists and people who do mainly other things in their lives. I am saying we have to redefine the whole terrain of politics in this country. That is a much larger conception than the one you are putting forth.

Andrea Kanterwitz People *are* actually doing things to change the cultural situation in this country or to provide alternatives. I am a member of the Alliance for Cultural Democracy, a national network of people who are doing work, art, and cultural projects in the communities, as a way of contributing to progressive movements. We have a small group in New York City, for instance, and one of the things we are talking about doing nationally to commemorate the anniversary of Columbus in 1992, is to use the opportunity to focus attention on the legacy of five hundred years of colonialism in the U.S.

Keith Piascezny My name is Keith Piascezny and I'm here from Detroit. I'm involved in an organization called Urban Center for Photography. I'm glad we got beyond culture as defined by the institution, museum, and gallery, because cultural participation is a part of everyday life. I wanted to return to something Martha Rosler said about strategies and about on what levels we can have an impact with our cultural participation. To what degree can we shape our culture through participation? Are there projects, are there collective actions, are there things we can do besides networking? People say, "Well, we are isolated, we are disempowered." But in New York City alone there must be a hundred artists' organizations that people can join. I think collective projects by artists are one way, one strategy, one method, to make a larger statement and have a larger influence on the culture. And you raised the question, how can we bring it into a social context? I say, back out of the museums, back into the streets, back into the communities.

In Detroit we did a project called "Demolished by Neglect." It was very interesting because a combination of fine-art artists, photojournalists, and non-fine-art photographers took part. This collective of photographers got together and talked about architecture that was demolished by neglect, and

Urban Center for Photography, *Demolished by Neglect,* 1987. An eviction notice on a burned-out house in Southwest Detroit juxtaposed against a portrait of the former residents.

how that affected our experience of living in the city, visually, psychologically, and socially. We came up with ways of representing those ideas photographically and had the photographs blown up to mural size and installed in various public locations. In many cases the locations were boarded-up facades of abandoned buildings, in some cases with permission, in some cases without permission. So it became sort of a renegade project at one point and received a lot of publicity about its controversial character. We called ourselves "photo-activists." We were doing photos and also getting very active and political.

Unidentified Speaker   How did people get involved in it?

Piascezny   Mainly through networking. At one point there were fifty or sixty people coming to the meetings. Through the universities or galleries,

Urban Center for Photography, *Demolished by Neglect,* 1987.

people heard about it and said, "I want to become involved with this, I want to do it." And some people didn't want to; they were nervous. They said, "I can't handle this, this is too crazy. You're going to get into trouble."

Avalos So how was the project funded?

Piascezny We received one grant from the Michigan Council on the Arts, and one grant from the Detroit Council on the Arts. There was a big controversy, because at one point the Detroit Council on the Arts announced that they were going to rescind the award because we had defaced public property. But they dropped that plan. They had to. There was no chance of getting their money back because it was already spent. It was mainly a bureaucratic maneuver on their part, I think. It was interesting, though.

Avalos Certainly that points up one of the concerns of any artist working in the public domain with tax-dollar support: the increasing eagerness of funding agencies at every level to impose censorship on projects. A related question: what was your public? Who was your audience?

Piascezny At one point it became a national audience when it was covered on National Public Radio.

Avalos But who was your audience originally?

Piascezny We sought to generate a new audience: passersby, the general public, anyone who would see the images on the street. There is a highly visible stalled renovation project in downtown Detroit called the Monroe Block; we initially wanted to put all our images together on that one site, a huge, boarded-up facade. The city said that our photographs were too negative, so they wouldn't allow us to do that. That was when we started defacing other buildings and putting them anywhere. Then the audience was wide open. Ultimately millions of people saw TV coverage of it.

Unidentified Speaker At the risk of sounding critical of these kinds of projects, I'm wondering about money. These are all like little things that artists want to do on the side but what about how we can radicalize the system of being artists—making money at it and still radicalizing and transforming it.

Avalos Yeah, I think that is an excellent question. Where is the funding for these kinds of projects? How many funding sources can you hit before you run out of money? Your example of the Detroit funding agency, I'm sure they would not be looking for you to come back with another project very soon. That's been my experience and I'm sure it has been the experience of a lot of people. What is the best way to fund these projects? Is there a way? You get a certain amount of rhetoric. There will be people who come forward and say there is such a thing as the First Amendment; in funding artists and art projects, there should not be a curatorial or censorial role for the funding agency. That should be handled through a third person and usually through the peer-panel process. What is the ideal way to fund these projects? Is there one?

Unidentified Speaker I was thinking more about how artists can make more money, then turn that back into making this kind of art, rather than always thinking of artists needing funding. After all, big money is being made by many artists. So artists who want to use that money to transform things should do that rather than always relying on public funding for these projects.

Avalos Okay, then, we are talking about the double dilemma of not only having to make the art but also having to find a new way to fund it.

Carole Ann Klonarides I don't know if anybody is aware but there is an exhibition right now in this city down at the World Financial Center that has twenty-eight artists in it concerned with the notion of the new urban landscape. For me, as a participant, I can say that this is the first time that a corporation is sponsoring an art organization in their own building and becoming a cultural institution. I'm interested to know if people are embracing and accepting Olympia and York as what you call "gatekeepers of culture." Having worked for a living in a straight job to pay for my art, I know that this is a constant problem: how to fund myself. It is a problem for a lot of artists: where does one go for support? I don't know where we go for money at this point, unless you want to acknowledge what that money represents.

Avalos Which is control.

Unidentified Speaker Well, isn't that what this gentleman said before: you have to redefine culture, and if you find that there are certain outlets that are unsuitable, you have to find other outlets. If an ethnic neighborhood has a certain art that is already an integral part of it, they will want to develop that and they will have their own display areas. If it is part of them, they will want it in their own community. You know you don't *have to* go to the museums. They aren't the only places to show art. You can put art in the shopping centers or the local factory. If you just make it part of the community—that is the important part.

Rosler Two questions about co-optation and critique, essential but difficult to talk about: one is, how do we feel about some of our most visible and exciting radical projects and radical artists being bought by collections like Saatchi? And how do we feel about some of the most visible projects being funded directly (not even through museums) by corporations like Olympia and York? I was waiting for someone in the vicinity of age forty to raise the question, "How do we make a living?" Because my experience with projects that I support very strongly, such as yours, David, or Paper Tiger, is that those projects tend to be fueled by the energy of young people. But after a while you run out of that energy and need to think of a way to support yourself without eating yourself alive.

The other question is one of critique. Most of the projects that we have heard about are populist, but most of what succeeds in the art world is referential to questions of representation. That does not go over well with the general public. What we find is that most artists who are interested in radical social critique tend to do it in a fashion that is not recognizably political or recognizably about the culture of everyday life or recognizably about the power of control or power relations. I find this tremendously problematic and rarely addressed. We must face the fact that most artists who are political at one point in their career wish to succeed and claim a space in the gallery and the museum as their turf. I don't know whether that is right or wrong. But I think that what gets tagged as political is work that appears in a gallery and simply is more political than the work hanging next to it which is apparently apolitical. Yet, it is not necessarily recognizable in the world at large as political.

Dan Wiley I can't resist speaking since Battery Park City was mentioned. This is a good example of art being used to cover over social or economic contradictions. I think it is problematic that Vito Acconci and Dan Graham have their work in the World Financial Center at Battery Park City, a project that symbolizes the economic polarization in New York City—the pushing out of people earning less money and the expansion of the essential business district. Initially Battery Park City was supposed to have public housing on the site, but with the fiscal crisis of the 1970s that idea kind of got lost. Then, when the plan got refunded it was made into an independent authority that could issue its own bonds. It was no longer accountable to the public at all. Suddenly the city said, we're still going to fund public housing but that public housing is going to be in other parts of the city—not here.

Avalos To get back to the agenda, the kind of privatization we are talking about—when a corporation uses its own building to exhibit work it has funded, or when the few take all the tax dollars, or when institutions are not used for the benefit of the whole society—makes us question our original idealism as artists. Is there something about being artists that makes us believe that this situation can be overcome? Is there a reason to go out and try to connect with our community? Or is the nature of consumerism, the nature of our community, a passive consumption of goods that are presented to us?

I think this is something that has to be considered in a participatory democracy. We have to inform arts-funding agencies of the ongoing need for the public to support artists, and we have to close the gap between what we do and how the public perceives us. These town meetings have included education and politics for exactly that reason. It is no longer possible for us to sit alone and talk amongst ourselves because the solutions are beyond us. We have to reach out.

Erma Bombeck

DINNER AT EIGHT (SECONDS)

I was reading a newspaper the other morning when a quote leaped out at me. Marty Friedman, editor of *New Product News,* said, "Fast food is too damn slow. No one has time for fast food anymore."

It is important for you to know I was eating an eight-second bagel from the microwave over the sink at the time.

All day I kept thinking about his prediction for food in the year 2001: oat-bran popcorn, pre-cooked chicken without preservatives in a vacuum-sealed bag that needs no refrigeration, robot cashiers, fast-food delivery, and video shopping.

He's probably right. We already eat breakfast from drive-in fast-food emporiums and lunch from street vendors and machines next to our desks. We allow six minutes for dinner from freezer to microwave to table, and if a pizza isn't delivered in thirty minutes, we don't have to pay for it.

Where are we going, and why are we in such a hurry to get there?

I am the product of the "dinner hour" generation. Showing up for dinner was a command performance, and the only reasonable excuse for getting out of it was a death certificate signed by three witnesses.

You were not permitted to leave the table to answer the phone or go to the bathroom.

The dinner hour had little to do with food. It was just something to do with your hands. The real purpose was to bring the family together at the end of the day. It was a combination therapy group/confessional/history course/critic's forum/supreme court.

Face it. A family is nothing more than a bunch of strangers thrown together by an act of birth. You sleep next to them for twenty years, but you don't know them. You share the same diseases and toothpaste, but that doesn't mean you know what they're thinking or feeling.

The whole world seems to be on fast-food forward, but in Mexico, South America, Spain . . . there is still respect for the art of family dining.

A couple of years ago, my husband and I watched a family having lunch in a small Italian village.

They laughed, discussed, argued, teased, and shouted at one another. The children talked and the parents listened. The parents talked and the kids listened. They must have sat there for more than two hours.

Look at it this way: it's just time. What are you saving it for? Something important?

Stuart Ewen

CONSUMPTION:

A PARTIAL TOTALITY

While many of the products of the marketplace were still financially and socially inaccessible to people, and where their accessibility required an increasing commitment to installment buying, still the ads portrayed the consumer market as an integrated and totalistic world view. Moreover, where resistance to the current direction and control of industry was manifest, it was ideologically severed from the vision of social experience proffered by the ads. The possibility of a world benefited by industrial technique yet respectful of popular determination and activity had been a central demand of working-class struggle for almost a century. Yet in *acceding* to the demand for industrial democracy, the machinery of corporate ideology had distilled out these critical questions. The ideologues of business, whose industry had altered the very process of industrial production, were cognizant of the need for wide-scale popular involvement in an expanding industrial culture. They responded by creating a cultural model by which that involvement was one of acting out the prescribed social roles of corporate planning. Art would flourish, but it would flourish within the aesthetic realms of business. Economy would dictate the creative dimension of industrial America, and the arenas of expression—newspapers, magazines, media, schools of design, etc.—were thus circumscribed.

Immigrants would be Americanized, a process identical to an abolition of their common memories and the replacement of them by a "mass" perception keyed to the vaulted aspirations for mass-produced goods. The concept of truth would be limited to the truths surrounding American goods and would reflect an ethical persuasion which might be constantly "outgrown" so as to conform to the overriding "rules for profit making."[1]

In the futuristic dreams of the ad men of the twenties, there soon would be a world in which ads would provide a common idiom of expression; language and communication would take on the role of constant selling; and the ongoing discontent with things *as they are* would seek amelioration according to that idiom. Dream and reality became equated in the world of ideas generated by the marketplace. Where reality did not conform to the dream, the reality was reformed (ideologically) so as to imply a world in which people didn't work and an industrial apparatus which had no factories.

In *Mythologies,* an interesting study of 1950s French culture, Roland Barthes has noted that much of modern industrial design is such that it seems to defy familiar mechanics and "natural law." Speaking specifically of the Citroën DS (automobile), Barthes notes that we can see the "beginning of a new phenomenology of assembling." He explains: "[It] is as if one progressed from a world where elements are welded to a world where they are juxtaposed and hold together by sole virtue of their wondrous shape." This, he adds, "is meant to prepare one for the idea of a more benign Nature."[2] Benign, partly because the element of human tension has been excised from it; a conception of products which denies not only the reality of human participation in production, but also the ability of human understanding to comprehend their mystified Nature. Within such a world, the product takes on a mysterious reality impervious to the understanding or action of the population.

What Barthes describes as a "new phenomenology of assembling" was not new to the context of the 1950s. The mystification of the production process, the separation of people (both as producers and consumers) from an understanding of this process, may be seen emerging early in the twentieth century. Yet the my-

stification is not one that limits itself to hiding the mechanics behind a "wondrous shape." In the productive process itself, one of the characteristics of "scientific management" beyond and perhaps more important than its efficiency, is its separation of the work process from an understanding of what is being made. In the American steel industry, as early as 1910, the "routing" systems of production tended to make the workers' understanding of mechanical process anachronistic. Samuel Haber, an historian, has culled the following insight into "scientifically managed" industry created by Frederick Taylor:

One of the most important general principles of Taylor's system was that the man who did the work could not derive or fully understand its science. The

result was a radical separation of thinking from doing. Those who under-
stood were to plan the work and set the procedures; the workmen were sim-
ply to carry them into effect.[3]

A phenomenon of industrial capitalism, the "separation of thinking from
doing" cut deeply into widespread labor demands for control over the workplace. The demand for such control had come from an historical tradition. It
had been based in a sense of self-defined workmanship as well as an experienced understanding of the contours of an environment fit to live and work
in. As technical "know-how" became imposed upon the worker in the form
of management from above, the self-perception of the worker as the source
of productive knowledge was historically undercut. Industrial skill became
located within the confines of industrial organization and management.

Whereas the first manifestations of this tendency took place on the shop
floor, it quickly spread to the arenas of consumption. Many early twentieth-
century consumer goods—the Model T is a good example—were products
of mass industry, and yet still assumed a level of mechanical know-how and

understanding on the part of the consumer. Ford's Model T was the consumer's to repair; it was a power plant which people could adapt to farm
tasks or to generating electricity. So too with other home and professional
equipment. One dentist interviewed has indicated that as late as 1938, when
he entered practice, he had the responsibility of servicing and repairing his
own equipment.

Yet by the 1920s both advertising and product design moved in the direction of separating products from the general knowledge of mechanics and
from technical understanding—moving in the direction of aesthetic and lin-
guistic mystification. The common development in usage of words such as
halitosis and *acidosis* placed the burden of definition in corporate hands.

The Gillette Razor Company in its advertising of the mid-1920s announced a razor with a new dimension, a *slanted head*. The ad was crammed with all sorts of technical data and jargon, but it was a totally mystified technical idiom. *The Journal of Applied Psychology,* doing a follow-up on the ad, noted that while subjects questioned were duly impressed with the superiority of the new shaving device, none could explain what was meant by the copywriter's text.[4]

Beginning in the twenties, the application of *art decoratif* (and later on, Bauhaus) styles to product design further intensified the process of mystification. While *art decoratif* had become passé as an expression of high culture, by the mid-thirties many mechanical products had internalized these designs—now called "streamlining."[5] In physics, streamlining was a design that was a "graphical representation of movement. . . . Streamline form is the shape given to a body . . . to the end that its passage through a material may meet with the least resistance."[6] As streamlining became applied to consumption and product design, physics became transformed into cultural allegory—a design which passes through the greatest amount of popular resistance.

Roland Barthes's commentary on the Citroën, then, is not merely a perception of the present, but one rooted deeply in the productive history of industrial capitalism in America. The "benign Nature" (as Barthes calls it) of industrial production is located in such mystifications. It is a benign Nature because it floats or appears to float by virtue of itself. It is a Nature apart from the experience of what is natural.

In the business ideology of the twenties, a benign Nature was being fashioned and publicized. It was a Nature girded by "Truth" and holding a dream of human happiness molded outside of the realm of human intercourse. Beyond selling goods, American industry was developing and selling a version of current history which extricated the most dangerous element— people—from its process. Change was something which took place on the commodity market, and which was then only mirrored in people's lives. Within such a conception of history and of nature lay the basic element of containment—an implicit denial of its public precept. The contained and orchestrated realities of consumer ideology were testimony to their political imperative. They addressed themselves more to the problem of discontent than they did to how to be content. In each case, the recognition of discontent attempted to channel these impulses into an acceptance of corporate solutions. When Filene spoke of teaching people "how to think" and separated this from any of the "class" traditions of thinking, he was confronting a problem broader than the particular historical *specter* of Bolshevism. He was confronting the problem of people looking amongst themselves for solutions to social ills. The hailing of a "machine civilization" which characterized the ideological formation of the consumer market cannot be separated from the corporate structure that was attempting to maintain control of the machine by forging a commensurate cultural life.

Consumerism was a world view, a "philosophy of life." But it was not a world view which functioned purely in the economic realm—selling of goods. While it served to stimulate consumption among those who had the wherewithal and desire to consume, it also tried to provide a conception of the good life for those who did not; it aimed at those who were despairing of the possibility of well-being in their immediate industrial environment.

As the ads cleaved all basis for discontent from the industrial context and focused on that discontent within realms that offered no challenge to corporate hegemony, they created a vision of social amelioration that depended on adherence to the authority of capitalistic enterprise. Such an adherence was not so much tied up in the actual flow of goods and services, but more in the flow of ideas that commercial propaganda was generating. Only in the instance of an individual ad was consumption a question of *what to buy*. In the broader context of a burgeoning commercial culture, the foremost political imperative was *what to dream*.

---

1. George Harrison Phelps, *Tomorrow's Advertisers and their Advertising Agencies* (1929), p. 39.

2. Roland Barthes, *Mythologies* (New York: Hill and Wang, 1972), pp. 88-89.

3. Samuel Haber, *Efficiency and Uplift*, quoted in Kathy Stone, "The Origins of Job Structure in the Steel Industry," *Radical America* 7, no. 6 (November-December 1973). Stone's article gives a good picture of the ideological and political function of technological development in industry.

4. Albert T. Poffenberger, "The Conditions of Belief in Advertising," *Journal of Applied Psychology* 7, no. 1 (March 1923), pp. 1-9.

5. Siegfried Giedion, *Mechanization Takes Command* (New York: Oxford University Press, 1948), p. 609.

6. Ibid., p. 607.

AIDS AND DEMOCRACY:
A CASE STUDY

Silence = Death. T-shirt distributed by ACT UP (AIDS Coalition To Unleash Power).

AIDS AND DEMOCRACY:

A CASE STUDY

Participants in the roundtable discussion of June 18, 1988:

Michael Callen, co-founder of People With AIDS Coalition
Jan Zita Grover, historian and critic living in Sacramento, California
Maria Maggenti, member of ACT UP (AIDS Coalition To Unleash Power)
Group Material: Doug Ashford, Julie Ault, Felix Gonzalez-Torres

Michael Callen   In terms of democracy, one of the most bizarre factors of the AIDS [Acquired Immune Deficiency Syndrome] epidemic is that the most directly affected by AIDS, people with AIDS themselves, are never involved, or rarely involved, in these discussions about what AIDS is. The People With AIDS Coalition came about in large part as a result of people with AIDS being frustrated with attending one too many forums where first a doctor said what it was like to have AIDS, then a nurse said what it was like to have AIDS, then an insurance person said what it was like to have AIDS. Almost simultaneously, it occurred to people with AIDS in different geographic regions that there was something wrong with this picture.

Fundamental to my understanding of democracy is the belief that people should be represented in situations where decisions are going to be made that affect their lives. I mean, you wouldn't have a commission on the status of women that had no women in it or a commission on minorities that had no minorities. I think we're sophisticated enough in this country now to recognize that such an approach would be fundamentally flawed. But I'm one of the plaintiffs in a lawsuit brought by the ACLU charging that the President's Commission on AIDS didn't have a person with AIDS on it and claiming that such an omission was illegal, a violation of our civil rights. Unfortunately, that argument was rejected by the court.

Maria Maggenti   That's right. Actual people with AIDS are never included in the process of definition, representation, strategy, or change. Of course, that's not without precedent. For years and years Americans have accepted the decisions of the Supreme Court where, to this day, irrespective of Sandra Day O'Connor's presence, you have individuals who have no idea what it would be like to have to make the decision to get an abortion.

All those problems have emerged again with AIDS, in terms of who actually does decide our fate. The lack of self-determination for women, for lesbians and gay men, and increasingly for people of color with AIDS is appalling. I know there are communities that have to deal with it. Dealing with AIDS signals the lack of access for these people at every step—economic, intellectual, medical, I mean, every tier. It just makes you realize that, despite the advances made by leftist activists over the past fifteen or twenty years, all the attitudes that everybody thought were unpopular, like racism and homophobia, are brought up again constantly by AIDS. Maybe these right-wing types were just quiet for a while, but were always present at the root of society.

Callen If you really want to be informed about AIDS, the latest breakthroughs, the things on the horizon, you've got to plug into the people with AIDS network—the various clubs and the underground network. The People With AIDS Coalition has set up a community-research initiative which conducts PWA-sponsored treatment research. And I'm very proud to say that the demographics of our latest trial are reasonably reflective of the demographics of AIDS in New York City, in terms of women, people of color, nongay, and bisexual cases of AIDS. We're trying to share our information and those research systems with all people affected by the disease.

Jan Zita Grover Scientific discourse is clearly the power discourse at the end of the twentieth century. It was so before AIDS and it will be so after AIDS. It's the only level at which a great many people will ever hear any information about AIDS. The notion of transmission categories, risk groups, risk practices, and so on, that all comes out of the discourse of epidemiology. But the discourses of people who are affected most directly by the epidemic, who are working within the epidemic, are not basically scientific discourses. They lie beneath the surface and they are difficult to find your way into.

I've been worrying a lot about that because I was trained as a historian, and my long-term goal is to write something about AIDS. So I'm particularly eager to see that there are records available that will allow for alternative histories produced around this epidemic. There is a great need for oral histories, for example, and for archives of material taken from nonofficial, nonscientific discourses, so that twenty-five years from now we can write histories from within, rather than having to deal with AIDS according to the official histories, which will almost exclusively use the scientific materials. In San Francisco, the Lesbian-Gay Historical Society is starting an AIDS history project.

Callen I know that both the Lesbian Herstory Archives and the Gay Archives have been very public about wanting to obtain AIDS stuff. I have in

Dorothea Lange, *Untitled*, 1942. Japanese grandfather awaiting war relocation bus, Hayward, California, May 8, 1942.

my own possession a tremendously valuable oral history. I take my tape recorder wherever I can, and I have some incredible stuff. I'm acutely aware of the historical value of this material, and I'm trying desperately to save it and find a place for it.

Maggenti In relation to AIDS the situation of lesbians has been almost completely ignored, although lesbians have always been active in the movement. But that's the way scientific discourse operates. When a doctor was asked why no studies were being done on transmission between lesbians, she said, "I didn't know that lesbians had sex." That's typical—the desexualization of lesbian women as contrasted with the oversexualizing of gay men. It's as if women have absolutely no sex.

This also makes it difficult to get information to lesbians who still are convinced that they have no real stake in this crisis. It's really painful. All the press coverage of the 1988 Stockholm Conference was relentless in asking, "What about heterosexuals? What about heterosexuals?" Everyone's worried about how to get information about heterosexuals. And this tiny voice in me says, "What about lesbians? What about lesbians?"

Grover Well, lesbians are used for signifying abstinence more than anything else around the whole question of AIDS—that's the role lesbians have in the question of AIDS. But what I really find fascinating is that the only two pieces regarding woman-to-woman transmission of AIDS in "the literature"—in other words, the scientific literature—are two letters to the editor, one in the *Annals of Internal Medicine* and one in the *New England Journal of Medicine*. Customarily, letters to the editor in these journals don't excite very much press attention, but in both of these cases (given the response to those two little letters), you would have thought somebody had just discovered the cause of life or something. Yet the letters themselves were completely ungrounded. One was written by a physician who never even saw the woman involved; it was just a sort of report from her about her activities. The other one had a little more information about the woman's specific sexual practices, but it was written in a sort of prurient way. So the *National Enquirer* picked that up. Both *Newsweek* and *Time* picked it up. The *New York Times* picked it up. These two little letters to the editor were suddenly treated as if they were big news.

Maggenti What did they say?

Grover The first letter was from a woman with ARC [AIDS Related Complex]. She was an IV [intravenous] drug user. But she was also a lesbian. This, by the way, is typical of the whole statistical construction of prostitutes; in most epidemiological studies, there's absolutely no distinction between sex workers who are IV drug users and sex workers who are not. Anyway, this woman had a lover who had "no risk factors" of her own. Eight weeks after the two women became involved, it appeared that the second woman developed an acute HIV [Human Immunodeficiency Virus] infection. This whole story takes up about thirty lines in the journal. It was just an anecdotal account by a physician.

What generated this huge response in the press, it seems to me, was the pure novelty, the fact that she was a dyke. It was the fact that they were *lesbians* that spun the letter out into the world at large. And the second case, there's just no way to make anything out of it at all: a doctor reported secondhand information from a woman who had since moved to another country.

Maggenti Well, as a lesbian who is a not a person with AIDS who has been involved in AIDS work for the past two-and-a-half years, I can say that there is a profound loneliness doing the work and not having a lot of lesbians involved. But I also feel as though my involvement is not predicated upon possible risk factors. I came to AIDS work, instead, as a member of the gay community, as a politicized person, and as someone who is interested in issues of social justice. But it's interesting to me that as we try to organize around AIDS as a political movement we come up against problems of how to reach people who are different from us. Especially in New York City, which is painfully stratified by class and race.

The idea of having a computer hookup to provide direct, instantaneous information from the Stockholm AIDS Conference was stupendous and wonderful. But when I think that at the same time so many people in this city are not even able to figure out where to go if they discover that they are antibody positive, it's incredibly depressing. That compounded with all the other problems that one might have as a poor person, as a female person, as a gay man of color who has tapped into the gay male community—these are overwhelming barriers.

In our own struggles, as strategies of intervention, it's interesting to note that we are presented with every other problem that already exists, and we try not to re-create those problems, the barriers of access and information, in the AIDS movement. And what I hope—when I think about the issue of history and what we'll be saying happened—is that they will say there was this unbelievable place in AIDS, made up of AIDS activists (people with AIDS, social-care providers, and many, many others) who were desperately trying to pull down those kind of walls that made the epidemic so frightening. That's the one place where I am consistently moved by doing the work that I do, and being around people who are doing it. Such amazing work.

Callen Sometimes I find myself—a white, gay man—in a minority, too. And I find myself put on the defensive about other people with AIDS. Here's a perfect example: the February issue of the *People With AIDS Newsline,* which, I think we've agreed, is a lifeline for people with AIDS. There are 14,000 copies printed a month and they go around the world. It includes people with AIDS writing about their own experiences with drugs, with treatment, with care providers, with AIDS. So the *PWA Newsline* is on the front line of information for all people with AIDS, irrespective of race, gender, etc. The cover of the February issue was a picture of me kissing Dan Turner. We're both long-term survivors and we were wearing headbands that said, "People With AIDS." You can't tell from the photo but it was taken seconds before we were arrested on the steps of the Supreme Court. For me, the picture had many layers of meaning—two long-term survivors, kissing, expressing sexuality, affection, about to be arrested protesting on the steps of the Supreme Court. Yet that picture, on the cover of the *PWA Newsline* set off an unbelievable wave of condemnation among other groups.

Catholic hospitals refused to distribute this particular issue. We also got a lot of letters, largely from lesbian and gay people working in the IV drug-use communities saying, in essence, "For months I've been trying to convince my clients to read the *Newsline*. It had a reputation for being gay and I'd just convinced them that it wasn't gay, and now you put this offensive picture of two men kissing on the cover. And now all my work has been undone." And in one particular office that I go to, run by a wonderful lesbian doctor, the box in which the *Newsline* is put has been taped up so that you can't see the photo on the cover.

Maggenti I think that the tension that emerges around AIDS is that it's not a gay disease, right? But, in fact, there are a lot of gay men who have AIDS. So, in fact, it's gay/lesbian people who are doing the work around it. And I think that needs to be recognized. Not to exclude anyone else, but to make the point that it hasn't been an all-inclusive kind of movement. I'm not saying that there aren't straight people doing the work. I'm not saying that. However, if I were in a black group as a white person, would I ask them to call it a multiracial group? I don't think so, if I were the only white person. Similarly, ACT UP isn't a gay/lesbian group. There are a couple of straight people who are doing work with us. Mostly straight women. I don't think there are any straight men who are doing the work that we're doing, direct action. And the way that shows up is as a tension. I mean, to me, it's going back to square one in the fight against homophobia.

Callen What's the solution? Let's stick with that example. What do you say to those people working with the IV drug-user community who say I will no longer put out the *Newsline* because I can't count on what it will say—it's offensive to nongay people sometimes. Over our three-year history we've gotten a lot of letters saying that the language of the *Newsline* is offensive because it talks frankly about gay sex. As editor, I have to make a painful choice because I want the information to circulate as widely as possible: do I self-censor? Do I not let gay men write in graphic detail about safe sex and what's going on in their lives sexually because I want all the rest of the information to get as widely distributed as possible?

Maggenti Let's look at it from the reader's point of view. I've spent a lot of time thinking about the question of at what level people actually make decisions and what influences their decisions in their life. And it's almost never general information that affects them. It's the authority of personal experience and the experience of people who are close to them or people that they see as influential in their own community. This is why so much of the transmission information that has been produced inside the gay community has tracked very well with what people are already doing or moving toward doing. But I think we have to take the next step and realize that information becomes either too general or too arcane as it spins out into radically different contexts. At the same time, it's a joke to say that gay men already know everything there is to know about safe sex. That's just not correct.

Grover I think that the real problem comes when someone else is imposing their set of standards, detoxifying something. You know, when the Centers for Disease Control gave some money to GMHC [Gay Men's Health Crisis] to develop a second videotape (following *Chance of a Lifetime*) to try to impress upon gay men that safer sex is really fun and sexy, it was such an extraordinary sanitized production. I don't think it's actually been distributed, has it? As soon as I saw the scene with a large hothouse cucumber sitting on a kitchen table, I thought, "Oh Christ, this is it." And it was: the safer-sex "here's-how-to-put-on-a-condom" scene. The string that came with getting the federal money was that the tape couldn't show an actual human erection. Instead, GMHC had to impress upon the viewer the notion of safer sex, had to stress condoms as a mode of risk reduction, and then had to show how you use a condom correctly, but they couldn't show a condom going on what it logically would go on. This is something for a specific audience? This is for gay men? I mean, this is a joke. A huge sad joke.

In contrast, how many of you have seen *Ojos Que No Ven*, the fabulous tape made by the Latino AIDS Project of La Familial de la Raza in San Francisco? It's a forty-seven-minute tape in the form of a soap opera about all these people who live on one block in the Mission District in San Francisco. It contains an enormous number of different kinds of transmission stories. But it's not didactic, and it's very funny. It's got a group of drag queens at one of the local Latino gay bars doing this kind of Carmen Miranda act, singing a song about transmission. It's just a wonderful tape, and the state of California was planning to distribute it. But they got very upset because one of the things the tape does show people is how to clean their works. It doesn't tell them they shouldn't be using drugs; it just says, "Well, if you're using, you should know how to stay clean." The segment concerns somebody who has gotten clean and doesn't want to use drugs anymore. He's been clean for three months and just doesn't want to get back into it. But the state dropped plans to distribute the tape because it dealt too evenhandedly and too nonjudgmentally with the notion that somebody might continue to use drugs.

Callen Maybe we should state right here what I take to be an assumption we all share: that this is no longer simply an example of that humorous American reputation for being puritanical or squeamish about matters of sex, but that the net result of these kinds of policies emanating from democracy is that people will die.

Grover In terms of education, in the city of San Francisco there has been no significant negative response to groups like Flying Wedge. This group of PWAs has been funded by both the public and parochial schools to go in and talk to kids in very blunt ways about what is known about HIV transmission, as well as introducing them to the fact that because somebody's going to die eventually doesn't mean either that they are contagious or that they're about to drop dead. Now, there have been no pickets, there has been no keeping the kids out of school when Flying Wedge is going to come in, or anything like that. And gay people have been elected to the school board in San Francisco. But I understand at the same time that what has been termed "the San Francisco model" is a model only *for* San Francisco—the danger lies in assuming that what is applicable or possible one place is equally so elsewhere.

Maggenti My work in the past year has been focused against the policies of the federal government, and directed more toward local politics. But the federal government still manages to set a tone, it is like the gestalt of the crisis for the whole nation. I see what's happening in San Francisco as a significant model that could operate on a local level in a lot of different places. What you are saying about San Francisco is wonderful. However, I don't see that being necessarily re-created in lots of communities.

Grover It really boggles me that San Francisco is seen as a model for someplace else. I live across the bay in Oakland. Oakland is to San Francisco as Brooklyn is to Manhattan: it's cheaper and there are more people living on that side. It's by and large a working-class city where about 45 percent of the population is black or Latino. And AIDS is an entirely different epidemic there than it is in San Francisco—epidemiologically, demographically, in every sense, it is absolutely different.

In any meaningful terms, I don't think that there is any such thing as *the* AIDS epidemic in the United States. It's a useful fiction for the federal government, the politicians, and the media, who so radically simplify everything, but in point of fact, there is no transnational AIDS epidemic except at the levels of federal policy, funding, and national media. Instead there is a series of local epidemics that are very different in terms of who is affected, what is funded, and whether official and voluntary responses are just stonewalling or something positive and effective.

Book cover, *Surviving and Thriving with AIDS: Collected Wisdom, Volume Two* published by the People With AIDS Coalition, 1988.

San Francisco is a city geographically twice the size of Manhattan. It's forty-six square miles—it's tiny. Still, 93 percent of the people who have been diagnosed with AIDS in San Francisco are gay men. And of those, about 70 percent are white gay men. This makes delivering care to PWAs a very manageable proposition in certain ways compared to what it is, actually, anywhere else. It's crazy for people to come there thinking that they are somehow seeing the future and that they can take it back to Tulsa. I mean, it's easy enough to understand where the notion of a quick fix comes from, and that initially may be very consoling, but it's also very crazy. You only have to look at Marin County, just north of San Francisco, a suburb that is even wealthier than the city—it doesn't have any AIDS program at all. But they have AIDS in Marin County. It's mostly IV drug-related—wealthy drug shooters. But they have no service delivery program in that county. And our program in Oakland is terribly, terribly underfinanced, yet there's a sizeable epidemic among women and children, IV drug users, and gay men.

Callen   Instead of relying on governments to lead the fight against AIDS, there should be more terrorist activity. We should use the mass media and letters to the editor. For any excuse at all we should write letters to the editors of all the major newspapers. That's what gets information across. Or we could place public announcements in the classified ads. If it gets the information out, we should use it—any means. We should use the tools that are already out there. We should take what people already read, go in, and start subversion.

Maggenti   I agree with you. But I think writing letters is a very culturally bound idea. I would have much more radical tactics. I mean, I would take from the fictionalized responses, like in Lizzie Borden's *Born in Flames* when they take over one of these TV stations with machine guns and tell the guys to put a tape in. More practically, I think that there are ways to get information out that bypass traditional forms of communication, and I think those routes are really valuable. That's where people do get information: on the street, or in communities. I think that's very valuable.

Felix Gonzalez-Torres   One obvious issue that AIDS raises is the clear need for this country to consider some form of socialized medicine and to recognize access to health care as a right. We are the only so-called civilized nation that doesn't have a national health-care program.

Callen   When people ask me why I think I'm still alive six years after my diagnosis, I say that, in part, it's because I've studiously avoided federally designed treatment protocols, few though they be. So when we talk about making access to medical care available equitably, I wonder whether that's a favor or not. A perfect example is AZT. I have interviewed more long-term survivors of AIDS than anyone I know; I went in search of long-term survivors outside the gay community. According to the current statistics, women with AIDS survive six months from diagnosis; IV drug-use cases with AIDS survive about a year after diagnosis. And one of the big reasons is that the health care in minority communities is almost exclusively city-clinic based. The people that I interviewed liked the clinic, they were satisfied. One woman said, "I was born at Harlem Hospital and that's where I feel comfortable getting my medical treatment. I wouldn't want to have only one doctor." It's a whole different way of looking at it. But the point is clinics follow the federal mandates, which aren't always right. Because federal subsidies now make AZT available, all of the minority people with AIDS were on AZT. That's what was being made available free to them at the clinic.

On the other hand, only one of the white gay men who was a long-term survivor was on AZT at the time of interview. And he approached it much more skeptically: he had a critique of the trials. So, if AZT is the poison that I suspect it is, this will be an example of where, although the people who fought for AZT subsidies and wanted it to be widely available did so in good conscience, it seems they encouraged its disproportionate use among minorities.

Grover   I think that points to a problem that lies deeper than whether or not one is getting treatment in a clinic. San Francisco General is a county hospital in which probably half of the gay white men who are treated in the ambulatory HIV clinic, Ward 86, are medically indigent and are on Medicaid/MediCal. But it seems to me that the underlying problem is people's attitude toward government-paid health care: whether they regard it as an entitlement or as a sentence. Because most gay white men who are medically indigent but who are using the services on Ward 86 are extremely skeptical and extremely well informed about AIDS treatment issues, they challenge the health care providers about what they are or are not getting and what they want. They set out quite deliberately to impress upon the house staff that they know as much as or more about their condition than the staff does. And it creates a very interesting and precarious and fascinating kind of balance between care providers and people who were formerly passive recipients of care.

But when you get somebody who is using that clinic who does not come to it with the notion that they are going to find out as much as possible about their condition or that they are not free to reject a particular treatment even if it's not what they want, then it's entirely different. It's the clinical setting per se—it's people's perception of where they fit into it, and whether they see health care as an entitlement or a form of begrudged charity that they cannot question.

Medical care, even if one doesn't have the money to pay for it, is an entitlement: in theory, we are all entitled to it. But that's a very different attitude from that of somebody who has always been the recipient of state care, who may not see it as an entitlement, and who may be much less likely to challenge treatment and say, "I don't want that garbage. Find something else for me."

Maggenti Just to change the subject a bit, I wanted to get back to the idea of what can be done in specific communities. For instance, the model of ACT UP, which is a direct action political group, does not work for everyone. We get individuals who come to ACT UP meetings and say, "We want to do ACT UP in Atlanta. So, can you send some people down and tell us how to do it?" And we say "Well, we don't work that way." And they say, "Well, I thought you had chapters." "Well, they're not really chapters. They're just people in a local area who have decided they want to get on the street about AIDS." And that's pretty much how we started. You just do it in any way that suits your community. And you figure out how that's supposed to work. It doesn't work all the time and it doesn't transcend all the issues in the culture, in the gay community, or in the communities in New York. It's just one possibility that's very empowering for the individuals who are involved. And I think that's very crucial. Any place where you do not feel small and do not feel isolated and alone with what you're experiencing is important and empowering.

Callen One of the curious things about the empowerment of the AIDS movement is the increasing institutionalization and the growing professionalization. I have an interesting example of this right now in the People With AIDS Coalition. The Coalition started with, you know, people with AIDS, and we decided that the most important thing that people with AIDS needed and wanted was information. So we started the newsletter, which I typed in my house, snuck into corporate America and xeroxed, and then handed out. That was three years ago. Our projected budget for July 1, 1988 to July 1, 1989 is $750,000. We only get $30,000 from government grants. We have no idea where the rest of the money is going to come from. We could fold next week. But what's interesting is that, as we've grown, we've been trying desperately to hold onto the grass-roots nature. But with a budget of $750,000, and that kind of growth, part of the problem—well, I can give you a perfect example because it involves my role as editor.

I produced the first two years worth of issues of the People With AIDS

Coalition newsletter for free. I typed every keystroke on my computer, and I did all the editing. Then the day came when someone from the coalition said, "You can no longer do this for free. It's costing us. We're paying for the cartridge, your time. While you're doing the *Newsline,* you're not doing something else, etc., etc.," So we have a situation right now at the coalition. There are several board members who receive money, completely below market for what they do, and so the board is fighting over whether it's appropriate for board members to even get any money at all. There are all these sorts of organizational issues. I mean, it's nearly splitting the coalition. So, we're at this very dangerous stage now in terms of organizational development where we're desperately trying to cling to our grass-roots effort. But, in order to do a *Newsline* and print 14,000 copies of it, it has now sort of become a big thing.

Maggenti   That's what is interesting. What grass roots means, at least what we understand grass roots to mean, is not "professionalized," even though everybody does very professional work to accomplish the work of grass-roots activism. That's true whether it's the Community Research Initiative or the *Newsline* or even ACT UP. In fact, ACT UP has to deal with this situation on a cyclical basis; it's why we don't get nonprofit tax status, the 501(C)-3. The IRS and the United States government would attach a lot of different strings if we were a nonprofit organization. They don't appreciate funding a group that wishes to take them over.

Callen   Perhaps my whole frustration with the science of AIDS is in fact a problem of democracy and science. I mean, it seems clear that the scientists can just vote on what the cause of AIDS is. If a majority of researchers vote that HIV is the cause, then we build social policy on it—whether it's actually the cause or not. It reminds me of a story—the only thing I ever got out of my religious childhood. Our minister once made an analogy about some kids who found a rabbit. They couldn't figure out if it was a boy or a girl rabbit. Their solution was to take a vote. That's the way science about AIDS is being done; it's based on these superstructure assumptions like about HIV and the germ theory (you know, for every disease there's a specific cause and all you have to do is find it and knock it out and the disease goes away). The problem is the idea that in democracy it's okay to build social policy on a scientific assertion just because it's the majority scientific assertion. Ideally, someone makes an assertion and then science tries to knock it down. If you can't knock it down, then it probably is the best explanation. But as I've said before, whatever is actually causing AIDS will continue to do so, irrespective of what a majority of researchers prefer to believe is the cause of AIDS.

Maggenti   Well, I guess I've always been skeptical about the scientific establishment. It's inherently exclusivist since very few people have access to scientific information. As Jan said, science discourse is a power discourse. It
seems to me that what ends up functioning is a power relationship, which
shouldn't have to be that way. The information is not necessarily so esoteric
that only a handful of individuals are able to make assessments about the
genesis of a particular disease or its components. There are places where, of
course, I don't know the language well enough to be able to talk to them
competently about epidemiology. But there are certainly other instances in
which the concerns you voice, you feel, and you know about your body are
not accepted by scientists or doctors. There's something wrong with a medical system that doesn't accommodate that type of information as a valid possibility for discussion around the illness or disease or infection. But I think
that that's intrinsic in the nature of science, which has historically not been
in any way community-based.

Grover   Well, supposedly we live in a free society because we have a right
to choose among nine hundred different name brands. Anybody's perfectly
free to dissent from the prevailing regime of truth, and many of us do. But
the catch is that in our dissent we don't have equally authoritative voices because the central, powerful discourse is the discourse of science and epidemiology. Now the interesting thing is that a lay person can read
epidemiology quite adequately and determine a given study's or method's
built-in biases. And since I can do that, it's been grist for my mill. But the
point is my own discourse is not a power discourse. So the fact that I pub-
lish my response to this stuff makes almost no difference at all because the
people who agree with me do not share the power discourse, either.

Gonzalez-Torres   To say that an already disenfranchised group is carrying a
cancer-causing virus and that it can kill people is a tremendously powerful
political tool and club to beat people with.

Grover   I've been thinking about one of the people from the Latino AIDS
Project, the woman who was responsible for putting together the production
team for *Ojos Que No Ven*. She pointed out that to talk about transmission,
it was not necessary to identify what it was that was being transmitted. And,
you know, for most of our purposes this is the salient and the central issue.
She said, "In the town where I grew up in Mexico, there are times of the
year when if you draw water out of the well, everybody gets ill. We had no
idea what caused it, but we had sense enough not to drink the water when
the water wasn't good." And she said, "It doesn't matter that we talk science

Martin Wong, *Big Heat*, 1988.

or not science in this video or in our community at all. If we know that there's a possibility of this somehow being conveyed sexually, then we have to convince people that they've got to protect themselves when they're having sex, and it doesn't matter what causes it." And I think from the level at which we are acting, as community activists or as artists, that's the important thing. It's profoundly important that somebody whose immune system is compromised figure out what the hell is behind that destruction. But at the level of community activism, it's not so important. It's important in terms of the politics of what gets funded and what doesn't.

Callen   Although you're essentially right, I think I can show you where diagnosis is important. I acknowledge that there's a transmissible component.
The difference between the multifactorial camp and the HIV camp is the
notion of whether a single sexual contact can kill you. In terms of construct-
ing risk-reduction strategies, that's what gets fudged all the time. The New
Right is saying "How can you be talking about condoms when condoms
have a 10 or 15 percent failure rate? You're talking about death, so you have
to tell people that they can't have sex at all. That is only logical." That is a
logical argument if you assert that a single sexual contact can transmit HIV
and that HIV is fatal.

If you think that HIV causes AIDS, then testing becomes rational. And
abstention for people who are positive becomes rational. It's not everybody
who'll do it. But once one says HIV is the cause of AIDS, then holding the
wall against mandatory testing becomes increasingly difficult. The multifactorial model that I favor suggests that different explanations apply to the different risk groups, that there are many different ways to arrive at the same
point. For example, as you mentioned, the major cause of pneumocystis prior
to AIDS is protein-calorie malnutrition in infants. So we know that malnutrition can cause pneumocystis and profound immune deficiency. We also
know steroids and chemotherapy can cause profound immune deficiencies.
That suggests to some of us—those of us who are multifactorialists—that
there are many ways to become immuno-suppressed. Once you're immuno-
suppressed, you tend to get pneumocystis, toxoplasmosis—the opportunistic
diseases you see will be similar.

The way AIDS is defined is as the incidence of a disease associated with
a profound submediated immune deficiency in the absence of another explanation such as steroids or chemotherapy. That is tantamount to suggesting
that there's only one cause of immune deficiency remaining to be identified
and that, by definition, is AIDS. If we can't explain why you have pneumocystis, then you have AIDS. The perfect example is Ann Hardy's study—
there are people with pneumocystis, cryptococcyl meningitis, Karposi Sar-
coma, who didn't have HIV. They were originally thought to have AIDS
but, now, what category are they in?

My point is that it is precisely antibody testing, the presence of a particular virus, from which all these social consequences flow. That is what the
New Right is seizing on. Now we can find out who's queer. There's a blood
test for it. And when we find out, we can isolate them, we can make them
lose their insurance, we can kick them out of their homes.

Maggenti   Right, but one of the ways in which you fight that is you say that
you are not for testing of people, that you are for the testing of drugs. You
can say that you are for providing the possibility of individuals having material lives that make them healthy and keep them healthy.

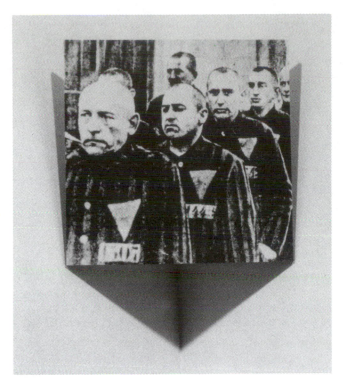

Steven Evans, *The Dark Quadrilateral*, 1987–88.

Grover You can say that, but look at the government's response. Testing was perfect. It's a great government thing. You can count on it. Think of the money that's gone into testing and you ask the question, what impact has that actually had on anybody's health or on the influence of AIDS?

Maggenti All of our social policies are linked to testing one way or the other.

Callen Right, I understand that. But what I'm saying is it's interesting to ask what social consequences flow from a particular belief such as the role of HIV in AIDS. Fear of particular social consequences affect one's preference for one explanation over the other. But believe me, my reasons for believing that HIV is harmless have nothing to do with the social consequences that I've seen flow from the belief that HIV is a necessary and sufficient cause of AIDS. But I do find it useful to discuss that.

Grover One of the things we ought to make clear here is that the definition of AIDS the Center for Disease Control devised is a surveillance definition for purposes of epidemiological reporting. It has been used in lots of other ways and a lot of very negative consequences have resulted from that, but it's

T. L. Litt, *Silvia at Silent Vigil,* Washington, D.C., October 1988.

important to place it and see why it evolved. It is not in any way meant to be a diagnostic tool. It was meant to say, this is X but it is not Y, this is Y but it is not Z. Initially, the definition was used simply for purposes of keeping track of the number of reported cases. It has since been treated as if it were a diagnostic tool and all kinds of unfortunate social and political consequences have accrued to it. But it was intended as a surveillance definition and conceived as a manufactured condition. It is not a disease, it is a set of characteristics of a state of immune exhaustion and that is not the same thing as a disease. A set of characteristics, clinical and serological, is not in any sense contagious. That's why I object, incidentally, to the term *AIDS test.*

Maggenti One thing that bodes well for the future is that when the anti-abortionists came to New York, and the women started organizing clinic defense and everything, all these men in ACT UP got involved. They were so excited about it. They were young enough that they didn't feel they shouldn't be involved in reproductive-rights work. Many women in the group had already done it and they were saying, "Oh, I really don't feel like doing clinic defense again." But all these young men were saying, "Oh, I want to do it, I absolutely want to do it, I want to be there." So there are places where I think new kinds of synapses or connections are being made that are really exciting and important.

Grover I have a lot of faith in the new generation.

Tom Stoddard

PARADOX AND PARALYSIS:

AN OVERVIEW OF THE AMERICAN

RESPONSE TO AIDS

Acquired Immune Deficiency Syndrome challenges more than medicine. Because it is deadly, because it continues to spread quickly, because it is linked to the controversial subjects of sex and drugs, and also because, in the developed world at least, it arose first among gay men and heroin addicts, it provokes deep and complicated feelings in nearly everyone, and those feelings, when extended across a society, have political and social consequences. As AIDS moves across the world, it tests each country's ability to act responsibly—or even sanely—in the face of catastrophe.

This short article will attempt to outline the way in which the United States of America has responded, or failed to respond, to the unique challenges of this modern epidemic. The article will look particularly at the way in which the government and the private or voluntary sector in the United States have divided up the tasks imposed by the emergence of AIDS, and then proceeded to perform those tasks, with the hope that the U.S. example will be instructive to other countries that have not yet had to face the brunt of the epidemic.

An analysis of this kind is particularly difficult with a nation as large, and as culturally and politically diverse, as the United States. This article will not attempt to relate the history of AIDS in the United States, even in summary form, but will instead identify patterns and themes in the country's overall response to the crisis since AIDS was first recognized in 1981.

The following four paradoxes will help to give the flavor of the American response to date for those readers who live outside the United States:

1. News about AIDS is everywhere in the United States. Newspapers, periodicals, television, and radio stations all report regularly on AIDS, dedicating far more attention to this subject than to any other health problem. Nonetheless, many Americans are still ignorant of such elementary facts about AIDS as the ways in which the Human Immunodeficiency Virus, which is believed to cause AIDS, is transmitted from one person to another. In a Gallup poll released in March 1988, nearly 40 percent of American workers accepted the proposition (which is totally without scientific basis)

that they might catch the virus through food served in the company cafeteria. The ignorance of the public is, to some extent, driven by fear, as in Arcadia, Florida, where unknown malefactors set fire to the home of three hemophiliac boys with HIV in their blood. The boys posed no threat to any of their playmates, but the neighbors seem to have been so fearful for their children that they simply could not accept the reassurances of the experts. The persistence of such irrational fears is coextensive with the amount of media attention.

2. Most political leaders in the United States have voiced their commitment to overcoming AIDS. President Reagan himself characterized AIDS as the nation's foremost health problem. Yet, seven years after the identification of the illness and four years after the discovery of HIV, there is still no national plan on AIDS. The primary burden of the illness has fallen, institutionally, on the fifty state governments and the localities within them, particularly those on the East and West Coasts, most of which lack the resources to address the issue adequately. President Reagan did, in 1987, create a special presidential commission on AIDS, or, as he put it, "the Human Immunodeficiency Virus Epidemic," but after the commission issued its final report in June 1988, he simply ignored its principal recommendations.

3. In the absence of decisive action by the government, particularly at the federal level, hundreds of private organizations have sprung into being to provide services to people with AIDS, and to others touched by AIDS. The prototype is Gay Men's Health Crisis in New York City, which began in someone's living room in 1981 and now, a mere seven years later, has an annual budget of more than $10 million and a staff of more than one hundred people. Although miraculous in their creation and heroic in their achievements, these organizations are limited in what they can do and more generally ill-equipped to address the future trends in the epidemiology of AIDS. AIDS is likely to become less a disease of the white gay men who were the first publicized persons to develop the illness, and more a disease of intravenous drug users, most of whom are poor and black or Hispanic. In New York City, for example, drug users and their sexual partners now account for a majority of the newly diagnosed cases. The name "Gay Men's Health Crisis" in itself suggests the difficulty that this organization will have in shifting its focus, assuming it should choose to do so. (New York City is also home to an organization called the Minority Task Force on AIDS, but the group has one-tenth the budget and one-tenth the number of employees of Gay Men's Health Crisis; it also receives considerably less attention from the press and the government.)

4. It is illegal for most private employers in the United States to fire, demote, or harass people with AIDS and people with HIV infection, unless an employee simply cannot do the job. Most states, as well as the federal gov-

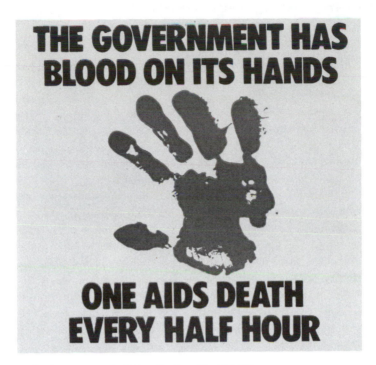

Blood on Your Hands. Sticker distributed by ACT UP.

ernment, have statutes forbidding discrimination on account of a worker's "handicap" or "disability," and increasingly these statutes have been interpreted to extend to AIDS. Consequently, while some employers faced with the issue of AIDS have acted stupidly or maliciously, and discrimination does without question exist, it is less than systematic—with one notorious exception. The federal government itself does discriminate against people with AIDS and HIV infection. The government now tests for HIV antibodies all applicants for military service, for the Peace Corps (which sends volunteers abroad to teach skills), and for residential placements in the Job Corps (which trains poor teenagers for employment), and rejects those with positive results. The government also requires tests of all Foreign Service officers and their spouses, all immigrants, and all prisoners subject to its jurisdiction. Thus, the federal government views itself as exempt from the rules imposed on other American employers.

As these four paradoxes imply, America has responded to AIDS with confusion and inconsistency. The picture is an extraordinary jumble of images, with signs of great courage and hope—the growth of Gay Men's Health Crisis, for example—beside symbols of failure—most prominently, President Reagan's virtual abdication of responsibility on the issue. The achievements have come largely from outside the government, as private individuals and organizations have discovered the problem and sought to address it. Within the government, especially in Washington, the response has been clumsy, feeble, and tardy. Official Washington has by now at least acknowledged publicly that AIDS is an epidemic, and one full of peril, but it is still unable to put together a strategy to overcome it. A nation that devised Project Apollo, the Marshall Plan, and the Manhattan Project has been unable to agree with itself on what to do about any aspect of the crisis posed by the Human Immunodeficiency Virus. The government cannot even achieve a consensus on what to tell ordinary citizens about the virus, with some officials urging warnings that are explicit and others advocating more circumspect messages for reasons of propriety, personal morality, or politics.

This failure of leadership is critical because of the enormity of the crisis in the United States. The United States is the epicenter of AIDS in the developed world. Apart from Africa, which has an epidemiology of its own, the United States was the first place in the world with a substantial AIDS caseload. And with currently more than seventy thousand identified cases, it still accounts for two-thirds of the world's caseload outside of Africa. The statistical future is even grimmer than the past. The federal government believes that at least one-and-a-half million Americans have HIV in their blood. Unless science can find a treatment more effective than those now available, most of these people will die premature, HIV-related deaths.

I should add that the American system of government does not lend itself to the efficient—or speedy—resolution of problems. The American federal structure favors stability over change, and diversity over uniformity. Basic services, including public education and public health, rest primarily in the hands of the states and localities, not the federal government. Even at the federal level power is dispersed. The president can propose legislation to Congress, but can rarely force his will on that body, particularly when (as now) it is controlled by the opposition. And the courts hold a potential constitutional checkmate over the actions of both the president and Congress that is unique to the West. Furthermore, the private sector plays a much larger role in American life than in any other developed country. Services that elsewhere belong to the public sector, such as gas, electricity, air travel, broadcasting, and telephones, are provided in the United States by private companies, often in competition with one another. Health care fails in this category. Most Americans obtain health care through private contracts with insurance companies and "health maintenance organizations." The government covers only the elderly and the very poor, and even for them not all forms of care. Under such a system, change comes about only with difficulty, even in the face of an emergency.

Any comprehensive national strategy on AIDS would necessarily center on four goals: the discovery of a cure; adequate care for the afflicted; the prevention of further spread of HIV; and the elimination of unfair discrimination against those connected with the virus. Sadly, in every one of these areas, the American response to date has been shortsighted and inadequate.

The Search for a Cure

Even in decentralized and highly privatized America, the task of finding a cure must be the responsibility of the federal government. The federal Department of Health and Human Services shelters several agencies designed to promote the development of new drugs and treatments, especially the Food and Drug Administration (FDA) and the National Institutes of Health (NIH). These agencies often work with private companies and universities in their investigations. Under ordinary circumstances, the system of drug development and approval works very slowly. Federal approval for sale of a new drug takes, on the average, eight years from the beginning of the first test. Until that time, the drug is generally unavailable to the public, even for a patient facing death whose doctor is prepared to use the drug.

Until recently these agencies had shown slight interest in AIDS, and very little concern over the slowness of the investigative process or the unavailability of a drug until the government gives final approval for its use. In 1986, some reporters and politicians raised questions about the federal government's approach to drug development in light of promising rumors about an antiviral compound known as Azidothymidine (AZT). Their inquiries, together with increasingly encouraging reports from the investigators, moved the FDA and NIH to accelerate rapidly the entire procedure for that particular drug, and AZT was eventually licensed for sale to some, but not all people with AIDS, in the spring of 1987. (It is now available on a wider basis, although its extremely high cost still makes it unavailable to some HIV-infected individuals who wish to use the drug.)

AZT may help to retard replication of the virus, but it is not a cure, and is toxic to some patients. Since its approval, private organizations serving people with AIDS have voiced ever louder—and ever angrier—dissatisfaction with the way in which federal agencies have approached other possible treatments. Indeed, a number of private organizations, such as Project Inform in San Francisco, now advise people with AIDS or HIV on substances not approved by the FDA, and some have surreptitiously helped them to get the drugs from other countries, or from illicit domestic sources. Frustration over federal indifference has also prompted the creation of private organizations that initiate or assist in the testing of treatments outside the typical research channels, such as the Community Research Initiative in New York. Private impatience has in addition greatly spurred charitable donations to a private organization called the American Foundation for AIDS Research (AmFAR), which awards grants of its own to scientists investigating possible treatments for AIDS. In the fiscal year 1985, AmFAR gave research grants totalling $1,512,278. In the fiscal year 1988—a mere three years later—it will give $7,200,000.

After several years of criticism and defiance, the FDA in particular has at last begun to bend. In July 1988, the agency's commissioner announced that people with AIDS would be permitted to import for their personal use small quantities of substances only available abroad. The next month he agreed to relax restrictions on an experimental drug for pneumocystis carinii pneumonia, the opportunistic infection that results in the most deaths from AIDS.

But these developments have come much later than they should have, or would have, had the White House taken an interest in the matter. Moreover, they cannot outweigh the persistent refusal of the federal government to adequately fund research into AIDS. Both the Institute of Medicine of the National Academy of Sciences, which is an independent organization funded in part by the federal government, and the president's own commission on AIDS have called for substantial additional federal funding of the national research and development agencies.

Whether these recommendations will be followed may become clearer in the course of 1989, but there is reason to fear yet more inaction. In the meantime AmFAR, the Community Research Initiative, Project Inform, and other private groups have sought to fill the gaps in federal activity. They, rather than any federal agencies, have pointed the way for those in search of a cure.

Care for the Sick and Infected

Almost alone in the developed world (South Africa is the other exception), the United States offers no comprehensive national health service to its citizens. Health care in the U.S. is a patchwork of programs, some private and some public, that serve some Americans reasonably well and some very badly or not at all. Most Americans assure health care for themselves and their families through participation in group health insurance plans offered by their employers. Those who are unemployed or self-employed, and those whose employers do not offer them a health plan, must provide for themselves or rely on whatever services, if any, are offered by their local government.

AIDS has not altered this basic fact of American life. But it has brought attention to the current inequities, and helped build support for public health insurance. (In the summer of 1988, Massachusetts became the first state to guarantee health insurance for all residents.) The changing epidemiology of AIDS will assist that process. AIDS, especially in the northeastern states, is increasingly an illness afflicting intravenous drug users and therefore the poor—those who, because they have no private insurance, must turn to the government. In a city like New York, with nearly a quarter of the country's AIDS cases and perhaps four hundred thousand people infected with HIV, the costs are soaring. Federal intervention may be the only possible solution short of abandonment of the city and its caseload.

While hundreds of private, local organizations have arisen across the country in the past seven years, to meet the needs of people with AIDS and people at special risk from AIDS, these organizations, with very few exceptions, do not and cannot provide medical care directly. Gay Men's Health Crisis in New York City was the first to do so and is still the model. The organization informs and counsels about AIDS, HIV infection, and their consequences. It links people in need with volunteer companions. It offers recreation and legal assistance. It produces brochures and films. It lobbies in the city council, in the state legislature, and to a more limited extent in Congress. It does not, however, run medical facilities or residences for people with AIDS, and would quickly sink under the workload if it attempted to. Furthermore, as its name indicates, it arose from and still addresses primarily the concerns of gay men. Because of its history, focus, and name, it is not well suited to meeting the needs of other people with AIDS or HIV infection.

The Prevention of Further Spread

In June 1988, the United States government mailed to every American household a pamphlet about AIDS. The language was generally straightforward, but at times euphemistic and equivocal; the pamphlet warned, for example, of "sex with someone you don't know well" without distinguishing between sexual acts involving penetration, which may be dangerous, and sexual conduct without penetration (so-called safer sex), which generally is not.

This pamphlet constitutes the principal effort by the federal government to inform the American people about AIDS. It has not been the sole attempt. The federal Centers for Disease Control have given money to private organizations to teach about AIDS, and the surgeon general has talked repeatedly and frankly to the press about AIDS. But the federal government's role has been largely incidental to the work of the private sector. Privately owned entities have taught the American people about AIDS: not-for-profit corporations like Gay Men's Health Crisis, small film companies like AIDSfilms, and the country's tangle of news outlets.

The disparate, decentralized nature of AIDS education in the United States has had its advantages. The U.S. is so massive and complex a country that AIDS affects different sectors of the population in different ways; the concerns, needs, and perspectives of gay men differ substantially from those of intravenous drug users. For instance, the sociology of gay men who live in

Salt Lake City does not conform to the patterns of the gay male subculture in New York City. But all the individual efforts taken together cannot substitute for a vigorous and cohesive national campaign to communicate certain basic themes to the country as a whole. And any national campaign on AIDS ought to convey more than medical facts and advice. It should, for instance, counsel against unfair treatment or stigmatization of people with HIV. By this broader standard, the federal government has failed totally. Apart from the surgeon general's avuncular admonitions, federal officials have been largely silent. President Reagan himself has been almost entirely absent from the national discussions about AIDS.

A full effort to arrest the spread of the virus would embrace, in addition to the dissemination of information, counseling and voluntary testing programs for people who fear they may be infected, and a campaign against the use of intravenous drugs. Projects of both kinds do exist in the United States, but without substantial federal support. A bill to fund HIV testing centers has yet to pass the Congress. And although the government does furnish money for drug treatment facilities, the inadequacy of its appropriations is appalling. In the state of New Jersey, for instance, where most AIDS cases arise from the use of drugs, the present drug treatment programs can accommodate only four thousand of an estimated forty thousand drug users.

The Elimination of Discrimination

The President's Commission on the Human Immunodeficiency Virus Epidemic called in its final report for a broad federal statute to outlaw discrimination against people with AIDS and HIV infection, and also for a presidential order forbidding discrimination within the federal government. James D. Watkins, who headed the commission, was adamant on this issue. In a press conference in June 1988 he characterized discrimination as "the most significant obstacle to progress in controlling the AIDS epidemic," arguing that so long as discrimination persisted, it would deter people from seeking testing, counseling, and care. The president, however, after he received the recommendation, first said nothing and then, five weeks later, referred the issue to the Justice Department for further "review."

The president's delaying tactics are not the worst of the government's sins. As mentioned earlier, the federal government itself discriminates against people with HIV infection. There are questions about the legality of the federal government's conduct; its Job Corps policy has already been challenged in federal court, in part on constitutional grounds. But federal discrimination persists, and serves by example to undermine any arguments against discrimination by others.

Unlike the federal government, many of the state governments have worked forthrightly to curtail discrimination related to AIDS, by enacting new laws or by interpreting existing statutes expansively. In 1986, California passed a law prohibiting employers and insurance companies from requiring the HIV antibody test. New York's Division of Human Rights has made clear that it believes the state's "disability" discrimination statute covers AIDS and the New York state legislature recently enacted a law generally barring disclosure of HIV test results without the permission of the subject.

Private groups have also fought AIDS-related discrimination. In 1983, Lambda Legal Defense and Education Fund, an organization promoting civil rights for gay people, brought the first AIDS discrimination lawsuit in the United States. In that case, Lambda prevented the eviction of a doctor from his office because he treated patients with AIDS. The successful legal precedent of that case has led to similar results in other courts across the country. The Citizens Commission on AIDS for New York City and Northern New Jersey, created in 1986 by fifteen private foundations, drew up a set of principles on AIDS in the workplace based on the concept of equitable treatment, and then set about obtaining endorsements from employers. As of December 1988, more than three hundred had lent their names to the commission's guidelines.

Fear of AIDS, often accompanied by misunderstanding, continues to foster discrimination against people associated with AIDS, even those who are not sick or infected. The attention of the state governments and of some not-for-profit groups has helped somewhat to check discrimination, but, as James D. Watkins has observed, federal inattention seriously limits the success of their efforts.

From this assessment of AIDS in the United States, two major themes emerge. The first and most powerful is the extraordinary lethargy of the United States government. At best, the government has been negligent. At worst, it has actually made the epidemic worse, standing in the way of forces and developments that might prove beneficial. The government need not have taken on all the tasks itself, but it should have at least planned, advised, and coordinated. This it has not done, although the cost to it of devising a preliminary national strategy on AIDS would have been insignificant in an annual federal budget of $1 trillion.

Why has the government been so irresponsible? The answer must be more than financial, for fiscal concerns, if taken seriously, generally militate for rather than against planning. This is especially true for AIDS: a truly effective prevention campaign now would substantially reduce future medical costs.

The explanation lies not in money but in politics. The populations most deeply affected by AIDS are outside the American mainstream: gay men,

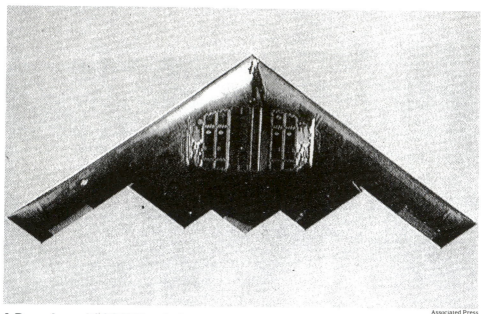

A Decade and $22 Billion Later, the Stealth Bomber Takes Off

The B-2 Stealth bomber, seen from underneath, as it lifted off the runway at Edwards Air Force Base, Calif., on its first flight. The radar-evading plane, the most technologically complex military aircraft ever flown, cruised for two hours at a maximum altitude of only 10,000 feet. The successful flight, however, had no discernable effect on the debate in Congress over the plane. Page 11.

and intravenous drug users and their sexual partners and children, who are largely black or Hispanic. They have few political representatives, and few advocates. They, and the lives they lead, are viewed with distaste and disapproval by many Americans. Some Americans even see people with AIDS as willing and culpable victims. In a national survey published in 1987, more than one-third of the respondents agreed with the statement "AIDS is God's punishment." James L. Kilpatrick, a well-known national newspaper columnist, wrote in June 1988: "My thought is that AIDS victims deserve about the same 'compassion' that society extends to those who smoke themselves to death or drink themselves to death." Sentiments of this sort, usually coupled with the notion that AIDS does not attack "normal" people, have sidetracked the calls for action of the president's commission and the experts on AIDS. They have also severely distorted the public debate on AIDS, confusing the issue with a variety of other concerns only vaguely related to the epidemic itself.

Official neglect is not, however, the sole theme to emerge over the first seven years of the epidemic. There is a brighter one. In the face of governmental indifference, hundreds of thousands of Americans, some acting on their own behalf, others for the benefit of relatives, friends, colleagues, or neighbors, have joined together to furnish the services not available from the government. In less than a decade, they have fashioned an alternative and unofficial national network relying principally on volunteer labor. They have also collected many millions of dollars to sustain their efforts.

With adequate support from the federal government, the private organizations that fight AIDS could have done more. Nonetheless, their growth and accomplishments tell a lesson: nongovernment organizations should have a major part of any effective national strategy against AIDS. Such organizations permit greater diversity and experimentation. They absorb changes in approach more rapidly than is ordinarily possible for government bureaucracies. They also give communities and populations more voice in the shaping of solutions. All in all, privately-run organizations shorten the distance between those who serve and those who are served. Most gay men do take seriously advice from Gay Men's Health Crisis, or its companion organizations across the United States. Similarly, drug users may not listen to the surgeon general or to the Secretary of Health and Human Services, but they do heed a former user employed as a counselor by a local organization.

Two lessons emerge from the polarity between government inaction and private initiative. One concerns politics. AIDS is unlike any other public health issue. In each individual and in the body politic, it spurs sentiments that are likely to interfere with a rational resolution of the crisis. AIDS requires special political leaders who will put public health concerns first, who will not shy away from controversy, and who will step forward to mold and inform public opinion. The second relates to the scope of government action. No government should attempt to confront the crisis entirely by itself, even if it possesses the necessary will and resources. Private citizens, and private organizations, can often reach those in need more quickly and more effectively than government agencies. Government should foster the development of these independent efforts with, among other things, money and advice.

May countries be guided, not by the sad example of the United States government, but by the ingenuity and compassion of those U.S. citizens who have taken it upon themselves to confront AIDS.

William Olander

WHERE WE ARE NOW:

HOMO VIDEO

On two previous occasions, the New Museum of Contemporary Art has presented work which specifically addressed issues of sexuality. The first was an exhibition devoted to art and gay sensibility; the second, an exhibition focused on more generalized, or perhaps more essential, ideas of sexuality, difference, and representation. Both were provocative expositions of contemporary art and critical theory. Both, however, in my opinion, with regard to homosexuality, were stunning failures.

The first, *Extended Sensibilities: Homosexual Presence in Contemporary Art,* organized by Daniel Cameron in 1982, failed precisely because of its emphasis on that pseudo-serious and intensely ambiguous field of sensibility—a world of camp and kitsch, gay cult and gay lifestyle, female goddesses and male transvestites, homosexuality viewed as *la vie bohème;* thus, Cameron could write of "Sensibility Content" as separate from sexuality; of "fun" as an "essential quality" of a homosexual aesthetic; of "the sordid possibilities in the gay sexual underworld."[1]

In *Difference: On Representation and Sexuality,* organized by Kate Linker and Jane Weinstock in 1984, the curators attempted to examine a much broader and more complex field of production "focused on sexuality as a cultural construction, opposing a perspective based on natural or biological truth."[2] Yet, in this exhibition of thirty-seven artists and forty-nine works in all media, only one work constructed from a recognizably homosexual viewpoint and a second from a more ambiguous position were included (Stuart Marshall's 1984 videotape *A Journey of the Plague Year* and Chantal Akerman's 1974 film *Je Tu Il Elle).* In the catalogue, written by six prominent critics and historians, each of whom is conversant with various modes of psychoanalytic theory, "homosexuality" is *never* mentioned, though "sexuality," "sexual difference," "masculinity," "femininity," "male," and "female" as socially and historically constructed concepts are discussed at length. Indeed, the one sentence devoted to Marshall's video does not reference homosexuality at all, but rather AIDS—the disease which

◀ Installation by ACT UP (AIDS Coalition To Unleash Power) in the New Museum window on Broadway, New York, *Let the Record Show. . .,* 1987.

has now assumed representational status with regard to male homosexuals. The lesbian component of Akerman's film was ignored in favor of a discussion of the heroine's lack of presence. "She has no reality," writes Weinstock—an unintentionally apt commentary on the organizer's view of homosexuality.[3]

So how is this third exhibition, so bluntly, almost vulgarly called "HOMO VIDEO," different? First, and foremost, it seeks to give back to homosexuals their *specific* difference, not in any conventional "gay is good" posturing or "Gay Pride" celebrating, but by recognizing that a different set of problematics is involved with regard to homosexuality than to heterosexuality from the points of view of politics, history, and an engagement with theory. For example, the key political strategy of homosexuality, distinct from any of the other liberation movements, has been, since the historic days of the late 1960s, "coming out"—the practice of revealing your sexual preference to family, friends, co-workers in order to consolidate some sense of personal and social identity and worth. There is no question that the significance of coming out for the homosexual liberation movement is incontestable but, as Jeff Minson has pointed out in a controversial piece in the now defunct journal *m/f,* two types of reservations severely complicate this issue in the 1980s.

In the first, the act of coming out fails to infiltrate and dismantle the materiality of homosexual oppression—the capitalist and patriarchal structures of Western society. Most homosexuals still subscribe to the ideology of the "personal is political" and go about their business forging a gay lifestyle which, in its most retro phase, assumes a new significance in relation to values of home, family, and country. The second reservation is even more complex: in Minson's words, ". . . to make homosexuality the defining characteristic of the entire person is to make the very assumption made by those hostile to homosexuality, e.g. in an employer's justifications for giving someone the sack purely on the grounds of their being a known homosexual."[4] Or, in 1986, in an insurance company's refusal to provide medical coverage to a gay man because he is known to be at risk for AIDS. Or in a doctor's refusal to artificially inseminate a woman who wants to be a mother because she is a lesbian. The problematic of coming out is just one instance of difference between gay men and lesbians, and straight females and males. It's also indicative and symptomatic of how much has changed since the glory days of gay liberation, how complex and contradictory it is in the 1980s to do battle against an ever-increasing attitude—despite both a liberal tolerance of homosexuality *and* its recent recriminalization—that deprives homosexuals of their specificity.[5]

If this program of videotapes has been motivated by genuine difference, it is not a difference for its own sake (again, this is not about seventies liberation tactics), nor is it necessarily about difference conceived in its currently institutionalized form of shifting signifiers, an ambiguous and unstable "I." (Only Lyn Blumenthal's *Doublecross* tackles this terrain directly and, in many ways, more effectively than many straight feminist tapes, by implicitly acknowledging first, that sexual difference cannot be separated from sexual preference and second, by taking as her subject the "strange history of our true sex"—the case of a young girl trapped within an indeterminate sexuality.) Here, difference is conceived primarily as political rather than merely ontological; heterogeneous, rather than essentialist; and homosexual in addition to heterosexual. There is no attempt to identify or characterize a gay aesthetic because built into this exhibition is the notion that genuine difference does not recognize such reductive gestures but rather, states from the outset that homosexuals are not the same as heterosexuals and do not desire clinical normalcy but, on the contrary, deviance; that gay men and lesbians are different from each other; and that within these groups, there is no male or female homosexual type. These are just some of the basic issues addressed by homosexual difference, cited primarily for one reason: to remind liberals and conservatives alike that neither tolerance nor persecution are going to make all homosexuals into compulsive imitators of normality, either by imitating the lifestyle of the dominant heterosexual class or by comforting themselves in the shelter of the pre-liberation closets.

Briefly, I want to try and describe the subjects and function of these thirteen videotapes. Two of them were independently produced for broadcast television and, not surprisingly, both address the crisis which has been wrought by the AIDS epidemic.

The first, Peter Adair and Robert Epstein's *The AIDS Show: Artists Involved with Death and Survival,* is, on the surface, a straightforward documentary produced with the support of San Francisco's public television affiliate, KQED. Its subject is a theatrical production mounted by San Francisco's gay stage company, Theater Rhinoceros, in 1984 and 1985, which is comprised of dramatized vignettes about the AIDS crisis—extremely human and emotional stories which chart, in many ways, a mini-history of responses to AIDS within both gay and straight communities. Although the tape is executed in a familiar and restrained fashion, by focusing on the theatrical revue, Adair and Epstein abjured the traditional role of the television documentary (there is almost no voice-over narration) in favor of allowing another work of art to speak for them. They refrained from the conventional editorializing of most broadcast documentaries in order *not* to make yet another "special" about AIDS. (That no network-produced program is included here indicates my own unwillingness to contribute to the spectacularization of AIDS which the media, in general, has produced and promoted.)

The second tape, Stuart Marshall's *Bright Eyes,* is an epic ninety-minute

production produced for Britain's Channel 4, a television network founded
in 1982, which is devoted to innovative, experimental, and independent pro-
gramming. *Bright Eyes* is divided into three equal and related sections: the
first, a complex historical analysis of how one forms a "true picture" of an
illness, including homosexuality and AIDS; the second, an evocative and almost poetic history of the modern persecution of sexual deviance; and the
third, interviews with a number of men and women involved with various
gay issues, including media coverage of AIDS, followed by the moving testimony of Michael Callen, an American PWA (Person With AIDS) and currently chairperson of the PWA Coalition, demanding additional government
funds for research and care. The two works could not be more different, indicative not only of the makers' particular aesthetic choices and political
views regarding their identical subject but also of their potential venues
(American versus British television) and audiences (presumably that for public television in the U.S. is larger but more homogeneous than the audience
for Britain's Channel 4).

AIDS, of course, is not the subject of every tape in this exhibition nor
have any of the other works, with the exception of Public Service Announcements, been made specifically for broadcast TV. Indeed, it is to the gay and
lesbian community's credit that the AIDS crisis has not excluded the continuing discussion of discrimination, censorship, sexual politics, and the
more complex subject of homosexual representation. These are the focuses of
the documentary tape, *Just Because of Who We Are,* by the lesbian collective
Heramedia; the short and funny tapes of Jerri Allyn and Suzanne Silver; and
John Goss's portrait of two Latino teenagers, Carlos and Cesar, on the loose
in California *(Wild Life).* Joyan Saunders's piece, *Here in the Southwest,*
goes so far as to end with a beautiful image of a young woman braiding another's hair, while a text trails over, stating: "Freud maintained that women
have never invented anything, with the possible exception of weaving. He believed they developed this craft by braiding their pubic hair in an attempt to
obscure their 'inferior' genitalia." And while many may believe that sex is
not to be figured in our postmodern critique of representation, Rick's cable
television program, *The Closet Case Show* (also called *City Heights* for the
closet cases in the audience), is there every week on Channel D to remind us
that there is a gay sex in the 1980s. Filled with good humor, one thirty-
minute segment, "How to Seduce a Preppy," is not merely a wonderful par-
ody of the conventional "how to" program (standard cable fare), but also an
insidious send-up and subversive commentary on lifestyle (both straight and
gay) *and* the best manual for safe-sex techniques that I've seen so far.

Because one agenda of this program is to show work that addresses
concerns of gay men and lesbians, while also speaking to the public at large,
the tapes that could be labeled "video art" intersect more than is customary

with the documentaries or works produced for broadcast. Thus, John Greyson calls one of his most recent tapes a "docu-drama," which, however, is more "realistic" than most of what appears on network or commercial TV. (A significant point of reference is the acclaimed made-for-television *An Early Frost,* the subject of which was the double predicament of many gay men who must reveal simultaneously to family and friends that they are homosexual and have been stricken with AIDS.) Greyson's tape, however, is not *about* AIDS but rather, about a trip that he made to the Soviet Union as a gay delegate to an international youth festival, which coincided in the summer of 1985 with the revelation that movie star Rock Hudson had AIDS. Such a sensational story could not be suppressed even in a country where deviant sexuality is neither acknowledged nor discussed but actively legislated against.

Richard Fung's tape, *Chinese Characters,* also falls over into the docu-drama category, in that it combines talking-head style interviews with fictionalized footage, and its subject—the role of pornography in the lives of certain gay men and the dominance, in the gay male subculture, of images of white, middle-class beauties to the exclusion of Asians, blacks, and Latinos—is one which easily could be the focus of academic treatment. Gregg Bordewitz's work also weaves together fact and fiction, with special attention paid to allegations that the Centers for Disease Control in Atlanta has seriously mismanaged the AIDS epidemic since the beginning. Finally, Lyn Blumenthal's tape (the preface to a longer work in progress) also takes as its ostensible subject a fact-based account of a young woman who sued a major drug company and her doctor for "lesbian damages" resulting from a drug-induced birth defect and the measures taken to correct it, which ended in a long history of confusion over sexual identity.

I began to think about this exhibition of videotapes during the summer of 1985, when I saw some rough footage of *The AIDS Show.* When I began to research the project seriously a year later, I initially thought that I would have to provide an almost retrospective view, i.e., that there was not going to be enough new material for a full-length program. I would have to include material that had already been seen in New York (a work like Daniel Brun's *Bleechin'* of 1980, which today assumes historical status as a document of the era pre-AIDS); work which was relevant to gay men and lesbians but not specific to them (e.g., Paper Tiger Television's *Ynestra King Reads "Seventeen"* of 1982); and/or work whose primary function was didactic ("safe sex" tapes), commercial (rock videos, like those made for the original Bronsky Beat or lesbian folk singer Phranc), or pornographic (one of the best I've seen is Michael Goodwin's *If You Had Friends Like Mine: The Goodjac Chronicles*). Happily, this was not the case, and as I write this, new tapes by gay men and lesbians are being brought to my attention every day (e.g., the work of a graduate student, Tom Kalin, in Chicago; a collaboration in Somerville, Massachusetts, producing a five-part lesbian soap opera called *2 in 20*).

What this means is obvious: while the political and social conditions for homosexuals become worse, gay men and lesbians continue to resist and, in fact, have escalated their resistance in the Reagan era—in response to AIDS, the Supreme Court ruling against homosexuals in *Hardwick* v. *Bowers,* the Meese Commission on Pornography. What is most promising is that there seems to be a genuine acknowledgment that the issues confronting us are not exclusive to gay men or lesbians but are our collective concern. What has begun to occur, as our lives are threatened from within and our freedom threatened from without, is that we have begun to address our "differences," at least those we have constructed within our own movement, and have shifted the countercultural emphasis of the earlier sexual liberation movements to a new politics which can more effectively link gay and lesbian concerns to each other and to the broader struggle against patriarchy, discrimination, and repression. Today's goal, as evidenced not only by these videotapes but equally by gay and lesbian fiction, history and theory, film and photography, is neither to affirm the dominant heterosexual practice nor the institutionalized subculture of gay life, whether female or male, but rather, to challenge the various ideological apparatuses which continue to harass, contain, and suppress the condition of homosexuality.

---

*The title of this program is borrowed from the title of an article by John Greyson, "HOMO VIDEO," *Jump Cut,* no. 30 (March 1985): 36-38.
1. Daniel J. Cameron, *Extended Sensibilities: Homosexual Presence in Contemporary Art* (New York: The New Museum of Contemporary Art, 1982), pp. 8, 13, 25.
2. Kate Linker, *Difference: On Representation and Sexuality* (New York: The New Museum of Contemporary Art, 1984), p. 5.
3. Jane Weinstock, "Sexual Difference and the Moving Image," in *Difference,* p. 42. There was at least one additional work by a lesbian filmmaker—Sally Potter's *Thriller* of 1979. For another critique of *Difference,* see Martha Gever and Nathalie Magnon, "The Same Difference: On Lesbian Representation," *Exposure* 24 (Summer 1986): 27-35. The authors comment: "Two notable sexual differences not represented were female and male homosexuality. This absence, of course, is not exceptional: in the proliferating texts on psychoanalysis and feminism, difference is decidedly singular—masculine or feminine—the same difference."
4. Jeff Minson, "The Assertion of Homosexuality," *m/f,* nos. 5-6 (1981), p. 19.
5. See Martin Dannecker, *Theories of Homosexuality,* trans. David Fernbach (London: Gay Men's Press, 1981), p. 9.

William Olander

THE WINDOW ON BROADWAY
BY ACT UP

Last March [1987], a small group of concerned men and women formed ACT UP, or the AIDS Coalition To Unleash Power. Their intention has been to fight, with any means necessary—"zaps," more organized demonstrations, posters, letter-writing campaigns, T-shirts, banners, stickers, placards, video screenings, flyers—the often uninformed and negligent response of federal, state, and local governments to AIDS. Since March, ACT UP has grown to almost three hundred strong; it meets informally (and often chaotically) every Monday evening; it is nonpartisan and grass roots; and at this moment, it is still one of the few AIDS activist groups in the country.

I first became aware of ACT UP, like many other New Yorkers, when I saw a poster appear on lower Broadway with this equation: "SILENCE = DEATH." Accompanying these words, sited on a black background, was a pink triangle—the symbol of homosexual persecution during the Nazi period and, since the 1960s, the emblem of gay liberation. For anyone conversant with this iconography, there was no question that this was a poster designed to provoke and heighten awareness of the AIDS crisis. To me, it was more than that: it was among the most significant works of art that had yet been done which was inspired and produced within the arms of the crisis. The poster was by ACT UP, and not surprisingly, many artists and arts-involved individuals are active in the organization. Last July, on behalf of the New Museum, I asked the group to do an installation in the Broadway Window. According to ACT UP, *Let the Record Show* . . . provides current information regarding the AIDS epidemic, as well as depicting the crisis in historical perspective. The intention is to make the viewer realize the depth of the problem and understand that history will judge our society by how we responded to this calamity, potentially the worst medical disaster of the century. Finally, the installation is more pointedly directed to those national figures who have used the AIDS epidemic to promote their own political or religious agendas. It is intended to serve as a reminder that their actions or inactions will soon be a matter of historical record.

In discussions about this project, inevitably the question, "But is it art?" arises. Though my own response is, "Not that again," it's a question that can be put to positive effect. That is, throughout history, all periods of intense crisis have inspired works of art whose functions were often extra-artistic. Let's cite just a few of the more obvious modern examples: Jacques-Louis David's *La Mort de Marat,* painted in 1793 for the revolutionary national convention; the achievements of the Russian avant-garde, which sought to eliminate class distinctions between artist and artisan and emphasize the materialist basis of art production; and the so-called political art of our own time—a work like Hans Haacke's *U.S. Isolation box, Grenada, 1983.* Of course, there is a propaganda aspect embedded in these works; for instance, David's masterpiece was to serve as a rallying point for the popular and middle classes sympathetic to the radical vision of revolution promoted by Jean-Paul Marat. The point is a simple one: not all works of art are as "disinterested" as others, and some of the greatest have been created in the midst, or as a result, of a crisis. Many of us believe we are in the midst of a crisis today. Let the record show that there are many in the community of art and artists who chose not to be silent in the 1980s.

Gran Fury, *All People With AIDS Are Innocent,* 1988. ▶

ALL
PEOPLE WITH AIDS
ARE
INNOCENT

TOWN MEETING!
AIDS AND DEMOCRACY: A CASE STUDY
ORGANIZED BY GROUP MATERIAL
Tuesday, January 10, 8 pm
DIA ART FOUNDATION • 155 Mercer St.
AGENDA

Meeting Chairperson: Maria Maggenti, member of ACT UP, (AIDS
                      Coalition to Unleash Power)

I. Welcome and introductory remarks by Maria Maggenti

II. Brief summary of issues raised during a panel on AIDS & Democracy: A
    Case Study organized by Group Material*

III. Open to the floor: Discussion on the following issues --

A. How does the AIDS crisis reveal the iniquities of democratic access to
power in the United States? How does this crisis provoke disenfranchised
communities to counteract their lack of traditional and acceptable power
in government and culture at large?

B. What systems of care provision, health maintenance, and education have
been created by the various communities? In what ways have these systems
of empowerment been formed? How do these grassroots responses parallel
successes and failures of previous social movements?

C. Is direct action an appropriate strategy for democratic participation?
When and where does it work? When and where does it fail? What is the
role of self-empowerment in the creation of a democratic society? What
are other possibilities for self-empowerment and representation?

D. What ideas can we come up with now that will include everyone in this
audience who wants to take action against the AIDS crisis?

Please come prepared to speak on these issues. The Town Meeting on "AIDS
& Democracy: A Case Study" will be recorded, transcribed and incorporated
into a publication organized by Group Material for the Dia Art Foundation.

*AIDS & Democracy panel held in June 1988: Michael Callen, Jan Grover,
Richard Hawkins, Maria Maggenti.

This project is supported in part by public funds from the National Endowment
for the Arts, a federal agency, and the New York State Council on the Arts.
"AIDS & Democracy: A Case Study" is also funded in part by a grant from Art
Matters, Inc. Admission is free. For more information call (212)431-9232.

AIDS AND DEMOCRACY:
A CASE STUDY

Chairperson, Maria Maggenti Before we begin I have a couple of remarks I want to make. One point that I have raised before in discussions of AIDS is the often overlooked fact that AIDS did not have to become a crisis. I believe it has become a crisis due to some very specific and calculated actions on the part of the United States government and the population at large. Those actions have to do with the individuals and groups that have been affected by AIDS: gay men, black and Latin people, IV drug users, and increasingly, women, most of whom are women of color. Perhaps the AIDS crisis simply reflects a crisis in democracy which existed long before the entrance of HIV into the bloodstream of the nation. As many people have said before, surely if AIDS had hit white-straight-male corporate America the way it has hit gay men and lesbians, poor people, and people of color, we would have had an immediate, sophisticated, and committed response to combat the disease. We most certainly would not have had the so-called second epidemic, a public response manifested as bigotry, prejudice, violence, discrimination, and hatred for people with AIDS.

What makes AIDS a political issue as well as a medical one is that it is not simply a virus that breaks the body's immune system; it represents what was already broken down in the immune system of the nation at large. It's a crisis that illuminates all the historically weak spots in American culture: our continuing racism, our homophobia, our sexism, and, of course, our inadequate and unequal health care delivery system. And looming over all of these issues is our inability or unwillingness to confront them and combat them as a way to save lives. What I hope we can do in this town meeting is not just discuss the issues but act on the discussion. I hope we can strategize about ways to end the crisis so that we create some lasting impact on the nation and so we don't have to end up in this place again.

Dewey Seed Hi. I'm a sculptor and also a certified home-care attendant for People With AIDS. There are 200,000 or 250,000 HIV-positive people in New York state. Recently in the newspaper it was reported that only 330 PWAs have home attendants assigned to them by the Human Resources Administration. That's a very small number, and if you realize that a home at-

So Long,
Farewell,
Auf wiedersehn,
Goodbye.

8 years and 42,000 AIDS deaths.

Don Moffett, *Goodbye*, 1988.

tendant often takes care of two PWAs then you can halve that amount and
you will get the number of home attendants in the state who are working
with PWAs. Now, that is incredible. What are the problems in getting people
to work with PWAs? There is a program in place, but that program is not
being fully implemented since the community and the public at large are un-
aware that there are openings and employment as home attendants. There
have been employment ads in the paper, in the *Village Voice* and in the *New
York Native*. But they have been discontinued in the *Native* because there
has been no response. Maybe the gay community is burnt out, maybe the
gay community can't deal with looking at advanced stages of AIDS. But the
gay community has to be aware of the needs of PWAs, and right now they
are not being addressed.

Maggenti Thank you. One of the questions that your statement addresses
has to do with the way the gay community has created its own system of
care provision. And as you point out, it's not a complete system. I happen to
think that the gay community has, in fact, taken care of its own for going
on eight years, but you're right, people do get burned out. And we need to
address the reasons why it would not be easy for our community to respond
to calls for social service provision or being health care providers for PWAs.

That's especially upsetting in light of the fact that as the disease progresses people will increasingly need hospice care and home-care attendants instead of hospital rooms at $800 a day.

Seed That's true. Also, because of the treatment advances for the opportunistic infections, PWAs are living longer, and the hospitals cannot cope with the numbers. Having spoken to social workers and nurses in various city hospitals, ones who are working with AIDS patients primarily, I know that in each hospital there are PWAS ready for release—and I don't mean low numbers—but who cannot be released until a home-care worker can be assigned to them. And they are waiting one, two, three months for release. In that waiting period they are in a situation where they can contract other infectious diseases. It is preferable that they be at home.

Tim Rollins My name is Tim Rollins and I'm director of the Art & Knowledge Workshop in the South Bronx. I'm a teacher and an artist. I just want to make a little report, and I should say that I have the kids' permission to say this. I've been working with the same twenty kids for about five to seven years. We're just talking about twenty average kids, but within the last four years we've lost six cousins, three uncles, two dads, one mom, and one mom is currently dying.

That is unkind in and of itself, but what is even more unkind is that to this date, even though it has been promised, there is no AIDS education whatsoever in many of these schools. The reason for this is not that the school bureaucracy is scared. They aren't so much scared of AIDS itself, as they are afraid that AIDS education would threaten the Brady Bunch scenario that they all imagine to be the ideal family mode. As a consequence, the kids are still pretending that nothing is happening.

I don't see any major change in sexual practices among either gay teenagers or heterosexual teenagers. Everyone is still acting like it's 1955, and they are really supported in this fantasy by the culture in general. Two concrete, practical things: one, the city Board of Education and the state education department must be forced by next September to implement a community-approved AIDS education curriculum. That means demonstrations. And second, we've got to get together and write, illustrate, produce, and distribute free of charge—probably by kids for kids to kids—our own AIDS education packet. We might have to set up four blocks from school and hand them to kids so they can learn for themselves.

Maggenti Thank you. Actually, Tim, last year when the AIDS Coalition To Unleash Power had nine days of actions, each day was devoted to a different issue and one day we went to the school. On Women and AIDS Day we went to the schools and did exactly what you said, set up tables outside the school and gave out safer-sex information. Some schools gave us their approval and some didn't, but we did it anyway.

Avrom Finkelstein Hi, I'm Avrom Finkelstein. I'm with the Silence = Death Project and Gran Fury. But of course those are collectives and tonight I'm just speaking for myself. I would like to speak about the inadequacies of culture and cultural response in relation to AIDS. Tonight, for instance, we are here in an art-funded space talking about AIDS, and I have to say that it makes me very sad that there are so few places where I can talk about AIDS aside from the street screaming with ACT UP or in some sort of cloistered environment like this. The arts community has contributed a tremendous amount, but it falls short of its true cultural responsibility in a crisis like this when the information it presents is so highly codified. I feel what the culture needs is more clear descriptions of what I consider to be a political crisis as well as a human crisis. What it doesn't need are cryptic descriptions of that crisis. I feel very disoriented and alienated when I walk into an art space and look at very elitist, very self-referential images that have potency and meaning but are largely about loss and issues that we all share. That is elevation, but there is another level of thought on which the art community falls short. That's a problem for me. When I enter an art space, I sense that there is somehow a kind of cultural distancing, for the viewers and from the viewers. Ostensibly galleries are there for people, museums are there for people who are not necessarily as educated in the highly codified language of the arts as are the people in this room.

A case in point is this evening's discussion. Why is it being documented? I think it is important for people to have access to any information on AIDS and in that respect I think it is a great idea. But my point is that by discussing these issues in codified ways and in these very elitist circles we are really serving the art patrons, the people who are funding this evening, the show that accompanies this, and a lot of other cultural events. The implication is that those people in some way will contribute to culture in a way that we as individuals are not able or that people who are not artists cannot.

I say this because I am in the awkward position of being one who identifies himself as an activist, one who happens to have created what I would consider guerrilla information, that is, the postering that we in Gran Fury have been doing. I've been approached by people in the media, in the art world, in the galleries, on the lecture circuits to discuss art and activism, and I have a lot of trouble thinking of our work in those terms. Even here, I have a lot of questions about the show being called "AIDS and Democracy." It really should have been "Art and AIDS" or "Art and Democracy." Why was it so personalized and so codified? I think we have to ask our-

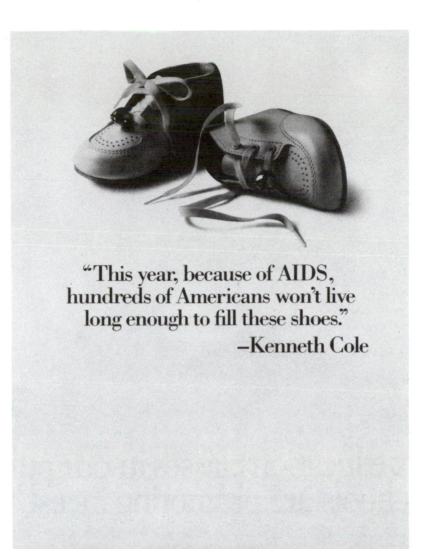

Kenneth Cole Productions Inc., advertisement, 1988.

selves such basic questions if we really want to call ourselves cultural activists in this crisis.

Maggenti What then would be a strategy for anybody who makes images whether they call themselves an artist or not? What are the concrete ways in which the so-called art world would move outside its insular, somewhat self-

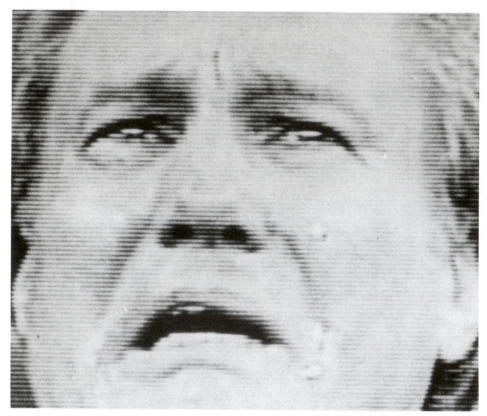

"Sex education classes in our public schools are promoting incest."

America has always been blessed with characters who claim to have all the answers.

The problem is, they don't always practice what they preach. And hypocrisy can be extremely harmful.

Take leading "pro-lifers," for example.

They want the government to outlaw abortion for every woman, even in the case of rape or incest.

Yet prohibition has never stopped abortion. It has only made terminating a pregnancy dangerous for the poor. And more expensive for the better-off.

"Pro-lifer" leaders claim they're ready to stop abortion by any means necessary.

Yet they violently oppose proven ways to avert abortion, like effective family planning programs and sex education that addresses young people's real-life problems and concerns.

According to Jimmy Swaggart, "Sex education classes in our public schools are promoting incest." While according to Phyllis Schlafly, "Sex education is a principal cause of teenage pregnancy."

Of course, enforcing ignorance and preventing young people from making safe, responsible decisions will only result in more unintended pregnancies and more abortions.

In fact, the "pro-lifers" couldn't do more to increase the number of abortions if they tried – while they push for measures that actually threaten women's lives.

Make time to save your right to choose. Before the "pro-lifers" start making your choices for you.

Take action! To join Planned Parenthood's Campaign to Keep Abortion Safe and Legal, please mail this coupon to: PPFA, 810 Seventh Ave., New York, NY 10019-5818.

NAME   T-3

ADDRESS

CITY   STATE   ZIP

Don't wait until women are dying again.

Ⓟ **Planned Parenthood** Federation of America

Planned Parenthood Federation of America, advertisement, 1988.

involved existence? In a crisis where, as Tim pointed out, most people still don't have basic information about HIV transmission, what are the ways in which artists can respond?

Finkelstein One strategy is exiting the art spaces. Publicly funded organizations that do support work and services for the AIDS crisis often don't have the advantage of being able to deal with it. They will be cut off from their funding. They can't do political advocacy. But as individuals ostensibly we have that right in a democracy. So I personally feel that guerrilla information is essential because what we have been handed as a party line for eight years is absolutely no education program. The education programs that have been discussed exclude the affected communities in any real way, or in any culturally sensitive ways. There is no access to any of that information and that is why when I walk into a gallery and I see some very cryptic references to personal loss or some sort of codified, aestheticized, or distanced vision of the way the culture's responding to the AIDS crisis, I feel angry and confused, because I think there is not enough concrete information. I mean, I think facts are in order. I think postering is in order. I think crimes are in order. Obviously I think the things I have been doing are in some way effective or contribute to consciousness-raising about the issues but I really think that clarity is the strategy.

Ann Northrop Hi, my name is Ann Northrop. I am an AIDS educator working for the Hetrick-Martin Institute for the Protection of Lesbian and Gay Youth, a social service agency here in Manhattan. My salary is paid by a contract from the city's Department of Health, and my job is to provide AIDS education all over the city to adolescents and to professionals who work with adolescents. I go into the city schools and into alternative schools and into alternative school programs all over the city and I talk to kids directly. I talk about AIDS, I talk about homosexuality, and I see what goes on in the city schools. I also happen to be the lesbian stepmother of the kid at LaGuardia High School who gave out condoms and AIDS information at my suggestion.

I want to talk about what happens with teenagers in this city and about the Board of Education. There is a woman named Gerri Abelson who is the person in charge of AIDS education at the Board of Education. And she has as sophisticated a knowledge of the subject as anyone I know in this city. She knows a great deal and she teaches me something every time I hear her speak. But the system of AIDS education in this city is nearly impossible, whether through lack of institutional commitment or lack of money or both. She has to train teachers who will then train students. The way teachers are trained in this city is that 300 or 400 of them are invited to an all-day conference at Kings Borough Community College in Brooklyn or Bronx Community College and they have a two-and-a-half-hour plenary session—all of them in a big auditorium in the morning. And Gerry gets up and gives them a lecture on AIDS. She tells them everything she knows about AIDS and that is a very great deal, but the idea that they could sit there and absorb that, let alone know it well enough to turn around and teach it to anyone, is ludicrous. The afternoon is spent going to one or two workshops—if they haven't cut out. They are simply not equipped to go back to school and teach this subject.

So their AIDS education—if they do any, and they often don't because it's too difficult—mostly consists of showing a twenty-minute tape and saying, "Any questions?" Of course, no one asks any questions and they go away and that's AIDS education. On the other hand, there is an enormous hunger for *real* information. It's like the Sahara Desert out there. I was one of the members of ACT UP who set up a table of AIDS information outside a high school on Staten Island, and I want to tell you, kids want this information. If you talk to them for two minutes they are asking so many questions you can barely answer them all. And you can talk to them for hours. Teachers, too, will stay after the bell and listen to you. Peer education is the other thing. These kids have got to learn from each other. It's not just a matter of us passing on information, it's a matter of condoms becoming the cool thing to do. It's a matter of sex automatically involving protection. The most prevalent method of birth control among teenagers in this city is still, believe it or not, withdrawal. So there is a great deal of work to be done and it involves changing their entire attitude toward what sex is about.

But now the good news. There is a school on the Upper West Side of Manhattan that I have gone into a couple of times. It's a special-ed school, only disabled kids. These kids are extremely bright but they are all very marginal and they are not allowed into mainstream schools. Also, it is sponsored by a Catholic agency, therefore they took a great chance in inviting me in to do this AIDS education. I go in there and talk to the kids by age level. I start with the youngest and work up to the oldest. This time I talked to the younger kids about their sexual habits and their condom use. They're still pretty leery of condoms and they're really not comfortable with them. But when I went to the oldest kids, they said, "Oh, yeah, we all use condoms." I said, "You're kidding me. You just know what I want to hear. All your friends say they don't use condoms. Don't give me that." And they said, "No, no, it's true. We used to be like that when we were younger. But now we're older and we know there is a lot of disease out there, and it isn't just HIV, it's herpes, it's gonorrhea, it's syphilis. And we don't want any of that. We know that using condoms is the right thing to do. In 1986 and 1987 we didn't use condoms but in 1988 we do."

So I want to tell you that kids can learn and the reason they haven't is because we haven't taught them. This kind of education has to be done—on a guerrilla basis or in any way you can. It can be done. My suggestion is this: start small, don't have large aspirations, and do it on an individual, one-to-one basis.

Martin Levin My name is Martin Levin. I'm a sociologist who writes about AIDS and sexuality in the lesbian and gay community. I'm also sero-positive. I buried my lover and I buried my best friend so I've really been touched by this epidemic, as have probably most of us in the room. I also train teachers on AIDS and teach a course on AIDS at one of the colleges here in New York City; I have been teaching this course for about two-and-a-half years. What I have been struck with is the common theme that runs through many of the comments tonight. People say that we've got to take an individual approach to the epidemic. Many people have been talking about what I call private responses: volunteering, doing guerrilla education, getting the information out in a community-based way, with individual participation. But what I am hearing in everyone's comments is that that is not satisfactory, that is not enough. We need to do more. We need to depict a collective response to the epidemic. We need to educate. We need to go outside the institutions. But then we need to do more.

With regard to the theme "AIDS and Democracy," for instance, we need to raise the question, Is there really democracy? We live in an elite, male-dominated, white-controlled society that has deliberately marginalized all of us with AIDS. They want us to die. As far as they are concerned, we're morally superfluous. They are more than content to see us pass on. I've always been struck by how the media really reflects that. In the early days of the epidemic we were all depicted as sex-crazed queers, drug-crazed junkies, and heterosexually promiscuous sluts. We were depicted in those terms and it was like, "Let these people die, they infected themselves." That was the media conveying the perspective of an elite. Now the attitude has shifted. Now they say, "We're compassionate, we'll help you die, and maybe we'll give you therapists who will help you adjust to your death." Of course, what is missing in this analysis—and I think even some of the establishment gay or AIDS organizations say this, "Let us help you die comfortably"—is the insistence that that is not enough. But what ACT UP and other groups like it are saying is, "That is not enough. That is just not enough." What needs to be mobilized is the raw naked power from the community.

Finally I don't know how much we can do as communities of the disenfranchised linking together to struggle around this epidemic, because this country is controlled by the class of the corporate elite. The *New York Times* today reported that in Reagan's budget only 10 percent of the taxes come from corporations. That's astonishing. Why shouldn't Burroughs Wellcome pay maybe a little bit more? And it seems to me that the other part of the analysis that people are getting at is that still, we need to force the institutions to deal with AIDS through whatever power we can mobilize. However we can create liaisons with other communities to direct us and solve this issue, we must do it. We need to do something in addition to a private community response. We need a collective endeavor. We need to mobilize whatever power sectors we can to confront an elite that would clearly like to see us dead.

Maggenti   One of the issues that has emerged in ACT UP and has certainly emerged historically in any social and political movement is that of coalition-building. How can we build a movement across barriers that exist in the culture at large?

Michael Miles   Just looking at the last election and considering that only 20 percent of America voted, I think that sort of sums up our democracy. Democracy only works when all the people are part of it. Americans on the whole, particularly in the last thirty years, have become incredibly lazy about everything, their lives, their attitudes, their commitment. We live here in New York, and I don't think we really get a clear picture of what it is like in Middle America. I am still appalled by the number of people who say to me, "ACT UP, what is that?" I have no tolerance for that in this day and age, for people who don't have a political mind and aren't willing to make some kind of commitment. We're faced with this epidemic that is not affecting most Americans so we have taken charge of our own lives, our own health, we're looking at alternatives. We're realizing that the establishment is not the answer. And most importantly, the establishment—the government and the health community—is now faced with people banging down their doors, who aren't doing what they are told, who are saying, "You are not the answer; there are alternatives and you cannot stop me from doing this." I still believe that the government can work. Unfortunately it is just full of the wrong people and it's not working now. Instead of demanding change we have to start demanding things that will lead to change. I still think the government can respond to our presence. We just have to be very smart about how we apply it and what we want out of it.

Robert Garcia   I'd like to address one of the questions on the agenda: "How does this crisis provoke disenfranchised communities to counteract their lack of

Fact sheet distributed at demonstration on September 26, 1988 by ACT UP (AIDS Coalition ▶
To Unleash Power).

The Reagan-Bush Record on AIDS:

NO CARE, NO CURE, NO COMMENT

Over 41,000 people have died of AIDS since 1981. By the time Ronald Reagan leaves office, more Americans will have died from AIDS than were killed in combat in the Viet Nam War.

These men, women, and children haven't been dying just from a virus, but from the administration's neglect and lack of leadership. Today top Republican officials and supporters eat lunch at a fundraiser in the Waldorf-Astoria. We are here to ask:

What have Reagan and Bush done about AIDS?

NO CARE:

▲ The Reagan administration has consistently underfunded federal AIDS research, education and testing efforts. In four of his eight budget proposals, the president has proposed spending less on AIDS than was spent in the previous year.

▲ The administration still has no coordinated policy for AIDS education. The Surgeon General called for a comprehensive education program in 1986, yet was not able to mail a flyer with the most basic information until four months ago.

▲ The president has rejected the call of his own AIDS commission for a federal anti-discrimination law protecting those with AIDS.

NO CURE:

▲ Over 100 drugs have been identified by people with AIDS and their doctors as showing promise against HIV (the virus thought to cause AIDS) and AIDS-related diseases. Yet these drugs are kept from men, women and children with AIDS despite the Food and Drug Administration's promises to speed up its drug approval process.

▲ In April, the AIDS research coordinator for the federal health institutes, Dr. Anthony Fauci, testified before Congress that a lack of staff was "almost exclusively" the reason why several high-priority drugs have not been tested.

NO COMMENT:

▲ In 1986 both the Surgeon General and the National Academy of Sciences issued reports calling for increased federal leadership in the fight against AIDS. The president didn't respond to either report. Seven years of the epidemic passed—and almost 21,000 people died—before Reagan made his first public address on AIDS in May, 1987.

▲ One year later, with almost 20,000 more people dead, the president received, with no comment, the final report of his own AIDS commission. The report has been handed to other federal agencies for further study while the administration ignores most of the report's recommendations.

When will the studying stop and the action begin?

AND WHERE WAS GEORGE?

As vice-president, George Bush has done nothing but support the administration's lack of action.

WHAT DOES BUSH THE CANDIDATE OFFER?

▲ At the GOP convention Bush's delegates killed an amendment to the party's platform which would have endorsed the presidential AIDS commission's report.

▲ Dan Quayle, Bush's pick for his running-mate, was one of a handful of senators who voted last year against a program to provide AZT—the only approved drug for AIDS—to people who couldn't pay for the $8,000-a-year drug themselves.

The next president will be faced with more people dying of AIDS each year than died during the first eight years of the epidemic combined. The next president must work to bring about:

▲ **accelerated drug-testing and drug-approval procedures**
▲ **a comprehensive AIDS education program**
▲ **increased funding for research and treatment**
▲ **an AIDS anti-discrimination law**

The next president must offer more leadership on AIDS than Ronald Reagan has. The next president cannot continue Reagan's criminal silence.

ACT UP

The AIDS Coalition to Unleash Power • 496A Hudson Street, Suite G4, New York, NY 10014 • (212) 533-8888

ACT UP is a diverse, non-partisan group of individuals united in anger and committed to direct action to end the AIDS crisis.

9/26/88

traditional and accepted power in government and culture at large?" I'm a gay Hispanic man, and I've been with ACT UP for a little over a year. From that experience I've learned two valuable lessons that have helped me deal with the AIDS crisis. They're lessons that were first learned through the women's movement. One is: "The powers that be render you invisible." Invisibility is a big issue here. Groups of people have been marginalized and then asked to go away and die quietly. The second lesson is: "The personal is political." My personal experience now reflects itself in an activist response to AIDS.

When AIDS first hit the gay community, I think it shocked all of us, and many of my friends still have not come out of that shell-shocked phase. But we did respond. It was a crisis, an epidemic, and the first thing to do was deal with how it was being transmitted. We were waiting for the government, the medical authorities, the people whom we supposedly trust, to tell us about AIDS and how it is transmitted. And nothing came out. Our community had to figure out transmission. The first true AIDS educators were actually bartenders passing out condoms in our communities. Suddenly we had other groups coming out with a booklet, "How to Have Sex in an Epidemic," and the government coming in and taking that away. Suddenly we had state educators and federal educators saying this is how it's done, this is the model for all people, for all communities.

The next step came after we learned transmission rates, people were dying all around us and we had to come together as a community. Once again we were looking for the government to provide services, to provide dignity and respect for the people who were dying. And we waited, and we waited, and no response came from the government. So our community rallied around and provided their own social services. A lot of social services were political acts. We got together and applied for federal funds to apply the buddy-support system and whatnot. Then suddenly we had the federal government coming in and agreeing to provide the money, but with strings attached. The attachment was "You'll do it our way." Power was denied us again. But a social service network did evolve, and now our community has to turn around and say to the government, "Where the hell were you?"

Once we had gone through these stages, suddenly we had ACT UP. We have groups to say the government isn't doing enough. ACT UP is one of the most empowering things that I know of because a lesson I have learned is that all I have—like everyone who has passed away, all they had in the final analysis—is my voice and my body. That is the only power that we have as a community, our voices and our bodies. There is obviously a need for us to get out and do what ACT UP is doing—a political response, direct action, so that people and the government respond. The government has to take a more effective stance in this crisis. We have to provoke the government into action. And the best way to do that is to directly confront them, to stop their business as usual, and say, "No, this is not going to happen."

Charles Frederick   I want to comment on coalition-building. We need to think about coalition politics a little differently than we have in the past. A coalition begins first and foremost as a state of mind. One of the things we have learned is that we all live with AIDS. Another is that a person with AIDS will not have a full identity in AIDS; their human identity and dignity supersede any disease. In our attempts at coalition-building, then, we must first understand the full human range of problems in this culture. People must come to understand that our common human identity is under attack from many places. And it is under attack because there are those who are in power who perpetuate a culture of racism, homophobia, sexism, classism, a culture that denies the poor a life. We must be able to stand up against all of those things. We must know that it is all one issue. That is the best way that we can create the coalition to deal with healing PWAs.

Yvonne Rainer   My name is Yvonne Rainer. I am a filmmaker. I'm not an activist with any particular organization, so I am in a way talking from a kind of utopian perspective. But it seems to me that the so-called AIDS crisis is part of the increasingly dismal state of health care in this country. I would like to know if there are any efforts to make connections between the various health activist organizations, like the National Women's Health Network or NARAL [National Abortion Rights Action League], for instance. I mean, the whole issue of abortion rights, it seems to me, is part of this spectrum of retrenchment and backing off from taking care of people's health needs. This also includes the aging, cancer patients, indigent people, and the more and more people in this country who have no health insurance. As we age, we all face rather dismal prospects unless we're in an upper-level economic situation. So, are there any efforts in the gay movement to make connections with other health organizations?

Maggenti   I'm sure there are people in the room who would be able to answer that. One comment I would like to make is that there is a distinction between NARAL in its current formation and the AIDS Coalition To Unleash Power as an activist organization. And the distinction is tactical. What I mean is that organizations that lobby in Washington are not necessarily in the same position to raise public consciousness as an organization that puts seven hundred people on Wall Street stopping traffic. So in terms of linking up activists, the notion of activism and what an activist does has many meanings. AIDS activists do one particular type of activism, people in service organizations do another type of activism, and the links between them are rather fragile sometimes.

Mitchel Cohen My name is Mitchel Cohen. I am from the Red Balloon Collective in Stony Brook. I am also very active with Northeast Student Action Network; we are working inside the hopefully newly emerging left student movement. I don't think there is any hope for empowerment outside of direct action. We must build alternative direct action communities in which people can begin to address various social problems and aspects of our lives and figure out how to fight for ourselves and for the new society. In that regard, I see ACT UP as an example, one of the foremost groups that are beginning not only to address the AIDS issue but to take direct action and to forge alliances. But in our student group when the question of coalitions comes up we wonder who do we coalesce with? The Democratic Party?

Unidentified Speaker Nothing that I have heard here tonight is directed toward that large, critical mass of people who are seriously at risk from AIDS in New York—predominantly gay men, addicts of color, whomever. Why aren't we talking about underground comic books or cheap videos on AIDS that I could give a friend who has just been diagnosed? Why not have at clinics or hospitals comic books like *How to Be an Uppity Patient?* There is something about performance, humor, graphic art that really could be used, and unfortunately we have thousands of directly HIV-related health consumers in New York. Not only is ignoring them morally wrong, but practically such things might be able to accomplish a lot more than lofty discussions about activism and strategy and democracy and art as a concept. Also, I can't imagine any way of separating the activist from the artist, because if you come to Sloan-Kettering tomorrow morning with a comic book for my patients that says how to talk back to your doctors, you might also get arrested. There is just no way to separate what I am talking about, the art/activism separation is ludicrous.

Elizabeth Tracy My name is Elizabeth Tracy. I'm a member of ACT UP. What we see as democracy in the United States is what might be called "top down" democracy. What happens in Congress or the Supreme Court, that democracy trickles down to us, not unlike Reagan's budgets. The democracy that is constructed around AIDS activism—ACT UP is a good case study— is a "bottom up" democracy. We have seized control of language and information. We have changed the way the media speaks about us, and about AIDS. In the AIDS crisis, I think nothing is as important as information, whether it is medical information or transmission information, and that is why we have struggles to retain control over it. For the most part information is still being held by a very small group of people, the medical elite and the governmental elite, and the dissemination of that is a means of activism. That is democracy in action, that is a "bottom up" democracy.

Maggenti Well, one thing about ACT UP as an example is that a majority of its members are very well educated and have a lot of resources at their fingertips in terms of language and access to information. So how does that relate to your point about getting information out and empowering your own community? You're actually starting out with a command of the language and an understanding of how the system operates. And that's not necessarily true for all the communities affected by AIDS. Right?

Tracy Right. But one way in which those people who do have access to information can spread it around is through the guerrillalike means of seizing control that we talked about before. Then maybe different communities, for instance Spanish-speaking communities, could take it and make it their own. Does it work? Will it work? I think there are a lot of barriers, but I think individuals cross those barriers. Whether or not whole groups are crossing those barriers is another question. Individuals doing it on their own will disseminate stuff to places where it will have a place to take root. There is a need for a constant give-and-take in this crisis, especially with information.

Sydney Pokorny I'm feeling really skeptical about ACT UP right now, because we have not had an action in three weeks. We have a lot of images left from posters and stickers, and that's great but I think we are getting carried away with the idea that the image is the action. The images that we are creating are still caught up in a whole ideological system that forms the basis of the structure of the AIDS crisis. When we went to the FDA [Food and Drug Administration], it wasn't simply the action of the individuals there, our bodies on the line. The media took that over and really told the story of what we were there for. It was really positive coverage, but to me that is a negative thing in a lot of ways. Yes, we have some control of the media but I think that we have to be a little more critical of the images that we are using and know that they are coming from Adland. Someday these images aren't going to work. Someday they are going to be just like everything else that is out there. They are going to lose the power to convey the information that we have. Direct action in the streets is something that we can claim as our own. Images are something that can be taken away from us very easily.

Maxine Wolf Look, a lot of communities have a lot more information than we have, and they know the system a hell of a lot better than we do. They have been fucked over by it for a very long time. They may not know the names of drugs, but they still think that a cure is going to be found by the American Medical Association. I think it smacks of condescension to think that we have information to give to people, that they don't have information to give to us. A lot of poor communities, women, and people who go to experimental drug trials and die instead of live don't trust that system. One of the "problems" that exists for a lot of communities is that they won't go near the system, but we are still deluded enough to think we can change it.

The second thing I would like to address is homophobia. I'm a person who knows that AIDS is a health care issue, but when the Marxist School has a forum and the only way they can talk about it is as a health care issue (they have never taught a course on gay studies and they cannot talk about AIDS and homophobia), then where is the progressive movement? I have been out there on the streets for those people for nearly thirty years but I never see them at a gay pride march. I never see them at our demonstrations. I don't see them talking about those issues. And part of that is that a lot of those people would not care if we died either. So not only is there an art community that is not doing anything, there is a whole progressive political community that has been sitting by for eight years and just this year discovered that AIDS is a health care issue. It took them eight years of homophobia to discover that AIDS is a health care issue. Great. As soon as they could get a changing mode of transmission and it started affecting blacks and Latinos it became a left issue. White gay people, black gay people (who they don't think exist), Latin gay people (who they don't think exist), gay office workers (who don't exist)—the left's inability to recognize these people has left us alone in this crisis to fight for ourselves. I would like to see those people who think of themselves as progressive move their asses down there and out on the line with us. We support their demonstrations but I did not see them at the FDA and I did not see them on Wall Street and I do not see them at most of the demonstrations that we do. They marvel that we have three hundred people coming to a meeting. They want to know how we do it. We do it because it is our lives on the line. It is not an abstraction and it is not halfway across the world. That's not to say that foreign policy issues are not important, but it has been far easier for the white, straight left to deal with Nicaragua than with gay people around the corner from them.

◄ Gran Fury, *Read my Lips*, 1988. T-shirt distributed by ACT UP (AIDS Coalition To Unleash Power).

I also want to say that to me the way that you coalition-build is to be who you are. I am not going to lie to anyone in any community about who I am. You don't go in with rhetoric, you don't go in with an agenda, you go in as a person. Lots of people say, "Just go to this community and pretend that you are not gay, because they won't understand." That is a condescension to the community I'm going into, and it's a condescension to me. And I am not going to do that. To me, that's not the way that you build a coalition. You get your ass out there on the street and you let other people who have been fucked over by this system know that you are willing to put your life on the line. And when you are willing to put your life and your body on the line to fight the same system that they have been fighting, you are not going to have any trouble working together. And if we are willing to be out there, we gain respect for the fact that we're willing to fight for our lives. That's why ACT UP has to be out on the street.

Vito Russo

A TEST OF WHO WE ARE

AS A PEOPLE

ACT UP Rally, Albany, New York, May 7, 1988

A friend of mine has a half-fare transit card which he uses on buses and subways. The other day when he showed his card, the token attendant asked what his disability was. He said, "I have AIDS," and the attendant said, "No you don't. If you had AIDS you'd be home—dying."

I'm here to speak out today as a PWA who is not dying *from*—but for the last three years quite successfully living *with*—AIDS. Members of my family who get all their information from reading the newspapers and watching television know two things about me—that I'm going to die and that the government is doing everything in its power to save me. They're wrong on both counts.

If I'm dying from anything it's from homophobia. If I'm dying from anything it's from racism. If I'm dying from anything it's from indifference and red tape. If I'm dying from anything I'm dying from Jesse Helms. If I'm dying from anything I'm dying from Ronald Reagan. If I'm dying from any-thing I'm dying from the sensationalism of newspapers and magazines and television shows that are interested in me as a human interest story only as long as I'm willing to be a helpless victim but not if I'm fighting for my life. If I'm dying from anything I'm dying from the fact that not enough rich, white, heterosexual men have gotten AIDS for anyone to give a shit.

Living with AIDS in this country is like living in the twilight zone. Liv-ing with AIDS is living through a war which is happening only for those people who are in the trenches. Every time a shell explodes you look around to discover that you've lost more of your friends. But nobody else notices—it isn't happening to them. They're walking the streets as though we weren't living through a nightmare; only *you* can hear the screams of the people dying and their cries for help. No one else seems to be noticing.

It's worse than wartime because during a war the people are united in a shared experience. This war has not united us—it's divided us. It's separated those of us with AIDS and those of us who fight for people with AIDS from the rest of the population.

Two-and-a-half years ago I read a *Life* magazine editorial on AIDS that said it's time to pay attention because "this disease is now beginning to strike the rest of us." It was as if I wasn't the one holding the magazine in my hand. Since then nothing has changed to alter the perception that AIDS is not happening to the real people in this country—it's not happening to *us* in the United States—it's happening to *them*—to the disposable populations of fags and junkies who deserve what they get. The media tell people they don't have to care because the citizens who really matter are in no danger. Twice, three times, maybe four, the *New York Times* has published editorials saying "Don't Panic Yet Over AIDS"—it still hasn't entered the general population and until it does we don't have to give a shit.

And the days and the months and the years pass by, and *they* don't spend those days and nights and months and years trying to figure out how to get ahold of the latest experimental drug and which dose to take it at and in which combination with what other drugs and from what source and for how much money because it isn't happening to them so they don't give a shit. And they don't sit in television studios surrounded by technicians who wear rubber gloves and refuse to put a body mike on them because it isn't happening to them so they don't give a shit. And they don't have their houses burned down by bigots and morons. They only watch it on the news and then they eat their dinner and they go to bed because it isn't happening to them so they don't give a shit.

They don't spend their waking hours going from one hospital to another, watching the people they love die slowly of neglect and bigotry because it isn't happening to them so they don't give a shit. They haven't been to two funerals a week for the last three, four, or five years so they don't give a shit. It's not happening to them.

We read on the front page of the *New York Times* that Dr. Anthony Fauci now says that all sorts of promising drugs for treatment haven't even been tested in the last two years because he can't afford to hire the people to test them. We're supposed to be grateful that this story has appeared. Nobody wonders why some reporter didn't dig up that story and print it eighteen months ago, before Fauci went public with his complaints before a congressional committee. How many people died in the last two years who might be alive today if those drugs had been speedily tested?

Reporters all over the country are busy printing government press releases. They don't give a shit—it isn't happening to them—meaning that it isn't happening to the real people, the world famous general public we all keep hearing about. Legionnaires' disease was happening to them because the people who got it looked like them, sounded like them, were the same color as them—and that fucking story about a couple of dozen people hit the front pages of every newspaper and magazine in the country and stayed there until the mystery was over.

All I read in the newspapers tells me that the mainstream heterosexual population is not at risk for this disease. All the newspapers I read tell me that IV drug users and homosexuals still account for the overwhelming majority of cases and those at risk. Then can somebody please tell me why every single penny allocated for education and prevention gets spent on ad campaigns directed almost exclusively to white, heterosexual teenagers who they keep telling us are *not at risk for this disease?*

Can somebody tell me why the only television movie ever produced by a major network in this country is not about a young man with AIDS but about the impact of the disease on his straight, white nuclear family? Why for eight years every single newspaper and magazine in this country has done cover stories on AIDS only when the threat of heterosexual transmission is raised? Why for eight years every single educational film designed for use in high schools has eliminated any gay positive material before being approved by the board of education? Why in the past eight years every single public information pamphlet and videotape distributed by establishment sources has ignored specific homosexual content? Why every bus and subway ad I read and every advertisement and billboard I see is specifically not directed at gay men?

Don't believe the lie that the gay community has done its job and done it well and has successfully educated its people. The gay community and IV drug users are not all politicized people living in New York and San Francisco. Members of minority populations, including so-called sophisticated gay men, are abysmally ignorant about AIDS. If it is true that gay men and IV drug users are the populations at risk for this disease we have a right to demand that education and prevention be targeted specifically to these people and *it is not happening.* We are being allowed to die while low risk populations are being panicked—not educated—panicked into believing that we deserve to die.

AIDS is not what it appears to be at this moment in history. It is more than just a disease that ignorant people have turned into an excuse to exercise bigotry they already feel. It is more than a horror story to be exploited by the tabloids.

AIDS is a test of who we are as a people. When future generations ask what we did in the war we have to be able to tell them that we were out here fighting. And we have to leave a legacy to the generations of people who will come after us. Remember that someday the AIDS crisis will be over. And when that day has come and gone there will be people alive on this earth—gay people and straight people—black people and white people—

men and women—who will hear the story that once there was a terrible disease—and that a brave group of people stood up and fought and in some cases died so that others might live and be free. I'm proud to be out here today with the people I love and to see the faces of those heroes who are fighting this war and to be part of that fight. To steal a phrase from Mike Callen's song, "Love is all we have for now—what we don't have is time."

Like the unsung, anonymous doctors who are fighting this disease and are so busy putting out fires that they don't have time to strategize, AIDS activists are stretched to the limit of their time and energy, putting out the fires of bigotry and hatred and misinformation when they need to be fighting for drugs and research money. We need luxury time to strategize the next year of this battle and we need our friends to join us so we can buy that time. And after we kick the shit out of this disease I intend to be alive to kick the shit out of this system so that this will never happen again.

ARTISTS IN THE EXHIBITIONS

Education and Democracy

John Ahearn
Angel Amarat with Rachel Romero
Mario Asaro with the Students of Class 7-333
Doug Ashford with the Students of Class F201
Jo Babcock
Rudolf Baranik
Joseph Beuys
Sam Binkley with the Students of Group C
Michael Boane with Hospital Audiences Inc.
Nancy Burson
Lance Carlson
Lynne Cohen
Eric Drooker
Educational Video Center
Barbara Ess
Oyvind Fahlstrom
Reverend Howard Finster
Peter Hallcy
Lewis Hine
Jenny Holzer
Jump Sneakers
Young K.
Dean McNeil
Meryl Meisler and the Drop Ins
Gerhard Merz
New Muse Summer Program with Onnie Millar
Ed Morales with Tom McGlynn, Diana
Caballero & Elaine Ruiz and the Committee
for a Multilingual New York, and Victory Arts
J. B. Murray
Tom Otterness
Luciano Perna
Adrian Piper
Keith Rambert with the Students of Class FZ01
Maria Reyes
Faith Ringgold
Rise and Shine Productions
Tim Rollins + K.O.S.
Dr. Seuss
Lorna Simpson
Caroline Stikker
Mitchell Syrop
Jon Tower
Robert Venturi
Douglas Walker
Andy Warhol
Gary Wilson with Rachel Romero

Politics and Election

John M. Armleder
Arnon Ben-David
Curtis Brown
Luis Camnitzer
Lynne Cohen
Kenneth Cole Shoes
Robbie Conal
Gregory Davidek
Sam Doyle
Kate Ericson & Mel Ziegler
Judy Fiskin
Mike Glier
Leon Golub
Hans Haacke
Ronald Jones
Margia Kramer
Bertrand Lavier
John Lindell
Jim Lutes
Christian Marclay
Dona Ann McAdams
Dean McNeil
Brad Melamed
Tony Mendoza
Kirsten Mosher
Antonio Muntadas/Marshall Reese
David Nyzio
Aric Obrosey
Norman Rockwell
Michael Rosario and Rachel Romero
Erika Rothenberg
Christy Rupp
Jana Sterbak
Caroline Stikker
Mitchell Syrop
Martin Wong
Wayne Zebzda

Cultural Participation

Vikky Alexander
Richard Armijo
Art Police
Tina Barney
Gretchen Bender
Daniel Buren
Nancy Burson

Luis Camnitzer
Lance Carlson
Don Celender
Lynne Cohen
Jane Dickson
Mary Beth Edelson
Reverend Howard Finster
Jeff Gates
Arnold Ginsberg
Bessie Harvey
Carmen Herrera
Jenny Holzer
Larry Johnson
Mike Kelley
Barbara Kruger
Ken Lum
Kirsten Mosher
Aric Obrosey
Richard Prince
George Romero
Peter Reiss
Alexander Remas
Erika Rothenberg
Fran Cutrell Rutovsky
Victor Schrager
Cindy Sherman
Haim Steinbach
Symbol Magazine
Mitchell Syrop
Richard Thatcher
Urban Center for Photography
Douglas Walker
Carrie Mae Weems
Judith Weinman

Aids and Democracy:
A Case Study

Joe Andoe
Gretchen Bender
Ross Bleckner
Teresa Bramlette
Ellen Brooks
Brian Buczak
Nancy Burson
Andrea Evans
Steven Evans
General Idea
Mike Glier
Gran Fury
Michael Jenkins
Ronald Jones
Tom Kalin
Jannis Kounellis

Barbara Kruger
Dorothea Lange
Louise Lawler
John Lindell
Nancy Linn
T. L. Litt
Robert Mapplethorpe
Tom McKitterick
Gerhard Merz
Don Moffett
Diane Neumaier
Tim Rollins + K.O.S.
Andres Serrano
Nancy Spero
Ben Thornberry
Martha Townsend

AIDS Videos

Nick Papatonis
1987 National March on Washington for Lesbian and Gay Rights

Jean Carlomusto & Maria Maggenti
Doctors, Liars & Women

Life Guard

David Thompson
The Names Project

Jean Carlomusto & Alexandra Juhasz
Prostitutes, Risk & AIDS

Ira Manhoff
Showdown in Atlanta

Gregg Bordowitz & Jean Carlomusto
Work Your Body

Ellen Spiro
ACT UP at the FDA

John Greyson
AIDS: Angry Initiatives/Defiant Strategies

Paper Tiger Collective
Simon Watney Says "No" to Clause 29

Testing the Limits Coalition
Testing the Limits

Artists/Teachers Concerned

84-44 60th Avenue

Queens, New York 11373

An organization of art educators that produces seminars, workshops, and exhibitions to progressively influence cultural and educational policy.

Artists For a Better Image (ArtFBI)

1440 East Baltimore Street #2E

Baltimore, Maryland 21231-1404

(301) 563-1903

A national information-gathering and advocacy group whose purpose is to promote a more realistic image of the artist by encouraging dialogue on the roles artists play in our society, how they are portrayed in the media, and how public reaction to art affects that perception.

Association for Drug Abuse Prevention and Treatment, Inc. (ADAPT)

236 East 111th Street

New York, New York 10029

(212) 289-1957

A volunteer, community-based organization working to decrease the spread of HIV infection by providing education, support, and needle exchange to intravenous drug users in New York City.

American Civil Liberties Union (ACLU)

132 West 43rd Street

New York, New York 10036

(212) 944-9800

A public interest law firm devoted to enforcing the Bill of Rights of the U.S. Constitution.

AIDS Coalition To Unleash Power (ACT UP)

496A Hudson Street

Suite G4

New York, New York 10014

(212) 989-1114

A diverse, nonpartisan group of individuals united by anger and committed to direct action to end the AIDS crisis. It utilizes various tactics to expose the health care system's failings and governmental negligence.

American Foundation for AIDS Research (AmFAR)

1515 Broadway

Suite 3601

New York, New York 10036

(212) 719-0033

Founded in 1985, AmFAR has awarded 26 million dollars in seed or start-up grants to more than 375 research teams and education projects.

Banana Kelly

965 Longwood Avenue

Bronx, New York 10459

(212) 328-1064

A nonprofit organization handling housing, training for high school dropouts, energy programs, and co-ops.

Body Positive

2095 Broadway

Suite 306

New York, New York 10023

(212) 721-1346

Provides educational seminars, support groups, counseling, and publishes a monthly magazine for HIV-positive members of the community.

The Center for Constitutional Rights (CCR)

666 Broadway, 6th floor

New York, New York 10012

(212) 614-6464

A legal and educational organization devoted to promoting rights guaranteed by the U.S. Constitution and the Universal Declaration of Human Rights.

The Center for Defense Information (CDI)

1500 Massachusetts Avenue, NW

Washington, D. C. 20005

(202) 862-0700

A national clearinghouse of information that traces excess spending and policies that increase the possibility of nuclear war; publishes *The Defense Monitor*, a comprehensive and accessible analysis of war costs.

Chalk Dust
409 Park Place
Brooklyn, New York 11236
(718) 779-2841
A collective of radical educators who seek to democratize the New York City school system by organizing through the teachers' union.

Committee in Solidarity with the People of El Salvador (CISPES)
P. O. Box 12156
Washington, D. C. 20005
(202) 265-0890
Formed in 1980, CISPES is the largest grass-roots organization in the United States whose goals are to educate and mobilize the public against U.S. intervention in Central America and to build support for the people of El Salvador. Their activities include: public protest, raising humanitarian aid, emergency campaigns to defend human rights, and congressional pressure.

Committee Research Initiative (CRI)
31 West 26th Street
New York, New York 10010
(212) 481-1050
A community-based research organization that tests promising new treatments for AIDS.

Democratic Socialists of America (DSA)
15 Dutch Street
Suite 500
New York, New York 10038
(212) 962-0390
Organization of over 5,000 people nationwide dedicated to the promotion of socialism through DSA local chapters.

Educators for Social Responsibility (ESR)
23 Garden Street
Cambridge, Massachusetts 02138
(617) 492-1764
A professional development organization for educators providing training and curriculum materials to aid teachers in developing critical thinking, decision making, conflict resolution, and social responsibility.

Gay Men's Health Crisis (GMHC)
129 West 20th Street
New York, New York 10011
(212) 807-6664
AIDS advocacy organization providing services for People With AIDS; among their programs are providing Buddies, financial help, and legal services.

Hospital Audiences, Inc.
220 West 42nd Street
New York, New York 10036
(212)575-7660
A nonprofit agency that brings artists into creative collaboration with patients in New York hospitals, health centers, and homeless shelters. It produces exhibitions for patient/artists and workshops for various professionals in the field to advocate culture in institutional life.

Jump Cut
P. O. Box 865
Berkeley, California 94701
A review of contemporary media that brings together a vast array of critical articles, interviews and analyses on the politics of popular culture.

The National Abortion Rights Action League (NARAL)
1101 14th Street NW, 5th floor
Washington D. C. 20005
(202) 408-4600
Promotes legislative and electoral change on abortion and pro-choice issues.

The National Rainbow Coalition
P. O. Box 27385
Washington, D. C. 20005
(202) 728-1180
A group formed with the intention of pressing for a progressive political agenda; among their plans are the fight for universal voter registration, well-enforced civil rights laws, a woman's right to choose, environmental responsibility, an end to wasteful military spending, and a foreign policy founded on human rights and real democracy.

Paper Tiger TV
339 Lafayette
New York, New York 10012
(212) 420-9045
Collective of media activists; produces half-hour videotapes for Public Access Television concentrating on media analysis and working with community and school groups.

People for The American Way
2000 M Street, NW
Suite 400
Washington, D. C. 20036
A nonpartisan constitutional liberties organization that operates on a national level. Through governmental lobbying, the distribution of publications and videotapes, and public mobilization, it works to protect civil rights, reproductive freedom, and public education from censorship.

People With AIDS Coalition
31 West 26th Street
New York, New York 10010
(212) 532-0290
Hotline: (212) 532-0568
Created by and for PWAs and PWARCs to promote a movement of self-empowerment. It publishes the *PWA Coalition Newsline*, a monthly newsletter that provides a forum for diverse opinions and includes treatment information, articles, memorials, and other resources.

Political Art Documentation/Distribution (PAD/D)
A progressive artists' resource and networking organization that is no longer operating. It published *Upfront*, a progressive cultural magazine and maintained an archive of socially conscious art work. The latter is now maintained by the Museum of Modern Art in New York.

Project Inform
347 Dolores Street
Suite 301
San Francisco, California 94110
(415) 558-9051
Toll free in California: 1(800) 334-7422
Toll free in the U.S.: 1(800) 822-7422
National HIV information treatment hotline offering information about up-to-date treatments for the HIV-infected; also handle referrals if they do not have the information.

Radical Teacher
Boston Women Teacher's Group
P. O. Box 102
Kendall Square Post Office
Boston, Massachusetts 02142
A socialist and feminist journal on the theory and practice of teaching.

The Southern Poverty Law Center
P. O. Box 548
Montgomery, Alabama 36195-5101
(205) 264-0286
An extensive legal service network for victims of civil rights violations that operates nationally. It produces pro-civil-rights publications and videotapes, monitors racist violence through Klanwatch, and counsels class-action suits against racist organizations.

Z Magazine
The Institute for Social and Cultural Communications
116 Saint Botolph Street
Boston, Massachusetts 02115
An independent political magazine of critical thinking on political, cultural, social, and economic life in the United States.

BIBLIOGRAPHY

ACT UP (AIDS Coalition To Unleash Power), ed. *The Women and AIDS Handbook*. New York: ACT UP, 1989.

Theodor W. Adorno. *Minima Moralia: Reflections from Damaged Life*. Trans. E. F. N. Jephcott. London: New Left Books, 1978.

Louis Althusser. *Lenin and Philosophy, and Other Essays*. Trans. Ben Brewster. London: New Left Books, 1971.

John Berger. *Ways of Seeing*. New York: The Viking Press, 1973.

Erma Bombeck. *Aunt Erma's Cope Book: How to Get From Monday to Friday . . . In 12 Days*. New York: McGraw-Hill, 1979.

Erma Bombeck. *The Grass is Always Greener Over the Septic Tank*. New York: Fawcett Crest, 1972.

The Boston Women's Health Book Collective. *The New Our Bodies, Our Selves*. New York: Simon & Schuster, 1984.

Bertolt Brecht. *Brecht on Theatre: The Development of an Aesthetic*. Ed. John Willet. New York: Hill and Wang, 1964.

Victor Burgin, ed. *Thinking Photography*. London: Macmillan Press, 1982.

Michael Callen, ed. *Surviving and Thriving with AIDS: Collected Wisdom*. 2 vols. New York: People with AIDS Coalition, 1986-88.

Erica Carter and Simon Watney, eds. *Taking Liberties: AIDS and Cultural Politics*. London: Serpent's Tail, 1989.

Noam Chomsky. *Problems of Knowledge and Freedom*. New York: Vintage Books, 1972.

Noam Chomsky. *Language and Responsibility*. New York: Pantheon, 1979.

Noam Chomsky. *Towards a New Cold War*. New York: Pantheon, 1982.

Alexander Cockburn. *Corruptions of Empire: Life Studies and the Reagan Era*. London and New York: Verso, 1988.

Douglas Crimp, ed. *AIDS, Cultural Analysis, Cultural Activism*. Boston: MIT Press, 1988.

Michael K. Deaver with Mickey Herskowitz. *Behind the Scenes*. New York: William Morrow & Co., Inc., 1987.

Guy Debord. *Society of the Spectacle*. Detroit: Black and Red, 1977.

Ariel Dorfman and Armand Mattelart. *How to Read Donald Duck: Imperialist Ideology in the Disney Comic*. Trans. David Kunzle. New York: International General, 1975.

Barbara Ehrenreich. *Fear of Falling: The Inner Life of the Middle Class*. New York: Pantheon, 1989.

Han Magnus Enzensberger. *Critical Essays*. New York: Continuum, 1982.

Stuart Ewen. *Captains of Consciousness: Advertising and the Social Roots of the Consumer Culture*. New York: McGraw-Hill, 1976.

Stuart and Elizabeth Ewen. *Channels of Desire: Mass Images and the Shaping of American Consciousness*. New York: McGraw-Hill, 1982.

Stuart Ewen. *All Consuming Images: The Politics of Style in Contemporary Culture*. New York: Basic Books, 1988.

Elizabeth Fee and Daniel M. Fox, eds. *AIDS: The Burdens of History*. Berkeley: University of California Press, 1988.

Paulo Freire. *Education for Critical Consciousness*. New York: Seabury Press, 1973.

Paulo Freire. *Pedagogy of the Oppressed*. Trans. Myra Bergman. New York: Continuum, 1981.

Lorraine Gamman and Margaret Marshment, eds. *The Female Gaze: Women as Viewers of Popular Culture*. London: The Women's Press, 1988.

Henry Louis Gates, Jr. *Figures in Black: Words, Signs and the "Racial" Self*. New York: Oxford University Press, 1986.

Henry A. Giroux. *Theory and Resistance in Education*. Granby, Mass.: Bergin & Garvey Publishers, 1983.

Christopher Gray, ed. *Leaving the 20th Century: The Incomplete Work of the Situationist International*. London: Free Fall Publications, 1974.

Arnold Hauser. *The Philosophy of Art History*. New York: Knopf, 1959.

Shirley B. Heath. *Ways with Words: Language, Life and Work in Communities and Classrooms*. Cambridge: Cambridge University Press, 1983.

Mark Hertsgaard. *On Bended Knee: The Press and the Reagan Presidency*. New York: Farrar, Straus & Giroux, 1988.

Jon Hendricks and Jean Toche. *The Guerrilla Art Action Group, 1969-1976*. New York: Printed Matter, Inc., 1978.

Dick Hebdidge. *Subculture: The Meaning of Style*. London: Methuen, 1979.

Edward S. Herman and Noam Chomsky. *Manufacturing Consent: The Political Economy of the Mass Media*. New York: Pantheon, 1988.

bell hooks. *Feminist Theory from Margin to Center*. Boston: South End Press, 1984.

bell hooks. *Talking Back: thinking feminist, thinking black*. Boston: South End Press, 1989.

Ivan Illich. *Deschooling Society*. New York: Harper and Row, 1971.

Gary Indiana. *Scar Tissue*. New York: Calamus Books, 1987.

Steven Jonas, M.D. *Health Care Delivery in the United States*. New York: Springer Publishing, 1986.

Douglas Kahn and Diane Neumaier, eds. *Cultures in Contention*. Seattle: Real Comet Press, 1985.

Ken Knabb, ed. *Situationist International Anthology*. Berkeley: The Bureau of Public Secrets, 1981.

Barbara Kruger, ed. *TV Guides: A Collection of Thoughts about Television*. New York: Kuklapolitan Press, 1985.

Thomas S. Kuhn. *The Structure of Scientific Revolutions*. Chicago: University of Chicago Press, 1970.

Lawrence W. Levine. *Black Culture and Black Consciousness: African American Folk Thought from Slavery to Freedom*. New York: Oxford University Press, 1977.

Lucy R. Lippard. *Get the Message? A Decade of Art for Social Change*. New York: E. P. Dutton, 1984.

Armand Mattelart and Seth Siegelaub, eds. *Communication and Class Struggle*, 2 vols. New York: International General, 1979-82.

Colin MacCabe. *Godard: Images, Sounds, Politics*. Bloomington: Indiana University Press, 1980.

Robin Morgan, ed. *Sisterhood is Powerful: An Anthology of Writings from the Women's Liberation Movement*. New York: Vintage Books, 1970.

Bill Moyers: World of Ideas. New York: Doubleday, 1989.

Brian O'Doherty. *Inside the White Cube*. San Francisco: The Lapis Press, 1986.

Bruce Perry, ed. *The Last Speeches of Malcolm X*. New York: Pathfinder Press, 1989.

Diane Ravitch. *The Great School Wars, New York City, 1805-1973*. New York: Basic Books, 1974.

Donald T. Regan. *For the Record: From Wall Street to Washington*. New York: Harcourt, Brace, Jovanovich Publishers, 1988.

Wilhelm Reich. *Listen, Little Man*. New York: Orgone Institute Press, 1948.

Wilhelm Reich. *The Mass Psychology of Fascism*. New York: Farrar, Straus & Giroux, 1970.

Wilhelm Reich. *People in Trouble*. Volume 2 of *The Emotional Plague of Mankind*. Trans. Philip Schmitz. New York: Farrar, Straus & Giroux, 1976.

Wilhelm Reich. *Sex Pol Essays 1929-1934*. New York: Vintage, 1972.

David Riesman. *The Lonely Crowd: A Study of the Changing American Character*. New Haven: Yale University Press, 1960.

Martha Rosler. *3 Works*. Halifax: The Press of the Nova Scotia College of Art and Design, 1981.

Richard Sennett. *Authority*. 2d ed. New York: Vintage Books, 1981.

Randy Shilts. *And the Band Played On: Politics, People, and the AIDS Epidemic*. New York: St. Martin's Press, 1987.

Ira Shor. *Culture Wars: School and Society in the Conservative Restoration, 1969-1984*. Boston: Routledge & Kegan Paul, 1986.

Ira Shor and Paulo Freire. *A Pedagogy for Liberation: Dialogues on Transforming Education*. South Hadley, Mass.: Bergin & Garvey Publishers, 1983.

Ann Snitow, Christine Stansell, and Sharon Thompson, eds. *Powers of Desire: The Politics of Sexuality*. New York: Monthly Review Press, 1983.

David A. Stockman. *The Triumph of Politics: How the Reagan Revolution Failed*. New York: Harper & Row, 1986.

E. P. Thompson. *The Poverty of Theory and Other Essays*. New York: Monthly Review Press, 1978.

Robert Farris Thompson. *Flash of the Spirit: African and Afro-American Art and Philosophy*. New York: Vintage Books, 1983.

Alexis de Tocqueville. *Democracy in America*, 2 vols. New York: Alfred E. Knopf, 1987.

Brian Wallis, ed. *Art After Modernism: Rethinking Representation*. Boston: David R. Godine Publishers, 1984.

Simon Watney. *Policing Desire: Pornography, AIDS and the Media*. Minneapolis: University of Minnesota Press, 1987.

Raymond Williams. *Culture and Society, 1780-1950*. New York: Columbia University Press, 1983.

Raymond Williams. *Keywords: A Vocabulary of Culture and Society*. New York: Oxford University Press, 1976.

Judith Williamson. *Consuming Passions: The Dynamics of Popular Culture*. London: Marion Boyers, New York:, 1980.

Bruce Wright. *Black Robes, White Justice*. Secaucus, N.J.: Lyle Stuart Inc., 1987.

PHOTO CREDITS

Title page and pages 4, 11, 125, 143, 206 courtesy Bettman Archive; page facing 1 courtesy The Museum of Modern Art, New York, Gift of Peter H. Deitsch; page 12 courtesy News & Observer Publishing Co., Raleigh, North Carolina; page 15 courtesy of T. L. Litt; page 19 courtesy of the artist; page 23 courtesy Group Material; pages 26 and 27 courtesy of Group Material, photos by Ken Schles and Noel Allum; pages 32 and 33 courtesy of the artists; page 36 courtesy of American Fine Art Co., New York; page 39 courtesy of Mr. Thomas Rockwell, photo by Oren Slor; pages 44 and 45 courtesy of Doug Ashford; pages 46 and 67 courtesy Brooke Alexander Inc., New York; page 49 courtesy of the artist; page 52 courtesy of Hospital Audiences Inc., photo by Oren Slor; page 62 courtesy of the artists, photo by Oren Slor; pages 68 and 127 courtesy of Photofest, New York; page 74 courtesy Eric Drooker, photo by Oren Slor; page 76 courtesy Impact Visuals, photo by Kathleen Foster; page 85 courtesy Random House, photo by Oren Slor; pages 88 and 91 courtesy Meryl Meisler and the Drop Ins; page 95 courtesy Photofind Gallery, New York; page 96 courtesy Rise and Shine Productions; page 98 copyright © 1974 by Mary Boyd Higgins as Trustee of the Wilhelm Reich Infant Trust Fund, courtesy Farrar, Straus & Giroux, Inc.; pages 106 and 107 courtesy Columbia Pictures; page 172 courtesy the artists; page 114 courtesy Impact Visuals, photo by Ansell Horn; pages 116 courtesy P.P.O.W. Gallery, New York; page 119 courtesy John Gibson Gallery, New York; page 120 courtesy the artist; page 131 courtesy the artist; page 134 courtesy CBS News; page 136 copyright © 1990 by News America Publications Inc., courtesy TV Guide® Magazine; page 142 courtesy Rick Reinhard; page 155 courtesy Copley News Service; page 156 Dallas Morning News, photo by William Snyder; page 159 courtesy Hudsons New York; pages 162 and 183 courtesy Fahey Klein Gallery, Los Angeles; page 39 courtesy H & L Enterprises, El Cajon, California, photo by Oren Slor; pages 167 and 282 courtesy Wessel O'Connor Gallery, New York; pages 168 and 169 courtesy Impact Visuals; page 173 courtesy the artists; page 174 copyright © 1990 by News America Publications Inc., Radnor, Pennsylvania, courtesy TV Guide ® Magazine and ABC, California; page 180 courtesy the artists; page 195 courtesy the artist; page 201 courtesy Public Art Fund; page 213 courtesy Solters, Roskin, Friedman, Los Angeles; pages 218 and 219 courtesy United Feature Syndicate, Inc.; pages 220 and 221 copyright © 1978 Dawn Associates courtesy Dawn Associates, The Laurel Group Inc.; pages 226 and 227 courtesy Urban Center for Photography, photo by Keith Piaseczny; page 232 courtesy Evan Estern; pages 234 and 235 photos by Oren Slor; pages 238 and 239 courtesy The NAMES Project, photo by Tom Alleman; page 240 courtesy Lorna Simpson; page 243 courtesy the National Archives; page 249 courtesy People With AIDS Coalition, New York, photo of the book by Oren Slor; page 255 courtesy Exit Art, New York; page 257 courtesy the artist; page 258 courtesy the artist; page 261 courtesy ACT UP, photo by Oren Slor; page 268 caption copyright © 1989 courtesy *The New York Times,* photo courtesy Wide World Photos; page 270 courtesy The New Museum of Contemporary Art, New York; page 279 courtesy Gran Fury and ACT UP; page 285 courtesy Kenneth Cole Productions Inc.; page 286 courtesy Planned Parenthood Federation of America; page 291 courtesy ACT UP; page 296 courtesy Gran Fury and ACT UP; page 313 copyright © 1977 the Estate of Robert Mapplethorpe, courtesy the Estate of Robert Mapplethorpe.

Robert Mapplethorpe, *American Flag*, 1977.